Cross-border Partnerships in Higher Education

Cross-border Partnerships in Higher Education looks beyond student and faculty exchanges to examine the myriad ways international colleges and universities work together as institutions. These partnerships have involved the creation of branch campuses, joint research and technology initiatives, collaboration in strengthening institutional management, testing, faculty development efforts, collaboration in quality assurance, and sharing of technology. Cross-national collaborations are a growing financial and informational resource for universities, and non-Western schools are increasingly taking part.

The volume provides an overview of the purposes and types of cross-border collaborations, an analysis of the benefits, and an examination of issues arising from these efforts. A cross-cutting goal is to provide a critical look at the models being employed, the challenges encountered, and the unintended consequences of such collaboration, both positive and negative. The book is intended for scholars and students of international higher education, higher education leaders and practitioners who are charting a course toward greater cross-border collaboration, and leaders in international development assistance organizations that are often asked to support such initiatives.

Robin Sakamoto is a Professor in the Faculty of Foreign Studies of Kyorin University, Japan as well as a lecturer at the University of Tokyo.

David W. Chapman is the Birkmaier Professor of Educational Leadership at the University of Minnesota where he teaches comparative and international education in the Department of Organizational Leadership, Policy, and Development.

International Studies in Higher Education
Series Editors:
David Palfreyman, OxCHEPS
Ted Tapper, OxCHEPS
Scott Thomas, Claremont Graduate University

The central purpose of this series of a projected dozen volumes is to see how different national and regional systems of higher education are responding to widely shared pressures for change. The most significant of these are: rapid expansion; reducing public funding; the increasing influence of market and global forces; and the widespread political desire to integrate higher education more closely into the wider needs of society and, more especially, the demands of the economic structure. The series will commence with an international overview of structural change in systems of higher education. It will then proceed to examine on a global front the change process in terms of topics that are both traditional (for example, institutional management and system governance) and emerging (for example, the growing influence of international organizations and the blending of academic and professional roles). At its conclusion the series will have presented, through an international perspective, both a composite overview of contemporary systems of higher education, along with the competing interpretations of the process of change.

Published titles:

Structuring Mass Higher Education
The Role of Elite Institutions
Edited by David Palfreyman and Ted Tapper

International Perspectives on the Governance of Higher Education
Steering, Policy Processes, and Outcomes
Edited by Jeroen Huisman

International Organizations and Higher Education Policy
Thinking Globally, Acting Locally?
Edited by Roberta Malee Bassett and Alma Maldonado

Academic and Professional Identities in Higher Education
The Challenges of a Diversifying Workforce
Edited by Celia Whitchurch and George Gordon

Cross-border Partnerships in Higher Education

Strategies and Issues

Edited by
Robin Sakamoto and David W. Chapman

Routledge
Taylor & Francis Group

NEW YORK AND LONDON

First published 2011
by Routledge
711 Third Avenue, New York, NY 10017

Simultaneously published in the UK
by Routledge
2 Park Square, Milton Park, Abingdon, Oxfordshire OX14 4RN

Routledge is an imprint of the Taylor & Francis Group, an informa business

First issued in paperback 2011

Typeset in Minion by Wearset Ltd, Boldon, Tyne and Wear

Library of Congress Cataloging-in-Publication Data
Sakamoto, Robin.
Cross-border partnerships in higher education: strategies and issues/Robin Sakamoto,
David W. Chapman.
p. cm. – (International studies in higher education)
Includes bibliographical references and index.
1. Transnational education. 2. Education and globalization. I. Chapman,
David W. II. Title.

LC1095.S65 2010
378.1'04–dc22

2010002842

ISBN13: 978-0-415-87648-3 (hbk)
ISBN13: 978-0-415-53026-2 (pbk)
ISBN13: 978-0-203-84926-2 (ebk)

CONTENTS

PART III: PARTNERSHIPS BEYOND THE CLASSROOM

Research

Faculty Development

Quality Assurance

PART IV: PARTNERSHIPS IN FIELDS OF PRACTICE

Health Care

Business Administration

Agricultural Extension

PART V: PARTNERSHIPS IN PURSUIT OF BENEFITS BEYOND THE CAMPUS

Sustainable Development

Poverty Reduction

Equity and Access

PART VI: CONCLUSION

ILLUSTRATIONS

BOX

FIGURES

TABLES

SERIES EDITORS' INTRODUCTION

This Series is constructed around the premise that higher education systems are experiencing common pressures for fundamental change, reinforced by differing national and regional circumstances that also impact upon established institutional structures and procedures. There are four major dynamics for change that are of international significance:

1. Mass higher education is a universal phenomenon.
2. National systems find themselves located in an increasingly global marketplace that has particular significance for their more prestigious institutions.
3. Higher education institutions have acquired (or been obliged to acquire) a wider range of obligations, often under pressure from governments prepared to use state power to secure their policy goals.
4. The balance between the public and private financing of higher education has shifted—markedly in some cases—in favor of the latter.

Although higher education systems in all regions and nation states face their own particular pressures for change, these are especially severe in some cases: the collapse of the established economic and political structures of the former Soviet Union along with Central and Eastern Europe, the political revolution in South Africa, the pressures for economic development in India and China, and demographic pressure in Latin America.

Each volume in the Series will examine how systems of higher education are responding to this new and demanding political and socio-economic environment. Although it is easy to overstate the uniqueness of the present situation, it is not an exaggeration to say that higher education is undergoing a fundamental shift in its character, and one that is truly international in scope. We are witnessing a major transition in the relationship of higher education to state and society. What makes the present circumstances particularly interesting is to see how different systems—a product of social, cultural, economic, and political contexts that have interacted and evolved over time—respond in their own peculiar ways to the changing environment. There is no assumption that the pressures for change have set in motion the trend toward a converging model of higher education, but we do believe that in the present circumstances no understanding of "the idea of the university" remains sacrosanct.

Although this is a Series with an international focus it is not expected that each individual volume should cover every national system of higher education. This would be an impossible task. Whilst aiming for a broad range of case studies, with each volume addressing a particular theme, the focus will be upon the most important and interesting examples of responses to the pressures for change. Most of the individual volumes will bring together a range of comparative quantitative and qualitative information, but the primary aim of each volume will be to present differing interpretations of critical developments in key aspects of the experience of higher education. The dominant overarching objective is to explore the conflict of ideas and the political struggles that inevitably surround any significant policy development in higher education.

It can be expected that volume editors and their authors will adopt their own interpretations to explain the emerging patterns of development. There will be conflicting theoretical positions drawn from the multi-disciplinary, and increasingly inter-disciplinary, field of higher education research. Thus we can expect in most volumes to find an inter-marriage of approaches drawn from sociology, economics, history, political science, cultural studies, and the administrative sciences. However, whilst there will be different approaches to understanding the process of change in higher education, each volume editor(s) will impose a framework upon the volume inasmuch as chapter authors will be required to address common issues and concerns.

In this sixth volume in the series, David W. Chapman of the University of Minnesota and Robin Sakamoto of Kyorin University offer a comprehensive overview of issues relating to cross-border partnerships in higher education. While the previous volume in the

Series by Anderson and Steneck focused on international scientific collaborations, this volume examines a much wider range of international partnerships among a much more diverse set of institutions. These cross-border partnerships may involve efforts such as faculty development, technology sharing, joint science and technology initiatives, the delivery of non-academic services, or quality assurance efforts.

Chapman and Sakamoto have enlisted an impressive list of international scholars whose chapters draw attention to this rapidly growing segment of college and university activity that already accounts for a multi-billion dollar industry. Far beyond the traditional partnerships that were typically defined by student and faculty exchanges, the authors in this volume illuminate today's much wider set of purposes, activities, and organizational arrangements that define the current state of cross-border partnerships. Attention is also devoted to understanding the motivations for such partnering. These include income generation, efforts to increase brand recognition, and promoting national strategic interests, among many others. Finally, the authors in this volume examine the contours of the expansion of these partnerships, showing that the landscape defining patterns of traditional partnerships are changing along with their focus and content. Increasingly we are seeing joint programs between partners such as China and Japan, China and Russia, and Hong Kong and Singapore, among others.

As with previous volumes in the Series, the above issues are located in different theoretical contexts. Its editors and authors have attempted to establish a dialogue between theory and praxis in order to further our understanding of the internationalization of higher education and, more especially, the role of international organizations in that process. At its best, this is what the study of higher education attempts to achieve.

David Palfreyman
Director of OxCHEPS, New College, University of Oxford

Ted Tapper
OxCHEPS, New College, University of Oxford and CHEMPAS, University of Southampton

Scott Thomas
Professor of Educational Studies, Claremont Graduate University, California

Part I
Framework and Overview

1

EXPANDING ACROSS BORDERS
The Growth of Cross-border Partnerships in Higher Education

ROBIN SAKAMOTO AND DAVID W. CHAPMAN

The international trade in educational goods and services has grown exponentially over the last decade. This growth has been both driven and made possible by increased global economic integration, new communications technologies, changing demographics, and the high value many students and families place on higher education. One fast-growing form of this international trade has been collaborations among colleges and universities in different countries around both instructional and non-instructional activities. The majority of cross-border collaborations are motivated by economic forces and focus in some fashion on the delivery of instruction. Most take the form of student and faculty exchange programs. Indeed, there are few highly regarded colleges and universities in any country that do not participate in some form of foreign study or faculty exchange. These programs are generally easy to understand since (a) instruction is central to the mission of virtually all colleges and universities, and (b) the financial mechanisms and benefits associated with the cross-border flow of student and faculty are relatively clear. The prevalence of these programs has spawned a considerable literature on instruction-focused cross-border collaborations (Beerkens 2002; Garrett and Verbik 2004; Heffernan and Poole 2004; Samoff and Carroll 2004).

However, higher education institutions increasingly have entered into a broader range of cross-border collaborations involving a wider set of purposes, activities, and mechanisms. In addition to the exchange of students and faculty, this trade sometimes involves the creation of branch campuses, joint research and technology initiatives, collaboration in strengthening institutional management, testing, faculty development efforts, collaboration in quality assurance, and sharing of technology.

The motivation for these new endeavors, while multiple and complex, often includes the hope that they will generate income. In many countries, the growing pressure on institutions to develop new income streams and generate more of their budget is intense (Salmi 2000; Chapman 2007; Asian Development Bank 2008). This increased emphasis on academic entrepreneurship (Slaughter and Leslie 1999) has led institutions to seek new products and services and enter into new partnerships, of which cross-border programs are but one subset (Fairweather 1988; Marginson 1995; Slaughter and Leslie 1999). However, these cross-border collaborations are often more difficult to establish and operate as they venture into less well charted areas.

While a common characteristic of cross-border partnerships is that all parties believe they are gaining something from the transaction, institutional leaders on each side may not be valuing the same aspects. Even in cross-border activities where both partners believe they benefit, collaborators may have different motivations for participation, assess the value of activities in different ways, seek different outcomes, and value the same outcomes differently. Cross-border partnerships often involve educators negotiating agreements, designing programs, and delivering services in settings and work contexts that are not fully familiar to them. As long as all parties benefit, such differences do not necessarily pose a problem. Nonetheless, these programs often encounter perplexing issues. As cross-border partnerships expand in number, size, and complexity, the need to more fully understand the ingredients of success increases.

This book examines the variety of ways that higher education institutions collaborate with counterpart institutions in other countries. Authors examine key issues that have emerged in the newer forms of cross-border instructional programs (such as branch campuses) and in the growing move toward non-instruction-oriented partnerships. These partnerships aim at such things as faculty development, research, joint science and technology initiatives, quality assurance, technology sharing, and delivery of non-academic services.

The volume will provide an overview of the purposes and types of cross-border collaborations, an analysis of the benefits, and an examination of issues arising from these efforts. A cross-cutting goal is to provide a critical look at the models being employed, the challenges encountered, and the unintended consequences of such collaboration, both positive and negative. The book is intended for scholars and students of international higher education, higher education leaders and practitioners who are charting a course toward greater cross-border collaboration, and leaders in international development assistance organizations that are often asked to support such initiatives.

GROWTH IN INSTRUCTION-ORIENTED CROSS-BORDER PROGRAMS

Cross-border education is a multi-billion dollar industry and, in many countries, growing rapidly (Shanahan and McParlane 2005: 220). Education programs, along with related goods and services, are already a significant component of the export market in many countries. The U.S. export of educational services was valued at $14.6 billion in 2006; education exports in the UK are over £9 billion (Jie 2008). Australia earns over A$2 billion annually from cross-border education products and services, larger than its most staple export, wheat (Bennell and Pearce 2002).

Most cross-border programs are focused on the delivery of instructional programs, generally through student and faculty exchange, joint or dual degree programs, and, occasionally, through branch campuses. The provision of these programs was long dominated by Western countries; that pattern is changing. More countries are entering into collaborations with non-Western partners, as evidenced by joint programs between China and Japan (Huang 2010), Hong Kong and Singapore (Lee 2010), and China and Russia (Aroda 2010).

For the most part, these programs are motivated by an interest in revenue generation, at least for those exporting the program. Satisfying the unmet demand and building educational capacity are reported more frequently by the importing side of the partnership. Other frequently mentioned motives include building an international reputation, student and staff advancement, meeting differentiated student needs, innovation through new delivery systems and providers, and enhancing mutual understanding (Organisation for Economic Co-operation and Development 2004a, 2004b; Martin 2007; Jie 2008). While instructional programs account for the greatest share of international collaboration, they are generally well understood. However, as cross-border partnerships take forms that involve greater investment in infrastructure and relocation of home campus personnel (as involved in construction and staffing of branch campuses), the stakes increase. These newer undertakings often involve greater financial and legal liability than typified student or faculty exchanges of the past.

THE EMERGENCE OF NON-INSTRUCTION-ORIENTED CROSS-BORDER PROGRAMS

Higher education institutions are increasingly entering into a broader range of cross-border collaborations involving a wider set of purposes, activities, and mechanisms. The motives for expansion in this domain include promoting brand recognition, increasing market share, and national strategic interests. In research, international collaboration provides a means of tapping multiple sources of funding and spreading financial risk (Godfrey 2008). In some respects, increased collaboration in non-instructional areas follows from the growth of collaborative instructional programs. For example, one reason research is increasingly a borderless activity is that researchers who met in graduate school continue to collaborate when they return to their respective countries.

While recognizing the variety of program designs, non-instructional cross-border programs are often typified by three characteristics. First, while instructional programs are usually tuition based, which provides a fairly stable source of funding, funding for non-instructional programs may come from a wider set of sources and be less predictable. Second, while instructional programs tend to be institutionalized and ongoing, non-instructional programs are more likely to be opportunistic, built around a specific activity. This fluidity can be an asset as it may be easier for such programs to adapt to changing external circumstances.

Finally, while instructional programs tend to originate as institutional initiatives, non-instructional programs are more likely to originate through activities of individual faculty members. Similarly, the life span of non-instructional programs often is linked to the continued interest of its faculty champion. One implication of this constellation of characteristics is the importance of frequent monitoring to ensure continued relevance, financial viability, and faculty support. In short, there is a special need to ensure that these programs continue to serve the best interests of the sponsoring partners.

FUNCTIONAL MODEL FOR THE ANALYSIS OF CROSS-BORDER PARTNERSHIPS

Non-instructional cross-border programs operate within a complex political, financial, and educational context, made more complicated by the likelihood that factors within each of these streams may be viewed differently by the partner institutions. Figure 1.1 provides an overview of a functional model that will be used to organize and analyze the material provided by the chapter authors.

This model posits that the willingness of higher education institutions to participate in cross-border partnerships is influenced by (a) organizational factors, such as anticipated payoffs balanced against their ability to absorb extra demands such programs would generate, (b) financial viability of the collaboration, (c) faculty interest in and

Organizational
- → centrality of content to institutional mission
- → sufficient comparative advantage
- → capacity of institution to absorb extra demands on faculty time and work
- → existing institutional relationships
- → anticipated prestige
- → organization depth of interest (number of faculty who want to participate)

Financial
- → internal financial viability
- → availability of external funding
- → sustainability of funding

Individual
- → faculty incentives for participation
- → international contacts of faculty
- → international experience of faculty
- → individual faculty interest

Context for collaborative venture
- → legal and regulatory context of higher education
- → protection of intellectual property rights
- → political stability

Participation in cross-border partnerships

Figure 1.1 Model of Factors Related to Higher Education Institutions' Participation in Cross-border Partnerships (Source: Authors).

incentives for participating, and (d) the larger political, legal, and regulatory environment in which the collaboration would operate.

Organizational Factors

The model begins with the organizational factors which pertain specifically to the institution or other provider. The cross-border collaboration must be seen as being well aligned with the stated missions of each partner institution. Similarly, there must be a sufficient benefit stream from participation, in terms of revenue, prestige, or valued outcomes. To the extent that faculty members will be absent from regular duties to administer and participate in the partnership, the institution must have the capacity to absorb those demands on faculty time and workload. Finally, the organization must have sufficient depth of interest as reflected in the number of faculty who want to participate.

Financial Factors

For all the other benefits that advocates can highlight, cross-border programs need to be financially viable. The institutional funding that supports these programs, while often coming from a variety of sources, must be viable, available, and sustainable (at least for the anticipated life span of the partnership).

Individual Factors

Often, early interest in non-instructional cross-border partnership emerges as an outgrowth of individual interest of faculty or staff, rather than as an organizational initiative. Unlike an instructional program in which it may not matter who directly teaches the course, cross-border collaborations are person-dependent and are moved or driven by individual researchers. Thus factors that promote cross-border partnerships at the individual level are that the faculty incentives for participation are satisfactory and that the faculty member has sufficient international contacts to begin the project. The faculty member should also have a degree of international experience and sufficient interest to keep the program operating.

Context Factors

Finally, sufficient attention to the context for the partnership venture must be addressed. Of particular importance are differences in the legal and regulatory contexts across partner countries. Differing regulations concerning academic freedom, protection for intellectual property rights, ethical treatment of human subjects, financial accounting rules, and ownership of jointly developed materials and products can lead to disagreements that threaten the success of otherwise successful partnerships. It is essential, then, that all partners be attentive to how different context factors faced by each participating institution shapes the nature of the collaboration. In some collaborative programs, context considerations also must include attention to the political stability of the country or region in which the program is operating. Partnerships in politically less stable settings require institutions to have clear exit strategies.

While individual chapter authors will draw on the conceptual and policy frameworks that underlay the particular cross-border partnerships on which they each focus, the functional model represented in Figure 1.1 provides the framework that will be used by the editors in looking across chapters.

OVERVIEW OF THE BOOK

This volume is organized into six parts. Part I examines the forms, dimensions, and recent growth of cross-border partnerships. It provides a framework for understanding the key terminology and issues raised in the remainder of the volume. As cross-border partnerships come to include a diversity of people, programs, providers, and services, it is necessary to understand the different perspectives and rationales that undergird these programs. Jane Knight addresses this in Chapter 2. She provides a historical overview of cross-border partnerships in higher education, distinguishes among the types of programs that have emerged, and examines the new challenges that professionals face as higher education is increasingly viewed as a tradable commodity in the international marketplace.

Part II examines the opportunities and issues that have emerged as colleges and universities have tried to move campuses, rather than students, across borders. Two chapters examine how differences in the design of these branch campuses reflect underlying differences in the vision, purpose, and operating procedures that can have important consequences for the outcomes of these programs. Patricia W. Croom, in Chapter 3, examines the growth of cross-border branch campuses in Japan and the United Arab Emirates. Her analysis of Education City in Qatar and Dubai International Academic City illustrate how initial design and implementation decisions during the start-up of a cross-border collaboration can have long-term consequences on the subsequent operation and eventual success of the effort. Among other things, she highlights the importance of finding the right local partner, regardless of the locale in which the collaboration is situated. In Chapter 4, Jason E. Lane draws on the experience of two Australian–Malaysian collaborations to explore the challenges universities face when they operate under more than one governmental jurisdiction, each with different laws, regulations, and operating procedures. He draws practical implications for university officials contemplating a joint venture that spans divergent legal systems.

Part III highlights non-instructional partnerships, in which the central activities of the collaboration extend beyond teaching or course credit generation. Chapters in this part provide examples of cross-border partnerships aimed at fostering scientific research, promoting faculty development, and advancing quality assurance and accreditation. Stéphan Vincent-Lancrin, in Chapter 5, provides an overview of partnerships aimed at fostering academic research. He argues that cross-border collaboration in research is a good strategy for receiving countries to develop capacity in domestic research and for sending countries to improve the quality of their research while also establishing relationships with the pool of new scientists in the hope this will give them an advantage in the global competition for talent. However, as Vincent-Lancrin points out, countries may encounter tension between seeking the short-term advantages of collaboration while better positioning themselves for longer-term goals and competition.

In Chapter 6, Ann E. Austin and Cheryl Foxcroft trace the development of a multi-year collaboration between Nelson Mandela Metropolitan University in South Africa and Michigan State University in the United States aimed at faculty development. They draw on negotiated order theory (Gray 1989) to analyze the characteristics of the collaboration that have been most essential in ensuring sustainability of both funding and faculty commitment over many years. Thuwayba Al-Barwani, Hana Ameen, and David W. Chapman, in Chapter 7, turn to the use of international partnerships in the service of quality assurance. On a per capita basis, Oman has had one of the fastest growing higher education systems in the world over the last 20 years. To ensure that new colleges and universities met international quality standards in the face of such rapid system expansion, the government "outsourced" some responsibilities for accreditation. This chapter traces how a well-conceived and largely successful effort to assure quality of national higher education institutions through a system of international affiliations ultimately led to unanticipated consequences that slowed the government's eventual effort to introduce its own national accreditation system.

Part IV shifts the focus to how cross-border partnerships have been used to strengthen selected fields of practice. Chapters examine partnerships in health care, public administration, and agricultural extension. In Chapter 8, Jane C. Shivan and Martha N. Hill, both of Johns Hopkins University, draw on a theory of mutuality based on Galtung (1975), Hayhoe (1989) and Xu, Xu, Sun, and Zhang (2001) as a framework for examining the long-term partnership in nursing education between Johns Hopkins University School of Nursing and Peking Union Medical College School of Nursing in Beijing. They provide an insightful analysis of the challenges of working across cultural differences to develop a sustainable partnership.

Shifting to collaborations in health, Peter Fong and Gerard Postiglione focus on efforts of universities in Hong Kong to establish Hong Kong as an international center for higher education exchange. They argue the value of these cross-border partnerships and illustrate their argument by drawing on the experience of three cross-border programs in business and public administration. Their analysis highlights the importance of common goals, shared power among partners, the need for a sound business plan, and the importance of program quality in the ability of programs to charge sufficient tuition to cover costs. The authors argue further that, even when those conditions are met, personal relationships are important in program success.

Gauri Maharjan and Robin Sakamoto, in Chapter 10, describe how a university in Japan is seeking to work with local farmers in Nepal to support agriculture at the community level. In particular, they describe the use of a web-based system for providing field diagnosis of plant diseases. Farmers in Nepal can take pictures of diseased plants, send them directly to agricultural experts at the Japanese university, and receive a diagnosis by return email. This system can provide diagnostic information far faster than previous methods for seeking expert advice. While not strictly a partnership of universities across borders, this chapter is included because it illustrates how universities are using technology in creative ways to link directly with communities in addressing high-value issues in national development.

Part V reaches beyond classrooms and beyond fields of practice to examine ways in which university partnerships contribute to even wider issues of national development. In Chapter 11, Ko Nomura, Yoshihiro Natori, and Osamu Abe introduce international multi-university networks as a more complicated form of cross-border partnership. They introduce the activities of a network in the Asia-Pacific region as an example of how universities can support larger national and international development goals, in this case, by promoting an ecological approach to sustainable development. The uniqueness of this particular network is that funding for its activities is provided by an agency that is not a higher education institution, which in turn brings new challenges to the network.

Both Chapters 12 and 13 explore how international development organizations have come to view cross-border partnerships in higher education as a mechanism for promoting national economic development and, to that end, the growing interest of these organizations in supporting these collaborations. Christopher S. Collins, in Chapter 12, draws on examples from Thailand and Uganda to highlight the role of the World Bank in funding cross-border initiatives. Drawing from these examples, Collins argues that lending and collaboration to build countries' human capacity for research and knowledge production in science and technology have great potential for solving poverty-related problems. He views the move of the World Bank to expand their lending for higher education as a positive step toward supporting this aspect of development. At the same time, he cautions that World Bank lending often introduces an additional voice about how such collaborations should be structured and operate. Further, while cross-border collaboration through World Bank lending can help to jump-start key development processes, countries have to weigh those gains against the consequences of the increased national debt incurred.

Jouko Sarvi, in Chapter 13, turns to the role of a regional development organization, the Asian Development Bank, in encouraging and financially supporting cross-border partnerships in higher education. He argues that the economic return to individuals (as well as countries) from higher education is substantial. Given the pressures of globalization, particularly as expressed in increased economic integration of countries and communication technologies that make geographic borders less relevant, cross-border collaboration is essential. Such collaboration can contribute to more balanced development across countries and more equitable opportunity for citizens within countries. Higher education can lead the way and organizations such as the Asian Development Bank can assist through the financial support and technical assistance it provides for international and regional cooperation.

Finally, in Part VI, Chapter 14, David W. Chapman and Robin Sakamoto offer a set of cross-cutting observations based on the issues and insights offered in the preceding chapters. Drawing on the framework introduced in Chapter 1, they suggest directions for the continued development of cross-border collaboration in higher education.

The overall message of this volume is that: (a) while cross-border partnerships in higher education are expanding rapidly, they are also taking on new forms which, in turn, raise new issues in higher education organization, management, and finance. (b) The rate of expansion and wider experimentation with a range of organizational forms of cross-border cooperation will continue, but this proliferation will pose challenges for colleges and universities trying to chart a sensible course into this terrain. (c) The dynamics that underlie motives, relationships, and operational strategies in these partnerships are different and, in many respects, less well understood by higher education leaders than those associated with more narrowly focused instructional collaborations. (d) Thoughtful analysis of institutional experiences to date provides a useful tool for those seeking to enter into new forms of cross-border partnership.

REFERENCES

Aroda, A. (2010). Borders bridging degrees: Harbin and Vladivostok's dual-degree programs. In D.W. Chapman, W.K. Cummings, & G.A. Postiglione (Eds.), *Crossing borders in East Asian higher education* (pp. 231–261). Hong Kong: Comparative Education Research Centre and New York: Springer Publishing.

Asian Development Bank (2008, June). *Education and skills: Strategies for accelerated development in Asia and the Pacific.* Manila, Philippines: Asian Development Bank.

Beerkens, E. (2002). International inter-organizational arrangements in higher education: Towards a typology. *Tertiary Education and Management, 8*(4), 297–314.

Bennell, P., & Pearce, T. (2002). The internationalization of higher education: Exporting education to developing and transitional economies. *International Journal of Educational Development, 23*(2), 215–232.

Chapman, D.W. (2007). Higher Education, Part 3. In V. Ordonez, R. Johanson, & D.W. Chapman (Eds.), *Investing in education in the Asia-Pacific region in the future: A strategic education sector study.* Manila, Philippines: Asian Development Bank.

Fairweather, J. (1988). *Entrepreneurship and higher education.* Washington, DC: Association for the Study of Higher Education.

Galtung, J. (1975). Is peaceful research possible? On the methodology of peace research. In J. Galtung (Ed.), *Peace: Research, education, action* (pp. 273–274). Copenhagen, Denmark: Christian Ejlers.

Garrett, R., & Verbik, L. (2004). Transnational higher education: Major markets and emerging trends. In Observatory on Borderless Higher

Education, *Mapping borderless higher education: Policy, markets and competition*. London: Association of Commonwealth Universities.

Godfrey, J. (2008, October). Oh, brave world: Finding the right assumptions. Paper presented at the Conference on Challenges and Tensions in International Research Collaborations, University of Minnesota, Minneapolis.

Gray, B. (1989). *Collaborating: Finding common ground for multiparty problems*. San Francisco: Jossey-Bass.

Hayhoe, R. (1989). *China's universities and the open door*. Armonk, NY: M.E. Sharpe.

Heffernan, T., & Poole, D. (2004). "Catch me I'm falling": Key factors in the deterioration of offshore education partnerships. *Journal of Higher Education Policy and Management, 26*(1), 75–90.

Huang, F. (2010). Transnational higher education in Japan and China. In D.W. Chapman, W.K. Cummings, & G.A. Postiglione (Eds.), *Crossing borders in East Asian higher education* (pp. 265–282). Hong Kong: Comparative Education Research Centre and New York: Springer Publishing.

Jie, Y. (2008). Cross-border higher education: An analysis of international inter-organizational collaboration. Unpublished manuscript, Minneapolis: University of Minnesota.

Lee, M. (2010). Internationalizing Universities: Comparing China's Hong Kong and Singapore (1996–2010). In D.W. Chapman, W.K. Cummings, & G.A. Postiglione (Eds.), *Crossing borders in East Asian higher education* (pp. 283–314). Hong Kong: Comparative Education Research Centre and New York: Springer Publishing.

Marginson, S. (1995). Markets in higher education: Australia. In J. Smyth (Ed.), *Academic work: The changing labor process in higher education* (pp. 17–39). Buckingham, UK: Society for Research into Higher Education and Open University Press.

Martin, M. (2007). The cross-border challenge of higher education: Comparing experiences. In M. Martin (Ed.), *Cross-border higher education: Regulation, quality assurance and impact* (Vol. 1, pp. 11–57). Paris: International Institute for Educational Planning.

Organisation for Economic Co-operation and Development (2004a). *Internationalization and trade of higher education—Challenges and opportunities*. Paris: Organization for Economic and Community Development.

—— (2004b). *Quality and recognition in higher education: The cross-border challenge*. Paris: Organization for Economic and Community Development.

Salmi, J. (2000). *Peril and promise: Higher education in developing countries: Summary of findings by the Task Force on Higher Education and Society*. Washington, DC: World Bank.

Samoff, J., & Carroll, B. (2004). The promise of partnership and continuities of dependence. *African Studies Association, 47*(1), 67–199.

Shanahan, P., & McParlane, J. (2005). Serendipity or strategy? An investigation into entrepreneurial transnational higher education and risk management. *On The Horizon—The Strategic Planning Resource for Education Professionals, 13*(4), 220–228.

Slaughter, S., & Leslie, L.L. (1999). *Academic capitalism: Politics, policies, and the entrepreneurial university.* Baltimore: Johns Hopkins University Press.

Xu, Z., Xu, Y., Sun, J., & Zhang, J. (2001). Globalization of tertiary nursing education in post-Mao China: A preliminary qualitative assessment. *Nursing and Health Sciences, 3*(4), 179–187.

2

HIGHER EDUCATION CROSSING BORDERS
A Framework and Overview of New Developments and Issues

JANE KNIGHT

There is no question that higher education is undergoing fundamental changes and that internationalization, particularly cross-border education, is one of the key shapers of this transformation. Over the last decade, cross-border education has significantly grown in scope, scale, and impact. Traditional universities, new types of commercial providers, government higher education agencies, and economic development boards are engaged in developing innovative cross-border initiatives in all regions of the world. There has been an exponential increase in the number and types of bilateral and multilateral academic partnerships facilitating international research work, curriculum design, faculty and student exchanges, and joint/double degree programs. New branch campuses, franchise and twinning arrangements, and distance education programs are being established. The most recent trend is the establishment of cross-border education hubs, academic cities, and education free zones in an effort to position a country as a regional center of excellence in education and a major player in the knowledge economy. These new developments are dramatic testimony to the fact that there is a new world of international academic mobility emerging.

The purpose of this chapter is to provide an analytical framework to understand these new developments, particularly the different types, modes, rationales, and providers of cross-border education, and to identify the emerging issues related to this unprecedented growth.

While students, professors, and researchers have been moving internationally for years, if not centuries, it has only been in the last two decades that there has been this renaissance in academic program and provider mobility. Moreover, it is only 10 years since education has been included in international trade agreements such as the General Agreement on Trade in Services (GATS). These fundamental changes warrant closer scrutiny.

The first section of the chapter traces the evolution of international education over the past five decades by analyzing the changes in language and key concepts to describe the international dimension of higher education. This provides the necessary context to look at cross-border education and the related terms of transnational, borderless, and trade in education services. In the following section, an analytical framework, which emphasizes the movement of academic people, programs, providers, projects, and policies across borders, is discussed. Of critical importance is the recognition that academic mobility happens through development cooperation projects, through educational exchanges and partnerships, and through commercial trade. Given the diversity of entities providing education, plus the various modes of program and provider mobility, three typologies are proposed to capture and clarify the major characteristics of each group. Building on this analysis, the most recent trends are introduced and labeled second generation cross-border education strategies. These include education hubs, academic cities, and gateways. The motivations, expectations, and appeal of cross-border education vary among different stakeholders (students, institutions, governments), and between sending and receiving countries. Therefore an in-depth look at the rationales driving cross-border education is provided to get a 360 degree view of the issues. Finally, the last section identifies some of the emerging issues and challenges such as equity of student access, quality assurance, accreditation, recognition of qualifications, GATS, and the brain train.

INCREASED DEMAND FOR HIGHER EDUCATION—THE CROSS-BORDER RESPONSE

In most countries, especially those in transition, the demand for postsecondary education including professionally related courses is increasing. This is due to changing demographics, more secondary school graduates, the movement to lifelong learning, and the growth of the knowledge economy. While demand is growing, the capacity of the public sector to satisfy this need is being challenged. Alternative ways to provide education are being developed. These include growth in private education, new developments in cross-border education, and a greater emphasis on distance education. *The Global Student Mobility 2025 Report* (Bohm, Davis, Meares, & Pearce 2002) predicts that the demand for international education will increase from 1.8 million international students in 2000 to 7.2 million international students in 2025. National and regional government agencies are investing in greater academic collaboration, exchange, and commercial trade (Currie 2005). All in all, there is a new era of cross-border education evolving, in reaction to and promotion of increased economic, cultural, and political globalization.

The mushrooming interest in the international dimension of higher education has spawned an increase in the number of terms used to describe these new developments. The term internationalization has only been used in the higher education system since the early 1980s but the discourse on the meaning and impact of internationalization continues (Knight 2008a; Wit 2002). Prior to this time, international education and international cooperation were the favored terms and still are in some countries. In the 1990s the discussion centered on differentiating the term international education from comparative education, global education, and multi-cultural education. Today, the relationship between cross-border, transnational, borderless, and international education is causing confusion and is the subject of much debate. Table 2.1 provides a longitudinal view of the evolution of terms related to the international dimension of higher education and illustrates that cross-border education and related terms have only emerged in the last 10 to 15 years.

International cooperation, international relations, and international education were the most common terms used 40 years ago. These concepts were usually defined in terms of activities such as development projects, foreign students, faculty exchange, and international academic/cultural agreements. About 25 years ago, the term internationalization emerged. It too was defined in terms of activities such as study abroad, language studies, institutional agreements, and area studies. As internationalization slides into the first part of the twenty-first century the emerging elements show an increasing orientation to students, research, programs, and providers moving across borders with more emphasis on commercial and market-driven activities than development projects. At the same time, there is substantial growth of multilateral academic partnerships focused on faculty mobility, benchmarking, and research networks, all of which are based on mutual benefits and collaboration. However, the current influence of the knowledge

Table 2.1 Evolution of International Education Terminology

New Terms (Last 15 Years)	Existing Terms (Last 25 Years)	Traditional Terms (Last 40 Years)
Generic Terms		
• Cross-border education	• Internationalization	• International education
• Education hubs	• Multi-cultural education	• International development cooperation
• Academic cities	• Inter-cultural education	
• Transnational education	• Global education	• Comparative education
• Virtual education	• Distance education	• Correspondence education
• Borderless education	• Offshore or overseas education	
• Internationalization "abroad"		
• Internationalization "at home"		
• Globalization		
Specific Elements		
• Education providers	• International students	• Foreign students
• Corporate universities	• Study abroad	• Student exchange
• Liberalization of educational services	• Institution agreements	• Development projects
• Networks	• Partnership projects	• Cultural agreements
• Virtual universities	• Area studies	• Language study
• Branch campus	• Double/joint degrees	
• Twinning and franchise programs	• Faculty exchanges	

Source: Adapted from Knight 2006c.

economy and the preoccupation with university rankings also means increased competition among universities that in turn is warping the selection of international academic partners.

Cross-border education refers to the "movement of people, knowledge, programs, providers, policies, ideas, curricula, projects, research and services across national or regional jurisdictional borders" (Knight 2005a). As cross-border education is often used interchangeably with transnational, borderless, and offshore education, it is interesting to juxtapose the concepts of borderless education and cross-border education. The former term acknowledges the disappearance of all types of borders—time, disciplinary, geographic—while the latter term actually emphasizes the existence of borders, especially geographic and jurisdictional. Both approaches reflect the reality of today. In this period of greater distance and e-learning education, geographic borders seem to be of little consequence. Yet, on the other hand, we can detect a growing importance of borders when the focus turns to regulatory responsibility, especially related to quality assurance, funding, and accreditation (Verbik & Jokivirta 2005).

Cross-border education is the preferred term for this chapter and given its complexity, a conceptual framework is proposed to help understand the major elements, modes of delivery, stakeholders, rationales, and implications for the larger picture of higher education crossing borders.

The GATS is a worldwide agreement managed by the World Trade Organization to further liberalize trade in services. Education is categorized as a service, in the same way that transportation, communication, health, and culture sectors are services. The GATS has identified four modes of trade or supply of services (Knight 2006b).

Mode One

Cross-border supply focuses on the service crossing the border, which does not require the consumer to physically move. Examples in higher education include distance education and e-learning.

Mode Two

Consumption Abroad refers to the consumer moving to the country of the supplier which in education means students taking all or part of their education in another country.

Mode Three

Commercial Presence involves a service provider establishing a commercial facility in another country to provide a service. Examples in higher education include branch campuses or franchising arrangements.

Mode Four

Presence of Natural Persons means persons traveling to another country on a temporary basis to provide a service. In the education sector, this would include professors or researchers.

In short, Mode One deals with the service moving, Mode Two deals with the consumer moving, Mode Three deals with the provider and investment moving, and Mode Four deals with human capital moving. There is no criticism implied regarding the central features of the four modes for trade services. On the contrary, it is quite an accomplishment to develop a generic framework to apply to the supply of commercial services for the 12 major service sectors and 160 subsectors included in GATS. The concern about these four trade modes focuses on the fact that they are now beginning to be seen as the four primary elements and methods of cross-border education and, as such, they do not capture or reflect the fullness of cross-border education activity—development cooperation, academic partnerships, as well as commercial trade. Using a trade framework to categorize activity is too limited and an education framework is needed.

ELEMENTS OF A CROSS-BORDER EDUCATION FRAMEWORK

One of the first questions to ask is: What are the defining factors for a conceptual framework of cross-border education? Many come to mind—what elements of education move, how does the movement occur, what are the key rationales, where is it happening, who is funding it, who is awarding the qualification, who is regulating it? Given the changing nature of the rationales driving cross-border education, the worldwide scope of delivery, and the diverse modes of provision, the "why, how, and where" are eliminated as defining factors. Instead, emphasis is placed on "what" moves across borders. Four different categories are suggested: people, programs, providers, and projects/service/new knowledge (Knight 2005b).

People

The first category covers the movement of people whether they are students or professors/scholars/experts. Students are mobile in a number of ways. They can take whole degrees in another country, participate in a study abroad exchange program, undertake field research work or an internship, register for a semester/year abroad program, etc. The funding for such education can be through exchange agreements, scholarships from public or private sources, and self-funding. Professors/scholars and experts can be involved in teaching and research activities, technical assistance and consulting assignments, sabbaticals, seminars, and other professional activities. These types of initiatives can be self or institution funded, part of exchange agreements, involve contracts and fee for service, or supported by public and private funding.

Programs

The program, not the student, moves in this category. The delivery of the program is often done through a partnership arrangement between international/foreign and domestic providers or can be an independent initiative by a foreign provider. The programs can be delivered by distance, face-to-face, or mixed mode. Franchising, double and joint degrees, twinning, and new forms of articulation and validation arrangements are most common. In some cases, the program and qualification awarded is provided by the source country institution/provider, but the teaching and support is done in part or totally by a local institution/provider. In other cases, the foreign provider takes complete responsibility for the delivery of the academic program but may have a local business partner investing in the operation. Distance delivery of a program involves yet another set of circumstances.

Providers

The key factor in this category is that the institution/provider moves to have physical or virtual presence in the receiving/host country. It is not the student who moves, the provider moves to serve the student. The movement of a provider can involve a more substantial range of programs and academic/administrative support services moving. A provider can establish a satellite campus or establish a full institution. In other scenarios the provider moves by purchasing/merging with a local institution. Virtual universities are yet another example of the provider moving across borders through distance delivery. The providers can include private and public, for-profit or non-profit, educational institutions, organizations, and companies. Both recognized bona fide institutions/providers and non-recognized rogue providers are included in this category.

Projects/Services/New Knowledge

There is a wide range of education related projects and services which need to be considered when analyzing cross-border education. Such activities could include joint curriculum development, research, bench marking, technical assistance, e-learning platforms, professional development, and other capacity-building initiatives especially in the information technology area. The production, transfer, and exchange of knowledge are critical components of the fourth category and is being done through innovative new research partnerships involving universities, governmental research centers, and private companies.

A second set of key factors relate to the fact that cross-border education occurs under different kinds of arrangements: (1) development cooperation/aid education projects, (2) academic collaboration and exchange, and (3) commercial trade initiatives. In contrast, the GATS framework only covers commercial trade types of activities.

Figure 2.1 presents the framework and illustrates two significant trends.

The first trend is the vertical shift downwards from student mobility to program, provider, and service mobility. It is important to note that the number of students seeking education in foreign countries is still increasing; but more emphasis is currently being placed on delivering foreign academic courses and programs to students in their home country. The second shift is from left to right signifying substantial

Category	Forms and conditions of mobility		
	Development cooperation ➔	Educational linkages ➔	Commercial trade ➔
People Students Professors/scholars Researchers/ Experts/consultants ↓	Semester/year abroad Full degrees Field/research work Internships Sabbaticals Consulting		
Programs Course, program, sub-degree, degree, postgraduate ↓	Twinning Franchised Articulated/validated Joint/double award Online/distance		
Providers Institutions Organizations Companies ↓	Branch campus Virtual university Merger/acquisition Independent institutions		
Projects Academic projects Services ↓	Research Curriculum Capacity building Educational services		

Figure 2.1 Framework for Cross-border Education (Source: Adapted from Knight 2008a).

change in orientation from development cooperation to competitive commerce, or, in other words, from aid to trade.

A DIVERSITY OF PROVIDERS AND ACTORS

The increase in worldwide demand for higher education has resulted in a diversity of providers delivering education across borders. The providers are classified into two categories: (1) the traditional higher education institutions who are normally oriented to teaching, research, and service/commitment to society, and (2) the "new or alternative providers" who primarily focus on teaching and the delivery of education services.

Traditional Higher Education Institutions

These include public non-profit, private non-profit, and private for-profit institutions. Many countries have a mixed system of publicly and privately funded higher education institutions. There is a definite blurring of the boundary between public and private institutions as public universities are now finding it necessary to seek private financing and are charging a tuition or service fee. On the other hand, in many countries private institutions are eligible for public funds and engage in social non-profit activities.

An important factor is whether the higher education institution is part of a home national education system and recognized by a national bona fide licensing/accrediting body. In cross-border education recognition/registration is critical to ensuring the legitimacy of the institution and the qualifications provided. The majority of traditional universities are bona fide institutions that comply with domestic and foreign regulations (where they exist). But, there is also an increase in rogue or low-quality providers who are not recognized by bona fide accreditation/licensing bodies in either the sending or receiving countries. "Rogue providers" are often accredited by self-accrediting groups or by agencies that sell accreditation (accreditation mills). In addition, there is a worrisome increase in the number of "degree mills" operating around the world (Garrett 2005). These are often no more than web-based companies that are selling certificates based on "life experiences" and are not delivering any education programs.

New or Alternative Providers

These are diverse in nature, but are typically described as a company or organization that provides education programs and/or services for profit purposes. They are more oriented to delivering education and training programs than undertaking research and scholarly activities. The new providers include publicly traded companies such as Apollo (USA), Informatics (Singapore), and Aptech (India), corporate universities such as those run by Motorola and Toyota, and networks of universities, professional associations, and organizations. These new types of cross-border providers can be bricks and mortar institutions or virtual universities and can complement, compete, collaborate, or simply co-exist with domestic higher education providers (and other foreign providers).

TYPOLOGY OF PROGRAM MOBILITY

Cross-border mobility of *programs* can be described as

> the movement of individual education/training courses and programs across national borders through face to face, distance or a combination of these modes. Credits towards a qualification can be awarded by the sending foreign country provider or by an affiliated domestic partner or jointly.

Franchising, twinning, double/joint degrees, and various articulation models are the more popular methods of cross-border program mobility (Knight 2005b). A short description of each follows.

Franchise

An arrangement whereby a provider in the source Country A authorizes a provider in Country B to deliver their course/program/service in Country B or other countries. The qualification is awarded by provider in Country A. Arrangements for teaching, management, assessment, profit sharing, awarding of credit/qualification, etc., are customized for each franchise arrangement and must comply with national regulations (if they exist) in Country B.

Twinning

A situation where a provider in source country A collaborates with a provider located in Country B to develop an articulation system that allows students to take course credits in Country B and/or source Country A. Only one qualification is awarded by provider in source

Country A. Arrangements for twinning programs and awarding of degree usually comply with national regulations of the provider in the source Country A.

Double/Joint Degree

An arrangement where providers in different countries collaborate to offer a program for which a student receives a qualification from each provider, or a joint award from the collaborating partners. Arrangements for program provision and criteria for awarding the qualifications are customized for each collaborative initiative in accordance with national regulations in each country.

Articulation

Various types of articulation arrangements between providers situated in different countries permit students to gain credit for courses/programs offered by all of the collaborating providers. This allows students to gain credit for work done with a provider other than the provider awarding the qualification.

Validation

Validation arrangements between providers in different countries allow Provider B in the receiving country to award the qualification of Provider A in the source country. In some cases, the source country provider may not offer these courses or awards themselves, which may raise questions about quality.

Virtual/Distance

Arrangements where providers deliver courses/program to students in different countries through distance and online modes. These arrangements may include some face-to-face support for students through domestic study or support centers.

It is clear that a critical factor in program mobility is "who" awards the course credits or ultimate credential for the program. As the movement of programs proliferates, there will undoubtedly be further changes to national, regional, and even international regulatory frameworks. The question of "who grants the credits/awards" will be augmented by "who recognizes the provider" and whether or not the program has been "accredited or quality assured" by a bona fide body.

Of central importance is whether the qualification is recognized for employment or further study in the receiving country and in other countries as well. The perceived legitimacy and recognition of the qualification at home and abroad, are fundamental issues yet to be resolved.

Given that several modes for program mobility involve partnerships, there are questions about who owns the intellectual property rights to course design and materials. What are the legal roles and responsibilities of the participating partners in terms of academic, staffing, recruitment, evaluation, financial, and administrative matters? While the movement of programs across borders has been taking place for years, it is clear that the new types of providers, partnerships, awards, and delivery modes are challenging national and international policies.

Typology of Institution/Provider Mobility

Cross-border mobility of *providers* can be described as "the physical or virtual movement of an education provider (institution, organization, company) across a national border to establish a presence in order to offer education/training programs and/or services to students and other clients." The difference between program and provider mobility is one of scope and scale in terms of programs/services offered and the local presence (and investment) by the foreign provider. A distinguishing feature between program and provider mobility is that with provider mobility the learner is not necessarily located in a different country than the awarding institution, which is usually the case in program mobility. Credits and qualifications are awarded by the foreign provider (through foreign, local, or self-accreditation methods) or by an affiliated domestic partner (Knight 2005b). Different forms of cross-border provider mobility are as follows.

Branch Campus

Provider in Country A establishes a satellite campus in Country B to deliver courses and programs to students in Country B (may also include Country A students taking a semester/courses abroad). The qualification awarded is from provider in Country A.

Independent Institution

Foreign Provider A (a traditional university, a commercial company, or alliance/network) establishes in Country B a stand-alone higher education institution (HEI) to offer courses/programs and awards. There is usually no "home" institution in Country A.

Acquisition/Merger

Foreign Provider A purchases a part of or 100% of local HEI in Country B.

Study Center/Teaching Site

Foreign Provider A establishes study centers in Country B to support students taking their courses/programs. Study centers can be independent or in collaboration with local providers in Country B.

Affiliation/Networks

Different types of "public and private," "traditional and new," "local and foreign" providers collaborate through innovative types of partnerships to establish networks/institutions to deliver courses and programs in local and foreign countries through distance or face-to-face modes.

Virtual University

Provider that delivers credit courses and degree programs to students in different countries through distance education using predominantly the Internet technology mode, generally without face-to-face support services for students.

The virtual and physical movement of providers to other countries raises many of the same registration, quality assurance, and recognition issues that program mobility does, but there are additional factors to consider if a network or local/foreign partnerships are involved. Setting up a physical presence requires attention being paid to national regulations regarding status of the entity, total or joint ownership with local bodies, tax laws, for-profit or non-profit status, repatriation of earned income, boards of directors, staffing, granting of qualifications, selection of academic programs and courses, etc. For some countries, it means that strict regulations are being developed to closely monitor, and in some cases restrict, new providers coming into the country. In other instances, incentives are being offered to attract high-quality institutions/providers to set up a teaching site or full campus. This is especially true where "knowledge parks," "technology zones," or "education cities" are being developed to attract foreign companies and education/training providers.

TYPOLOGY OF PROJECTS AND SERVICES MOBILITY

The extreme diversity of international projects and services and the accelerated pace of change merits careful monitoring and analysis, but this category is not conducive yet to a rigorous typology or framework. Most noteworthy is the rapid increase in the number and type of activities related to the production, transfer, and application of new knowledge. Higher education's role in the knowledge enterprise brings unprecedented opportunities and innovative types of international and commercial partnerships between universities and private companies. The trend to move from bilateral academic collaboration to competitive knowledge networks reflects the shift toward commercialization and competitiveness in international higher education. This is not to neglect the existence of academic exchanges, linkages, and partnerships, but the quest for new sources of funding and greater international prestige is increasingly dominant in the proliferation of cross-border projects and services. For instance, many of the new international networks of research universities are based on the premise of increased collaboration to gain individual competitive advantage.

SECOND-GENERATION CROSS-BORDER ACTIVITIES

These typologies demonstrate that it is no longer students and scholars who move across borders, so do programs, providers, and services. But, countries propelled by the need to establish a firm footing in the knowledge economy, are moving to second-generation cross-border education strategies such as regional education hubs, economic free zones, education cities, knowledge villages, gateways, and hot spots. While these initiatives include familiar strategies such as branch campuses, they are of another magnitude as they try to co-locate foreign universities with private companies, research and development enterprises, and science and technology parks to collectively support and develop new knowledge industries. Universities play a pivotal role in the new knowledge enterprise through developing a skilled workforce by attracting and educating local and regional students and through research and innovation.

The development of "international education cities" and "regional education hubs" are new territory for the higher education sector. That being said, it is important to recognize that it is not necessarily the higher education sector that is sponsoring or guiding these new education initiatives. In many cases, branch campuses of foreign institutions are seen as tenants. Economic development boards, tourism authorities, science and technology parks, and multinational investment companies are capitalizing on higher education institutions/providers as key players in the preparation of future knowledge workers and the production of new knowledge in partnership with the private sector. Countries such as the United Arab Emirates, Singapore, Korea, Bahrain, Mexico, Botswana, Hong Kong, Malaysia, and Japan are investing in and actively promoting themselves as regional education hubs, cities, or gateways. The success and sustainability of these new developments is yet to be determined. No matter how distasteful academics may find the treatment of education as a commodity, the development of these hubs and education cities are positive proof of education being seen as a commodity to be acquired and used to gain a competitive advantage in the knowledge economy. That being said, it is mandatory that the quality of the knowledge product or service is maintained and the integrity of an earned qualification assured.

RATIONALES AND IMPACT OF CROSS-BORDER PROVISION

An examination of the driving motivations and expected outcomes related to the increase in cross-border education requires a 360 degree view of the issues. This involves giving serious consideration to the diverse and often contradictory perspectives and expectations that different groups of stakeholders may have. This is not a linear task of analysis as the viewpoints differ depending on whether you are a student, a foreign provider, a local HEI, a governmental body and whether you are in the country that is sending or receiving the programs and services. In short, the analysis of rationales and impacts is rather complex.

RATIONALES AT THE NATIONAL/COUNTRY LEVEL

In the past several years, much has been written about the changes in rationales for internationalization in general and cross-border education in particular (Altbach & Knight 2007; Vincent-Lancrin 2005). Four rationales for cross-border education proposed by the Center for Education Research and Innovation at the Organisation for Economic Co-operation and Development (OECD) include mutual understanding, skilled immigration, revenue generation, and capacity building (OECD 2004a). Another approach broadens these rationales to be more inclusive of both sending and receiving countries and to address the political and prestige-oriented motivations related to the cross-border education (Knight 2007).

Human Resources Development: Brain Power

The knowledge economy, demographic shifts, mobility of the labor force, and increased trade in services are factors which are driving nations to place more importance on developing human capital and recruiting and training brain power through cross-border education. Understanding the impact of "brain drain," "brain gain," and the phenomenon of "brain train" (students moving to study and work in several countries to gain more international experience), are critical to building benefits and avoiding risks of increased student mobility. This phenomenon affects small and large, developed and developing countries in different ways. The term "brain chain" may be more appropriate as it is usually the larger and more developed countries that benefit most from brain gain and it is the smaller less developed nations that are at the bottom of the brain chain and experience more brain drain. For some countries, there are increased risks of brain drain when international student recruitment policies are linked to aggressive immigration policies. Therefore, smaller countries which attract cross-border programs and providers often see the imported programs as effective means to lessen the chances of their tertiary education graduates staying abroad after they have finished their studies.

International Prestige and Rankings

The knowledge economy makes higher education a much more important political and economic player. The competitiveness imperative is propelling universities to improve their international prestige and reputation. Being a "world-class university" is on top of the agenda for many institutions, even though world class is not universally defined and is often in the eyes of the beholder (Altbach & Balan 2007). The presence of national, regional, international, and discipline/profession specific rankings allows universities of all types to be deemed "prestigious" by some self-appointed ranking body whether it be newspapers, consumer guides, universities, or private companies. However, all that is being said about the "hollowness" of the university ranking game does not diminish the attention and competition to be seen as a prestigious or "world-class" institution.

Income Generation: Commercial Trade

For sending countries there is a strong motivation to use cross-border education as a means of generating income from fee-based education programs and services. New franchise arrangements, foreign or satellite campuses, online delivery, and increased recruitment of fee-paying students are examples of a more commercial approach to internationalization. While more emphasis is now being placed on economic and income-generating opportunities, it is usually not seen as the primary motivation by traditional higher education institutions. Yet, the fact that education is now one of the 12 service sectors in GATS is positive proof that importing and exporting of education programs and services is a potentially lucrative trade area especially for the commercial companies (OECD 2004a).

Nation Building: Capacity Building

While some countries are interested in the export of education for income generation, there are others that are interested in the importing of education programs and institutions for nation-building purposes. The fact that the increased demand for education cannot always be met by domestic capacity makes the importing of foreign programs and providers an attractive option to help increase access to education and to build national capacity and improve the quality of the higher education system (Vincent-Lancrin 2007).

Social/Cultural Development and International Understanding

There are mixed views and sometimes conflicting opinions related to social/cultural rationales. For students who stay in the home country while studying for a foreign qualification, there is always the question about how relevant and culturally appropriate course content and teaching/learning processes are when they are imported from other countries. An alternate opinion emphasizes the advantages for students who live and study in a different country than their own. Such an experience opens their eyes and increases their international understanding and cross-cultural skills, while at the same time learning about how their own country relates to the rest of the world. These kinds of experiences and insights are difficult to replicate in virtual or cross-border provision.

STUDENT AND PROVIDER/INSTITUTION PERSPECTIVES

It is equally important and revealing to examine the rationales and anticipated impacts from the viewpoint of the students enrolled in cross-border courses/programs and the institutions/providers involved in delivering the education. Table 2.2 presents differing perspectives on several key factors.

These are but a few of the aspects that contribute to the complexities of delivering courses, programs, and service in other countries. The next section of the chapter introduces emerging issues involved in this dynamic arena of cross-border education and identifies some of the challenges with respect to access, quality assurance, accreditation, recognition of qualifications, trade agreements, and brain drain/gain/train.

EMERGING ISSUES AND CHALLENGES

Student Access

Demographic changes, lifelong learning, changing human resource needs created by the knowledge economy, as well as increasing number of graduates from secondary level education are increasing the unmet demand for postsecondary education and training. Does cross-border education help countries satisfy this growing demand for further education? Many would answer yes and that increased access for students is a driving motivation for all forms of cross-border education. But there remains the critical issue of equity of access and whether it will be available only to those who can afford it or have the language skills (primarily English). No precise data exist on the rate of participation of students in cross-border programs at the national or international levels. Only a few countries such as Australia, Hong Kong, United Kingdom, Singapore, and Malaysia collect reliable data on enrollments in cross-border education programs. This is an area requiring further national and international attention as without solid data it is challenging to develop appropriate policy and regulatory frameworks.

Quality Assurance of Cross-border Education

It must be noted that, in the last decade, increased importance has certainly been given to quality assurance at the institutional and national levels. New regional quality networks have also been established. The

Table 2.2 Different Perspectives on Rationales and Impacts of Program and Provider Mobility

Rationales and Impact	Enrolled Students in Receiving Country	Institution/Provider in Sending Country	Institution/Provider in Receiving Country
Increased access/supply in home country	Ability to gain foreign qualification without leaving home. Can continue to meet family and work commitments.	Attracted to unmet need for higher education and training.	Competition, collaboration or co-existence with foreign providers.
Cost/income	Less expensive to take foreign program at home as no travel or accommodation costs. Tuition fees of quality foreign providers may be too high for majority of students.	Strong imperative to generate a profit for cross-border operations. Fees could be high for receiving country.	Varied rationales and impacts depending on whether institution/provider is competing or cooperating with foreign providers.
Selection of courses/programs	Increased access to courses/programs in high demand by labor market.	Tendency to offer high-demand courses which require little infrastructure or investment.	Need to offer broad selection of courses which may not have high enrollments and/or have major lab or equipment requirements.
Language/cultural and safety aspects	Can have access to courses in foreign and/or indigenous language. Remain in familiar cultural and linguistic environment. Post-9/11 students have stronger concerns about safety and security.	Language of instruction and relevance of curriculum to host country important issues. If foreign language used additional academic and linguistic support may be needed.	Provide courses and programs according to local cultural and linguistic norms.

Quality	Can be exposed to higher- or lower-quality course provision.	Depending on delivery mode, quality may be at risk. Assurance of relevant and high-quality courses may require significant investment.	Presence of foreign providers may be a catalyst for innovation and improvement of quality in courses, management, and governance.
Recognition of qualification	Foreign qualification has to be recognized for academic and employment purposes.	May be difficult for academic award and for institution to be recognized in foreign country.	Recognized home providers have an advantage and are attractive to foreign providers for award-granting powers.
Reputation and profile	Due to massive marketing campaigns international profile is often mistakenly equated with quality of provider/program.	Profile and visibility are key factors for high enrollments and strategic alliances.	Home (domestic) providers are challenged to distinguish between those providers with high/low profile and high/low quality.

Source: Adapted from Knight 2007.

primary task of these groups has been quality recognition and assurance of domestic higher education provision by public and private higher education institutions. However, the increase in cross-border education by institutions and new private commercial providers has introduced a new challenge (and gap) in the field of quality assurance. Historically, national quality assurance agencies have generally not focused their efforts on assessing the quality of imported and exported programs, with some notable exceptions. The question now facing the sector is how to deal with the increase in cross-border education by traditional higher education institutions and the new private commercial providers who are not normally part of nationally based quality assurance schemes (OECD 2004b).

It is probable that sectors, in addition to education, will be interested in developing international quality standards and procedures for cross-border education. International Standards Organization standards, or other industry-based mechanisms such as the Baldridge Awards are examples of quality systems that might be applied or modeled for cross-border education. The education sector has mixed views on the appropriateness of quality standards being established for education by those outside the sector; some see merit to this idea and others see problems. At the same time, there are divergent opinions on the desirability and value of any international standards or criteria for quality assurance as this might jeopardize the sovereignty of national level systems or it could contribute to standardization, not necessarily the improvement, of quality standards.

New Developments in Accreditation

The increased awareness of the need for quality assurance and/or accreditation has led to several new developments in accreditation, some of which are helping the task of domestic and international recognition of qualifications, some of which are only serving to hinder and complicate matters. First, it is important to acknowledge the efforts of many countries to establish criteria and procedures for quality assurance recognition systems and the approval of bona fide accreditors. At the same time, it is necessary to recognize the increase in self-appointed and rather self-serving accreditors, as well as accreditation mills that simply sell "bogus" accreditation labels.

Market forces are making the profile and reputation of an institution/provider and their courses more and more important. Major investments are being made in marketing and branding campaigns in order to get name recognition and to increase enrollments. The possession of some type of accreditation is part of the campaign and assures prospective students that the programs/awards are of high standing. The desire for accreditation status is leading to a commercialization of quality assurance/accreditation as programs and providers strive to gain as many "accreditation" stars as possible in order to increase competitiveness and perceived international legitimacy. The challenge is how to distinguish between bona fide and rogue accreditors, especially when neither the cross-border provider nor the accreditor are nationally based or recognized as part of a national higher education system (Knight 2006a).

At the same time, there are networks of institutions and new organizations that are self-appointed and engage in accreditation of their members. These are positive developments when seen through the lens of trying to improve the quality of the academic offer. However, there is some concern that they are not totally objective in their assessments and may be more interested in generating income than to improving quality. While this can apply both to cross-border and domestic provision, it is particularly worrisome for cross-border provision as attention to national policy objectives and cultural orientation is often neglected.

Another development that is worrisome is the growth in accreditation mills. These organizations are not recognized or legitimate bodies and they more or less "sell" accreditation status without any independent assessment. They are similar to degree mills that sell certificates and degrees with little or no course work. Different education stakeholders, especially the students, employers, and the public need to be aware of these accreditation (and degree) mills which are often no more than a web address and are therefore out of the jurisdiction of national regulatory systems.

Recognition of Qualifications

Increased academic mobility raises the issue of credential recognition to a more prominent place in international education policy. The credibility of higher education programs and qualifications is extremely important for students, their employers, the public at large, and of course for the academic community itself. It is critical that the qualifications awarded by cross-border providers are legitimate and will be recognized for employment or further studies both at home and abroad. This is a major challenge facing the national and international higher education sector in light of new cross-border providers and programs.

The General Agreement on Trade in Services (GATS) and Higher Education

GATS has been a wake-up call for higher education leaders around the world. Higher education has traditionally been seen as a "public good" and "social commitment." But with the advent of new international trade agreement, higher education has also become a tradable commodity or, more precisely, in terms of GATS, an internationally tradable service. GATS is often seen as the catalyst for the increased growth in commercial higher education between countries. Many educators would argue that GATS is responsible for these new developments. But, others would contend that the opposite is true by pointing out that one of the consequences of increased private for-profit education at national and international levels has actually led to education being a multi-billion dollar business and thus a profitable sector to be covered in trade agreements (Knight 2008c). Academic mobility (students, programs, providers) is considered by many as a huge commercial business and is expected to increase exponentially as the demand for higher and continuing education escalates (Larsen, Momii, & Vincent-Lancrin 2005). GATS has been seen by many as presenting new opportunities and benefits, and by others as introducing new risks. Thus, while international academic mobility is not new, the presence of international trade law to regulate is new and causing vigorous debates within the higher education community.

Brain Drain/Gain/Train

Brain power is an increasingly important issue for many countries due to the growing mobility of professional/skilled workers. The increase in cross-border movement of scholars, experts, and teachers/professors is due in part to the increasing competitiveness for human capital in the knowledge economy. The higher education sector is affected by this mobility both positively and negatively depending on whether a country is experiencing a net brain drain or gain. It is important to be aware of the long-term implications in terms of human resource capacity in specific fields, for instance medicine, at both the national and institutional levels (Agarwal, Said, Sehoole, Sirozie, & Wit 2007).

While "brain drain and brain gain" are well-known concepts, research is showing that international students and researchers are increasingly interested in taking a degree in Country A, followed by a second degree or perhaps internship in Country B, leading to employment in Country C and probably D, finally returning to their home country after 8 to 12 years of international study and work experience. Hence, the emergence of the term "brain train" (Knight 2008b). In the final analysis, whether one is dealing with brain gain, brain drain, or brain train, this phenomenon is presenting benefits, risks, and new challenges for both sending and receiving countries. From a policy perspective, higher education is becoming a more important actor and is now working in closer collaboration with immigration, industry, and the science and technology sectors to build an integrated strategy for attracting and retaining knowledge workers. The convergence of an aging society, lower birth rates, the knowledge economy, and professional labor mobility, is introducing new issues and opportunities for the higher education sector while, at the same time, encouraging unprecedented competition for recruiting the best and the brightest of students and scholars.

CONCLUDING REMARKS

Words like diversity, innovation, complexity, confusion, opportunities, and challenges have been used repeatedly in this chapter to describe the development and evolution of cross-border education. The mobility of students, professors, knowledge, and values has been part of higher education for centuries but it has only been in the last two decades that there has been a significant growth in the mobility of programs, providers, and services. This presents many new opportunities: for increased access to higher education; for strategic alliances between countries and regions; for the production and exchange of new knowledge through academic partnerships; for the movement of graduates and professionals; for human resource and institutional capacity building; for income generation; for the improvement of academic quality; and for increased mutual understanding. The list of potential benefits is long and varied. But so is the list of potential risks. Risks can include: an increase in low quality or rogue providers; a potential decrease in public funding if foreign providers are providing increased access; non-sustainable foreign provision of higher education if profit margins are low; foreign qualifications not recognized by domestic employers or education institutions; elitism in terms of those who can afford cross-border education; overuse of English as the language of instruction; and national higher education policy objectives not being met. These present major challenges to the education sector. It is important to acknowledge the huge potential of cross-border education but not at the expense of academic quality and integrity.

REFERENCES

Agarwal, P., Said, M., Sehoole, C., Sirozie, M., & Wit, H. de (2007). The dynamics of international student circulation in a global context. In P. Altbach and P. McGill Peterson (Eds.), *Higher education in the new century, Global challenges and innovative ideas* (pp. 109–144). Rotterdam, the Netherlands: Sense Publishers.

Altbach, P., & Balan, J. (Eds.) (2007). *World class worldwide: Transforming research universities in Asia and Latin America.* Baltimore: Johns Hopkins University Press.

Altbach, P., & Knight, J. (2007). The internationalization of higher education: Motivations and realities. *Journal of Studies in International Education,* *11*(3–4), 290–305.

Bohm, A., Davis, D., Meares, D., & Pearce, D. (2002). *The global student mobility 2025 Report: Forecasts of the global demand for international education.* Canberra, Australia: IDP.

Currie, J. (2005). Privatization and commercialization: Two globalizing practices affecting Australian universities. In A. Arimoto, F. Huang, & K. Yokoyama (Eds.), *Globalization and higher education* (pp. 23–27). Higashi-Hiroshima, Japan: Research Institute for Higher Education, Hiroshima University.

Garrett, R. (2005, July). *Fraudulent, sub-standard, ambiguous: The alternative borderless higher education* [Briefing Note]. London: Observatory on Borderless Higher Education.

Knight, J. (2005a). *Borderless, offshore, transnational and cross-border education: Definition and data dilemmas.* London: Observatory on Borderless Higher Education.

Knight, J. (2005b). Cross-border education: An analytical framework for program and provider mobility. In J. Smart (Ed.), *Higher education: Handbook of theory and research practice* (pp. 345–396). Dordrecht, the Netherlands: Springer Academic Publishers.

Knight, J. (2006a). Cross-border higher education: Issues and implications for quality assurance and accreditation. In Global University Network for Innovation (Ed.), *Higher education in the world 2007: Accreditation for quality assurance: What is at stake?* (pp. 134–146). Basingstoke, UK: Palgrave Macmillan.

Knight, J. (2006b). *Higher education crossing borders: A guide to the implications of GATS for cross-border education.* Paris: Commonwealth of Learning and UNESCO.

Knight, J. (2006c). *Internationalization of higher education: New directions, new challenges. 2005 IAU Global Survey Report.* Paris: International Association of Universities.

Knight, J. (2007). Cross-border tertiary education: An introduction. In S. Vincent-Lancrin (Ed.), *Cross-border tertiary education: A way towards capacity development* (pp. 21–46). Paris: OECD.

Knight, J. (2008a). *Higher education in turmoil: The changing world of internationalization.* Rotterdam, the Netherlands: Sense Publishers.

Knight, J. (2008b). The internationalization of higher education: Are we on the right track? *Academic Matters: OCUFA's Journal of Higher Education,* October/November, 5–9.

Knight, J. (2008c). The role of cross-border education in the debate on education as a public good and private commodity. *Journal of Asian Public Policy, 1*(2), 174–188.

Larsen, K., Momii, K., & Vincent-Lancrin, S. (2005). *Cross-border higher education: An analysis of current trends, policy strategies and future scenarios.* London: Observatory on Borderless Higher Education.

Organisation for Economic and Community Development (2004a). *Internationalization and trade of higher education: Opportunities and challenges.* Paris: OECD.

Organisation for Economic and Community Development (2004b). *Quality and recognition in higher education: The cross-border challenge.* Paris: OECD.

Verbik, L., & Jokivirta, L. (2005). *National regulatory frameworks for transnational higher education: Models and trends.* London: Observatory on Borderless Higher Education.

Vincent-Lancrin, S. (2005). *Building capacity through tertiary education.* London: Observatory on Borderless Education.

Vincent-Lancrin, S. (2007). *Cross-border tertiary education: A way towards capacity development.* Paris: OECD.

Wit, H. de (2002). *Internationalization of higher education in the United States of America and Europe: A historical, comparative, and conceptual analysis.* Westport, CT: Greenwood Publishers.

Part II
Moving Campuses (Instead of Students) Across Borders

3

MOTIVATION AND ASPIRATIONS FOR INTERNATIONAL BRANCH CAMPUSES

PATRICIA W. CROOM

As the worldwide demand for higher education continues to grow, developing nations are keen on upgrading their country's ability to compete in the new knowledge economy. In many nations, domestic institutions of higher education cannot provide enough seats (Wende 2003) and increasingly use "transnational" or "cross-border" higher education as a means of satisfying the otherwise unmet demand. While some institutions are experimenting with such arrangements as twinning or "bookend" programs, in which a student completes a portion of the curriculum at a home country institution and a portion at the partner institution abroad, others are going a step further and opening full masters or undergraduate programs abroad. Students attending such campuses located in a host country (such as Singapore) may never set foot on the soil of the source country (such as the United States).

International branch campuses typically target nationals of the host country, and in some cases, international students from the larger world region. Decisions to expand overseas often involve working with some kind of partner in the host country, such as a private investment group or government-related entity. The degree of institutional investment in international branch campuses varies depending on the scope of vision and what resources the partner and home institution bring to the table. Indeed, the partnership relationship itself is a key factor in establishing and sustaining many, if not most, branch campus relationships. In many countries, such as India, an in-country partner is required (Green, Kinser, & Eckel 2008; Neelakantan 2008) in order to offer higher education programs on the ground at all.

In nearly every case, a strong partner can help the source country institution navigate the local bureaucracy, establish facilities, identify suppliers and staff, create relationships with companies, and recruit students. While the potential benefits of partnership may seem obvious, the long-term needs and importance of identifying the right partner may at times be underestimated or oversimplified. In some ways, such international partnerships can resemble a marriage, in that the initial romance, optimism, desire, and focus on the "wedding" (in this case announcement and campus launch) can hinder a hard-line assessment of long-term risks and interests. Over time, however, the realities of continuing the partnership and managing the ongoing adjustments to changing circumstances can strain even strong partnerships. A former instructor who lived through several changes in partners for Temple University's campus in Japan during its early years noted that each time a partnership failed and another partner took over it was like going through a divorce.

Like divorce, a failed partnership can also be expensive to an institution's pocketbook and even reputation. For example, the University of New South Wales closed its campus in Singapore just one semester after opening, creating "huge egg on their faces as a provider in South-East Asia," according to New South Wales Greens Party education spokesperson John Kaye (Alexander 2007). UNSW Asia, as the institution was called, expected to enroll 500 students the first year and eventually reach an enrollment of 10,000 students as a research-based institution (Cohen 2007a). Despite significant investment from the Singapore government, the institution was unable to break even, and reportedly agreed to repay Singapore as much as $22 million (Cohen 2007b). A short time earlier, Johns Hopkins University closed its biomedical research center in Singapore Center amid considerable controversy after it was also not able to meet targets for faculty and doctoral students (Jaschik 2006). As these examples show, even with significant partner support, such agreements can have financial and non-financial impacts if the arrangement does not go as planned.

This chapter examines the critical role of partnership in opening and sustaining an international branch campus. The chapter reviews the Japanese branch campus partnership experiences from the 1980s and 1990s to establish a lens for considering branch campus partnerships in other areas of the world today. The chapter then focuses on contrasting arrangements for institutional partners in Qatar's Education City and Dubai International Academic City, and concludes by considering the implications for institutions considering such arrangements in the future.

DEFINITIONS

A branch campus is a form of cross-border, program mobility in which an entire degree program of the originating "source" country is offered across borders in another "host" country. While some element of online coursework may be involved, this definition of an international branch campus entails a physical presence of the source institution in the host nation from admission through graduation. This physical presence may vary from a relatively small instructional site to a large campus setting with athletic facilities, residence halls, etc. In this chapter, the term "branch" is used loosely and does not imply a specific definition such as that used by some regional accreditation organizations. In particular, this definition does not imply a separate governance structure; in fact, most U.S. institutions noted in this chapter operate "branch campuses" as instructional sites under the programmatic and organizational auspices of the home campus rather than as independent entities. Further, many kinds of institutions may establish branch campuses, including vocational programs, for-profit enterprises, and traditional non-profit universities. This chapter examines only the latter category, traditional not-for-profit universities, when applying the term "international branch campus."

DRIVERS AND RATIONALES

Establishing an international branch campus requires not only interest on the part of the source institution, but also a hospitable climate in the host country—economically, politically, and operationally. Some countries impose significant restrictions on whether and how foreign universities may operate within their borders (Bjarnason 2005). Such restrictions, in fact, were behind inclusion of higher education in the most recent round of General Agreement on Trade in Services (GATS) negotiations in Doha, driven especially by for-profit educational enterprises (Bottari 2007). Although negotiations in this area have stalled, the fact that cross-border higher education even entered these negotiations is indicative of the perceived market potential in this arena.

The Organisation for Economic Co-operation and Development (OECD 2004) classifies drivers and rationales for the worldwide growth of cross-border education by policy rationales, institutional rationales, and student rationales. The first two of these, policy and institutional rationales are most relevant for the discussion of partnership between sponsors and providers, although of course without students these ventures could never survive. A successful venture requires an alignment of policy rationales, often embodied through a host-country partner, with rationales of the source country institution.

National policy rationales are either explicitly or implicitly established at the government level. Where not explicit, policies may become evident through the actions of subsidiary organizations charged with their implementation or the actions of private partners working within the established regulatory framework. OECD (2004) lists four categories of policy rationales underlying cross-border education: mutual understanding, capacity building, revenue generation, and skilled migration. Mutual understanding has undergirded study abroad and exchange programs now for decades. The Fulbright program exemplifies such policy in the United States.

Many branch campus ventures today, however, are premised on the need for educational capacity building; governments and other sponsors view attracting established universities as a way to quickly build lagging capacity for higher education while at the same time garnering immediate prestige and respect through partnerships with well-known institutions. Establishing new universities from scratch, especially within a developing country, is typically a slower prospect; it may take many years to build the recognition needed to attract students and top-tier faculty members. An international branch campus, on the other hand, can immediately draw on the reputation, accreditation, and resources of the source institution.

A third rationale is revenue generation. For example, revenue is a key driver behind the large influx of international students in Australia as well as many Australian offshore campuses. International students pay full fees, and provide a large injection of funding into the otherwise declining budgets of Australian universities. In addition, attracting international students from outside one's borders is a form of export, in that students from abroad consume various products and services during their stay in the country, thereby boosting the local and national economy.

The fourth rationale, skilled migration, is often tied to a country's desire to make its economy more competitive. Universities help fuel a knowledge-based economy through research and development; in today's world, leading-edge research requires attracting top scholars from all corners of the world. Competition for the "best and the brightest" worldwide does not cease upon graduation, however. Many countries create paths to allow these international scholars to stay on and help fuel innovation and development throughout their careers.

Institutional rationales are also an important part of the equation in such efforts. For any successful long-term partnership, both parties must find they are gaining something worthwhile in exchange for the effort and risk. According to OECD (2004), "a significant share of the development of cross-border education has been institution- rather than solely policy-driven" (28). That is, institutional objectives play a significant role in shaping cross-border ventures, including international branch campuses. OECD notes two common reasons for institutional interest in cross-border education: the search for quality and prestige, and domestic funding issues. Green, Eckel, Calderon, and Luu (2007) add to this list a desire to advance internationalization and quality as well as the service mission.

In a climate where the Times Higher Education—QA World University, Shanghai Jiao Tong University, and other such rankings take on increasing importance, "competition has increasingly required gaining (or maintaining) a worldwide reputation for quality" with a "strong international dimension" (OECD 2004: 28–29). With international reputation a part of this game, the recent chain of institutions opening or looking at opening a branch campus leaves the impression many are "keeping up with Joneses," hoping not to be left behind in the quest for international partners and strategic locations.

Meanwhile, the move to mass education and contracting government support has left many Western universities struggling to maintain a strong funding base. As a result, institutions of higher education, especially public universities, are increasingly looking for ways to diversify sources of income. Many institutions seek to bring international students to their campus to enhance revenue. Like corporations, others hope to find new revenue sources abroad and look to an international branch campus as another external income stream. Although revenue often does not materialize as expected, in the right circumstance an international campus may provide enough external funding so as to provide an opportunity to be "mission-centered and market-smart," that is, a situation in which revenue allows a relaxation of existing financial limits, thus allowing greater mission attainment (Zemsky, Wegner, & Massy 2005). Mission attainment may take the form of internationalization, quality improvement, research opportunities, and service. Of course, the wrong arrangement may have just the opposite effect, pulling down mission attainment.

The OECD (2004) notes, "The growth of cross-border education activities has been driven by educational institutions and providers, students and policy makers, whose rationales for delivering or receiving cross-border education may be quite different but are largely compatible" (25). Compatibility of goals is indeed a core feature of any kind of partnership. However, goal compatibility has not always occurred in international branch campuses. The following section reviews the experiences of Japan two decades ago to put in perspective the emerging partnerships and branch campuses in the Middle East.

HISTORICAL PERSPECTIVE: THE EXPERIENCE IN JAPAN

As an early hotbed for branch campus expansion, Japan provides an interesting parallel to the Middle East today. Branch campuses in Japan in the 1980s developed concurrently with Japan's emergence as an economic powerhouse. Western nations turned their attention to Japan to grab a piece of the perceived economic pie. Further encouraging branch campuses were a growing emphasis on internalization within Japan, surplus Japanese capital that encouraged Japanese investors to find new opportunities, and rural Japanese communities looking for ways to reverse or at least counter the flight to major cities (Chambers & Cummings 1990). Meanwhile, many U.S. institutions faced falling enrollments and sought new sources of revenue. In this context, a "climate of opportunism" (Magner 1990) encouraged many U.S. institutions to establish branch campuses in Japan as a spectrum of private Japanese investors and local governmental authorities lured institutions overseas by providing funding and facilities. During the late 1980s and early 1990s, more than 30 U.S. institutions established a branch campus in Japan (Brender 2004; Ohmori 2004) although by the start of the new millennium only a handful remained (McMurtrie 2000; Brender 2004).

In a 1990 report, Chambers and Cummings surveyed around 100 institutions that had at least contemplated programs in Japan and found many institutions did not fully understand the cultural context in which they were operating and made decisions based on "assumptions and myths" (12). Many made decisions quickly, sensing the market for students would fade within 5 years (Chambers & Cummings 1990). Other problems included naïve negotiations, unmet educational expectations, lowered standards and institutional commitment, awkward governance structures, problematic costing mechanisms, financial and legal manipulation, and power and control issues among partners. The financial control exercised by foreign partners and some unsavory business ethics hindered some institutions in Japan (Magner

1990). Moreover, the Japanese government did not recognize degrees from U.S. institutions, the traditional aged student population plummeted, and potential students were faced with a culture that viewed anything outside of the normal schooling path as deviant (McMurtrie 2000; Rubin 1996). Finally, the "bubble burst" in the Japanese economy during the 1990s, halting the generosity of partners and leaving families with less disposable income for U.S. higher education (Rubin 1996). While not all of the ensuing problems in Japan could have been foreseen, some were predictable. The lack of up-front investigation, negotiation, or alignment of intentions on the part of some institutions resulted in later problems.

Chambers and Cummings (1990) provided a number of guidelines for future ventures and underscored the importance of understanding the partner's motives, then clarifying who retains which rights and documenting this contractually. Although this kind of investigation and consideration happens in many cases today, in others the recent explosion of branch outposts makes one wonder how carefully such issues have been evaluated. Have we really learned from the Japan experience? Will today's branch campuses succumb to the fate of those in Japan?

CURRENT BRANCH CAMPUS INITIATIVES

Twenty years after the rush to open campuses in Japan, again it seems every few months another institution is announcing plans to open a branch campus abroad. This time, however, the greatest hotbeds of action are Southeast Asia and the Middle East (McBurnie & Ziguras 2007b). In these regions, as was the case in Japan earlier, private and governmental in-country partners are encouraging Western universities to open programs on their soil. Today, areas such as Malaysia, Hong Kong, Singapore, and the United Arab Emirates (UAE) aim to create centers of higher education to meet domestic demand, add to the local revenue base by attracting foreign students, and promote a knowledge-based economy in the region. Institutions pursuing such opportunities across the globe offer a number of reasons in the announcement of such ventures, including opportunities to internationalize faculty and students, enhance their service mission abroad, gain prestige, and diversify revenue (Green et al. 2007). These justifications echo three of the OECD (2004) policy rationales described earlier: mutual understanding (internationalization), capacity generation (service mission), and revenue. Despite the potential gains, establishing a branch campus remains "one of the riskiest ventures a university, college or school can embark on" (McBurnie & Ziguras 2007b: 36).

BRANCH CAMPUSES IN THE GULF REGION

The situation today in the Middle East bears some similarities to Japan in the 1980s. The nations in the region are fast developing and well resourced. Businesses are flocking to cities such as Dubai and Abu Dhabi to have a part in this expansion. Private investors and government-related organizations, not to mention sheikhs directly, aim to attract foreign institutions to quickly add higher education capacity as well as prestige to their cities and states. One significant difference with Japan is that higher education in the Gulf region has a relatively young history, dating back only four decades. And there are profound cultural differences between Japan and the Middle East. Nevertheless, taking a closer look at current international branch campus activity in the Gulf region of the Middle East provides insight into the role of partnerships today as Western-based institutions expand overseas.

Thirty-five years ago, the now emerging metropolises of the Gulf region were little more than small fishing villages. The discovery and extraction of oil in these countries changed the landscape dramatically through development and international investment in this lucrative region. Today, the Gulf countries have trade surpluses measured in trillions of dollars (Rodenbeck 2008). Yet, many of these nations, with national budgets heavily based on oil revenues, are actively diversifying their economies by expanding into international finance, tourism, transportation, and other service and knowledge-based industries. A few years ago, few Americans had heard of Dubai. Today, Dubai has achieved notoriety for its grand visions and bold real-estate development, including man-made islands in the shapes of palms, the tallest building on earth, an indoor ski run, and plans for an entertainment park larger than Disneyworld. Other centers, including Abu Dhabi and Doha also have large developments underway. Hundreds of corporations in finance, media, and transportation and service industries have opened offices in the region in order to capitalize on double-digit growth rates.

As a result, Western institutions of higher education have shown growing interest in the region. Over the last 10 years, the Gulf countries have become increasingly engaged in cross-border education (Krieger 2008). For instance, dozens of institutions have set up shop in Dubai, many at Dubai International Academic City, described later. Elsewhere in Dubai, the Rochester Institute of Technology, Harvard Medical International (a branch of Harvard Medical School), and the London School of Economics are all involved in educational programming in Dubai (Krieger 2008). Other Emirates are similarly engaged; New York University plans to open a large branch campus in Abu Dhabi in 2010, while George Mason University began operations in Ras Al Khaimah in 2006. In Qatar the Qatar Foundation, headed by Her Highness Sheikah Moza Bint Nasser Al-Missned, has established Education City, an enclave of elite, U.S. higher education institutions. Kuwait, Oman, and others are also working with Western institutions to expand their higher education capacity. Meanwhile, following a different model of expansion, Saudi Arabia's King Abdullah University of Science and Technology (KAUST), while a national Saudi university and not a branch campus, has enlisted the University of California at Berkeley, Stanford University, and University of Texas at Austin to help it design curriculum and hire faculty members for what it hopes will be leading graduate programs and research centers (Fischer 2008). In sum, not unlike Japan in the 1980s, the lure of prosperity and growth in the Persian Gulf, along with attractive offers from willing partners, are sirens for higher education looking to expand abroad.

The largest single driver from among the four OECD categories of policy rationales noted earlier is capacity building. The Middle East and North Africa have among the largest populations under the age of 25 as a percent of population, with 45% under the age of 14 (World Bank 2008). Advanced education is viewed as an essential element in successfully diversifying Gulf economies. Until recently, however, domestic capacity has not been able to handle the growth desired. Moreover, countries such as Qatar and Saudi Arabia are attempting to very quickly ramp up the quality of education, illustrated by involving very highly ranked institutions to jump-start their efforts of capacity building. In Qatar and the UAE this expansion is driven by policies aimed at preparing a larger share of nationals to take part in the workforce, referred to as "Qatarization" and "Emiratization," respectively. These very wealthy nations, in effect, are able to buy facilities and talent in an effort to quickly raise the level of higher education needed to support not only that nation and its citizens but the larger region as well. The desire for capacity building to support a growing population differs significantly from the declining population and established higher education system found earlier in Japan.

Despite the general trends, each partnership is different. The next section describes such differences through the examples of Education City in Qatar and Dubai International Academic City in the UAE.

EDUCATION CITY IN QATAR

Education City in Doha, Qatar, is an initiative led by the Qatar Foundation, an organization closely tied to the Qatari royal family. This large, gated compound is located on the outskirts of Doha, and consists of not only institutions of higher education, but also a primary and secondary private school, faculty housing, athletic facilities, the Al Jazeera Network Children's Channel, and offices of the Qatar Foundation. The Qatar Foundation is opening a large, modern research facility in the Qatar Science and Technology Park, adjacent to Education City, that will help bridge commercial and academic research and provide an incubator for new technology (Qatar Science and Technology Park 2008). In addition, the Qatar National Conference Centre, an impressive, modern facility, will open in 2011 and will also attract business and industry to Doha and Education City (Qatar National Conference Centre 2009). All of these efforts aim to put Doha on the map in terms of higher education, research, and commerce.

Six U.S. universities are operating programs in Education City: Virginia Commonwealth University (design), Carnegie Mellon (computer science, business, and information systems), Weill Cornell Medical College, Georgetown School of Foreign Service, Texas A&M (engineering), and Northwestern University (journalism and communications). In addition, Education City houses the Qatar Faculty of Islamic Studies. Education City is characterized by large open spaces and striking, modern architecture. Virginia Commonwealth University was the first U.S. institution to open in Education City in 1998. The remainder opened between 2003 and 2008, and are thus relative newcomers to the Gulf. No other foreign universities operate within the compound, and only a handful of other Western institutions have any form of branch campus in Doha. The Qatar Foundation covers most of the operational costs of the U.S. institutions operating in Education City, from facilities to faculty salaries. The institutions charge the same tuition in Qatar as they would to international students at the home campus, although the Qatar tuition dollars flow through the Foundation. The Foundation provides visibility and support in joint recruiting efforts.

"Qatarization" and capacity building appear to be significant drivers behind the creation of Education City. The Qatar Foundation, on its website, describes its mission to "prepare the people of Qatar and the region to meet the challenges of an ever-changing world, and to make Qatar a leader in innovative education and research" (Qatar Foundation 2008b). Qatar has one national university, but Education City provides additional capacity and prestige, aiming to provide students with a "world-class academic education" and a "first-class experience in all aspects of their lives at Education City" (Qatar Foundation 2008a). With the support of the Qatar Foundation, 46% of the students in Education City are Qatari citizens (Qatar Foundation 2008a), although approximately 75% of the population of Qatar is ex-patriot (Oxford Business Group 2008).

Revenue generation, on the other hand, is not prominent in the Education City strategy. Indeed, money seems to be no problem at all. The Qatar Foundation has spent lavishly on new buildings for institutions that house a student body measuring only a few hundred. In May 2008, Her Highness celebrated the graduating classes by flying in the London Philharmonic and Italian tenor Andrea Bocelli and gave graduates a watch or diamond ring. Rather, Qatar appears to target quality, image, and prestige in order to attract top institutions and researchers to its campus. The Qatar Foundation has maintained close, highly selective control over the selection of programs and institutions to operate there. All are top programs in their field, and, so far, only American institutions. If institutions wish to add a new program, however, they need permission of the Qatar Foundation. Otherwise, the universities report considerable operational freedom, although budgets must be approved annually by the Qatar Foundation.

Certainly, a failure in a branch campus venture in Qatar would hold potential financial and reputational risk. However, the enormous support and commitment of the Qatar Foundation have kept the investment on the part of institutions relatively low. To the extent these campuses align with institutional mission, the freeing of resources through the Qatar Foundation may provide a "market-smart and mission-centric" (Zemsky et al. 2005) strategy.

DUBAI INTERNATIONAL ACADEMIC CITY

Similarly, Dubai International Academic City (DIAC), a project of TECOM Investments, brings together a number of higher education institutions with plans for shared facilities and services among them. DIAC grew out of an earlier venture, Dubai Knowledge Village, which houses a number of branch campuses and other organizations involved in some manner of education, training, or human resource-related services. DIAC was established in 2007 to better address the specific and increasing need for higher education in Dubai. DIAC is in its early stages of development, but includes a contiguous plot of land of 25 million square feet (DIAC 2007). The DIAC website reports that DIAC houses nearly 30 postsecondary institutions from multiple countries and continents, and claims to serve approximately 12,000 students (DIAC 2008). These range from the French Fashion University Esmond to the Jain School of Management from India. Michigan State University (MSU) opened four diverse undergraduate programs as well as a few graduate offerings in DIAC in August 2008. With this new venture, MSU became the first not-for-profit research-oriented university in Academic City (AME Info 2008). DIAC plans to continue adding institutions and eventually serve a student body of approximately 35,000 (DIAC 2007).

The DIAC web pages describe an interest in promoting a knowledge-based economy for Dubai: "This thriving knowledge community was founded as part of a long-term economic strategy to develop the region's talent pool, to accelerate its move into a knowledge economy" (DIAC 2008). DIAC operates through a more corporate model as the world's only Free Zone dedicated to higher education. DIAC (2008) argues that the benefits for DIAC partners include 100% foreign ownership, a 100% tax-free operation, and 100% repatriation of profits (DIAC 2008). DIAC is one of the ventures of TECOM Investments, a division of Dubai Holding, which operates with close ties to the Dubai government. TECOM develops and manages businesses that promote the growth of knowledge-based industries in Dubai in five areas: information and communication technology, education, media, biotechnology, and energy (Knowledge Village 2008).

While the DIAC web pages note the need to build a knowledge economy, the strategy to do so is different in Dubai than Doha. Dubai is very multi-cultural, with just over 80% of its residents being expatriates (UAE Interact 2008). Not surprisingly, the student population at DIAC is diverse as well, with a relatively small proportion of the students being Emirati. It is important to note that not all the degrees from DIAC institutions are accredited by the UAE government, due perhaps in part to UAE accreditation issues discussed later in this chapter. Capacity building at DIAC, so far at least, does not predominantly target the Emirate population, in contrast to Education City's role in advancing the education of Qatari citizens.

Furthermore, despite the desire to develop a knowledge economy noted in websites, overall, DIAC reflects the highly commercial, growth-oriented environment that characterizes Dubai. In many ways, DIAC's logo and other marketing materials resemble those of many other real estate developments sprouting up across the desert in Dubai. In contrast to Education City's quiet solicitation of institutions, DIAC has been actively recruiting institutions at conferences for several years, with glossy brochures noting the market potential in Dubai and grandiose plans for future development. Marketing itself is certainly no stranger to U.S. higher education institutions today. In this case, however, the marketing is targeted at attracting institutions to invest in DIAC more than on attracting students to attend DIAC institutions.

Unlike the Qatar Foundation, which highly subsidizes Education City, institutions pay rent to DIAC and cover most expenses themselves. For instance, whereas the Qatar Foundation provides high-speed Internet connections to Education City, institutions in DIAC must each pay the monopoly provider for the relatively basic educational access available currently in the region. In the future, DIAC intends to build common residence halls, athletics facilities, a library, and research facilities. While in Education City such costs would be borne by the Qatar Foundation, capital investment for DIAC may be directly or indirectly supported by DIAC institution leases, or other revenue sources upon which DIAC and its parent TECOM might draw. Although institutions in DIAC pay rent and cover many costs within their own budgets, in some cases, institutions may work with the sponsoring organization to gain start-up financing (Michigan State University 2007).

In the main, DIAC reflects a model in which the source country institutions in many ways operate more independently from the sponsor, DIAC and its parent organization TECOM, than in the example of Education City in Qatar. As a result, the sponsorship agreements with DIAC provide significant operational freedom, perhaps greater yet than in Education City. Universities have full control over their budgets, as well as hiring and academic programs. DIAC, in addition to facilities support, helps institutions by connecting them to suppliers, businesses, and authorities within Dubai, including acquiring the necessary residency visas for faculty and students.

As the majority of the occupants operate on a for-profit model, revenue generation plays a much greater role than is often true in Education City. Michigan State University, as the first not-for-profit, internationally ranked university in DIAC, heralds in a new type of institution. Much like an anchor store at the mall, the presence of MSU, as a Research-1 institution, has the potential to raise the reputation and visibility of DIAC.

IMPLICATIONS OF PARTNERSHIP

Qatar and Dubai have each created higher education centerpieces that at first glance might appear similar in focus. As the previous descriptions reveal, however, the philosophies behind these endeavors have striking distinctions that illustrate the critical role partners play in an overseas branch campus. These differences will undoubtedly affect the way in which these ventures evolve in the coming years, including the relationship between universities that open branches and the sponsoring organizations in the country that are so anxious to invite these institutions to their soil. The differences fall into five categories: capital investment, environmental adjustment, institutional recognition, influence, and vision.

As noted, the capital investment differences between DIAC and the Qatar Foundation are profound. The Qatar Foundation is investing significantly and takes a lead role in the Education City facilities. DIAC, on the other hand, offers the basic building shell and the university is relatively free to design the interior of these facilities at its own cost. In both cases institutions have brick and mortar facilities and the sponsors have each promised a host of shared facilities. So far, Education City is much further along in developing these facilities, though DIAC may catch up in the coming years.

The future ability to react to a changing environment and educational demand differs in Education City and DIAC as well. In Education City the Qatar Foundation has selected institutions to operate in particular specialty areas, thus providing a monopoly position for the specific majors offered within Education City to date. Yet, institutions there may not independently decide to offer an entirely different program without permission of the Qatar Foundation. Further, competition in Qatar outside of Education City is currently much lower than in Dubai, where multiple providers are already operating overseas campuses in various outposts, in a more competitive environment. In DIAC, although programmatic offerings must have approval of the Dubai Knowledge and Human Development Authority, in practice there is relative freedom to add offerings to adapt to changing market needs and interests, including non-credit and certificate offerings.

Another important programmatic difference between the environments in Education City and DIAC is the role of institutional recognition. Qatar only began developing any form of higher education accreditation in the mid-2000s by initiating a self-study at the University of Qatar modeled somewhat after a U.S. accreditation review (Lezberg 2003). There is no national system of accreditation. Rather, the University of Qatar process focuses on external program-level accreditation through Western organizations where these exist (Qatar University 2008). The lack of a national standard eases entry into the Qatar market for accredited U.S. institutions and programs. The Ministry of Education in the UAE, on the other hand, has developed an involved and demanding national accreditation process that includes detailed programmatic review and having an operating board within the UAE (Ministry of Higher Education and Scientific Research 2007). These requirements can pose significant obstacles to foreign universities. UAE accreditation is not required to get a license to operate within the DIAC Free Zone. However, Emiratis wishing to work in the government may find obstacles in employment from an institution not accredited within the UAE and are not currently eligible for substantial government scholarship money. The partner, in this case, can provide a certain amount of operating freedom; however, they are not able to waive these strict requirements for accreditation.

The degree of influence a partner can provide to an institution engaging in cross-border education also has far-reaching impact on the relationship and its potential to open doors and break down obstacles for the institution. The Qatar Foundation, with its direct tie to Her Highness, is well positioned to exert this kind of influence, directly and indirectly, as long as the Foundation and government continue to support this strategic direction. Qatar is one of the richer oil-producing nations in the Gulf. For the foreseeable future, funding is likely secure. Beyond financial investment, ties to Qatari leadership bring not only money, but a high degree of influence through many aspects of the operation. In a culture where personal relationships and respect for the royal family are paramount, the support of Her Highness, through the Qatar Foundation, is immensely significant. In Dubai, TECOM, under which DIAC operates, is one of several entities of Dubai Holding. Dubai Holding, in turn, is one of several holding companies that serve as arms of the Dubai government, thus somewhat loosely tied to the Sheikh himself. Additionally, with its more commercial focus, TECOM's revenue is dependent on real estate, transportation, entertainment, and finance, making it potentially vulnerable to economic downturns. Just how the 2008–2009 economic downturn will play out in Dubai remains to be seen; however, a prolonged downturn could impact what influence DIAC and TECOM wield as well as their ability as partners to support DIAC institutions over time.

Finally, Education City and DIAC differ in terms of overall vision. Both envisage a large campus with shared facilities for students and faculty and seek to be centers of higher education. Education City's vision, however, is narrow and deep, focusing on elite education for future leaders. DIAC, on the other hand, looks to educate tens of thousands of students through a variety of postsecondary education paths.

In sum, these models of partnership, although operating in a region with many similar cultural and economic dynamics, illustrate significant differences that impact the scope of cross-border operations and relationships, now and in the future. Neither of the models is inherently better than the other. The important issue is that institutions looking to establish education sites overseas understand these differences and take into account how the opportunities align with their own goals, resources, risk assessment, and, most importantly, institutional mission and vision.

THE MIDDLE EAST AND JAPAN

Having examined the partnerships in Education City and DIAC more closely, we now return to the question of whether and how the rapid expansion in the Middle East bears a likeness to the experiences of Japanese branch campus partnerships in the 1980s.

In 1990, Chambers and Cummings advised institutions to conduct an entirely neutral evaluation of the prospective market in the target region before entering. It is unclear whether institutions considering Qatar or the UAE are doing this. Even so, such forecasts are difficult in a region with a limited history in higher education and rapidly changing economics and demographics. It is common for partners to promise an ample population of students, but the institution itself must assess whether it believes this to be true for its own needs. Though young, branch campus programs in the UAE are so far largely surviving, although the start-up efforts can be difficult. Australia's University of South Queensland closed its campus in Dubai after only a few years of operation (McBurnie & Ziguras 2007a; University of Southern Queensland 2004). In the Emirate of Ras Al Kheimah, George Mason University, with an enrollment of only 180 out of its 2011 target of 2,000 students, decided to close its campus in May 2009 after 3 years of operation, citing disagreements with its partner regarding funding and control (Lewin 2009). On the other hand, the University of Wollongong has been in Dubai for 15 years and attracts an enrollment of 3,500 students (University of Wollongong in Dubai 2009). Clearly, the longer-term capacity to attract students both locally and internationally to the region is still evolving and difficult to forecast.

Chambers and Cummings (1990) also emphasized a need to accurately plan the cost of operation and identify the financial resources of the partner. Identifying expenses can be a challenge in a new country, especially for institutions for which this is the first branch operation. Even Carnegie Mellon University (CMU), now operating in seven countries, ran into major unanticipated costs when its auditors determined its management of currency transactions insufficient. As a result, Carnegie Mellon spent $6 million retrofitting its accounting systems to handle multiple currencies (Green et al. 2008). While this need was not a direct impact of the Education City venture alone, the cumulative impact of CMU's expanding overseas operations resulted in significant costs that the institution probably did not initially take into account. Additionally, it can also be awkward to question the finances of a partner in a culture in which relationships and trust play such a central role, especially when the partner may be indirectly part of the government itself.

Indeed, cultural issues pose interesting parallels between the Middle East and Japan. While there are many differences beyond the scope of this chapter, the nature of business relationships in both cultures stands in contrast to the U.S. Having an appropriate and supportive overseas partner requires understanding and working within the local culture. While relationships are not insignificant in the United States, business relationships operate around a set of cost negotiations, procedures, and detailed contracts. In contrast, Japan and the Middle East both place much more value on relationships. In the Gulf, one can accomplish much with "wasta," or, roughly translated from the Arabic, connections. Having a partner with *wasta* can open doors that may otherwise take years to establish. Also, much like in Japan, Gulf business partners would rarely be direct like Americans and tell someone "No" to a request. Rather, they might say yes, or "Inshallah" (God willing) and do their best. These kinds of behaviors can baffle U.S. faculty and staff new to the Gulf region, leading to conflicts and challenges in establishing relationships and campuses, much as cultural misunderstandings were evident in some of the Japanese branch campus arrangements. It is critical that the U.S. and other foreign institutions approaching partnerships in this region understand the cultural innuendos and assess critically, if quietly, their partner's commitment and ability to deliver as promised, lest they succumb to the same fate as some Japanese institutions abroad.

Finally, as noted earlier with the Asian Financial Crisis of 1997, Japanese families faced economic conditions that made private higher education an unattainable luxury. The dire economic situation, combined with the falling numbers of Japanese high school graduates created a difficult market indeed. Although the Gulf anticipates increasing numbers of high school graduates, the Economic Crisis that began in 2008 still poses an uncertain future. Already in 2009, there is a slowing of development in Dubai and other areas. It is too early to know how long this downturn will last and what prolonged effects it may have on areas such as Qatar and Dubai. However, this change in events highlights how economic risk can threaten overseas operations, an issue multinational corporations have managed for years. Indeed, higher education institutions are still new in the role of multinational; through such branch campus endeavors, those pioneering universities have much to learn and share.

CONCLUSION

In summary, what can we conclude about the future of international branch campus partnerships sprouting up in the Gulf region, considering the historical experience in Japan? The Gulf today certainly differs from Japan, although the high interest in the region does carry a similar Gold Rush feel. Institutions that believe cities like Abu Dhabi and Dubai have nearly unlimited money may be more apt to see the upside potential and minimize the downside. Much like Japan in the 1980s, the region today holds a certain luster for corporations and higher education alike. As in Japan, this allure is heightened by attractive offers from sponsors. However, since many negotiations are not publicized, the number of institutions that have carefully considered offers and rejected them remains unclear. Higher education institutions are still very new in this transnational role and have much yet to learn in navigating these complex situations. While environmental factors can pose significant challenges, the role of the partnership in such enterprises arises as a key element, for both the best of circumstances and through potentially difficult scenarios.

Despite the attention in this chapter to costs and risks, the decision to expand abroad, in the Gulf as well as in other regions, may be driven by factors other than rationally analyzing and choosing from alternatives. McBurnie and Ziguras (2007b) observe "a hard-headed economic weighing of the risks against the likely financial benefits is unlikely to produce a compelling argument for an institution to establish an overseas campus" (37). As discussed earlier, other drivers may be at play. Gioia and Thomas (1996) note that when looking to establish competitive advantage, "perceptions of an institution's prestige or ranking come to the fore, often taking precedence over measurable substance" (352). In fact, McBurnie and Ziguras (2007b) suggest prestige may outweigh any near-term economic analysis in the decision to open an overseas campus.

In this context, institutions exploring the Gulf region need to be self-aware and move beyond the romance of the early relationship and consider carefully the prospects of marriage. International branch campuses are long-term ventures and partnership is an essential element. As one American Council on Education roundtable participant advised, "Throw away your short-term goals, they are irrelevant. The decision to venture abroad should be viewed as a long-term commitment" (Green et al. 2008: 21). Institutions need to know what they are seeking and why, and pick locations that align with their goals. Then, institutions need to get beyond the initial introductions to ensure they have a partner with a complementary vision, and whose resources (financial and social capital) are sufficient to reach that vision. Certainly, as in the case of Temple University in Japan, some institutions can and will flourish in the Gulf. Just as in a marriage, however, succeeding requires a lasting commitment to a relationship that benefits all. Just like our parents advised us many years ago, choose your partner carefully.

REFERENCES

Alexander, A. (2007, May 24). Red faces, millions lost as uni closes campus. *Sydney Morning Herald*. Retrieved January 2, 2009, from www.smh.com. au/news/national/red-faces-millions-lost-as-uni-closes-campus/2007/ 05/23/1179601495596.html.

AME Info (2008). *Michigan State University hosts orientation day for prospective students*. Retrieved December 26, 2008, from www.ameinfo. com/147266.html.

Bjarnason, S. (2005, November). Facts, figures, and trends. Paper presented at the Global Meeting of Associations, Alexandria, Egypt. Retrieved January 4, 2009, from www.unesco.org/iau/conferences/alexandria/gm_ papers/observatory.pdf.

Bottari, M. (2007). *U.S. trade negotiators push to bind U.S. higher education "services" to World Trade Organization jurisdiction, jeopardizing public subsidies as well as other educational policies*. Retrieved November 3, 2007, from www.citizen.org/documents/Higher%20Education%20 Memo.pdf.

Brender, A. (2004, October 15). Japan recognizes U.S. and other foreign universities on its soil. *Chronicle of Higher Education*. Retrieved October 28, 2006, from http://chronicle.com/cgi-bin/printable.cgi?article=http:// chronicle.com/weekly/v51/i08/08a03802.htm.

Chambers, G.S., & Cummings, W.K. (1990). *Profiting from education: Japan– United States international educational ventures in the 1980s*. New York: Institute for International Education.

Cohen, D. (2007a, June 22). A failure amid success. *Chronicle of Higher Education*. Retrieved September 21, 2007, from http://chronicle.com/weekly/ v53/i42/42a04001.htm.

Cohen, D. (2007b, December 13). Settlement in Singapore over failed university. *Inside Higher Education*. Retrieved December 13, 2007, from www.insidehighered.com/laoyout/set/print/news/2007/12/13/singapore.

Dubai International Academic City (2007). *Educating the future* [brochure]. Retrieved December 26, 2008, from www.diacedu.ae/files/DIAC%20Corporate%20Brochure.pdf.

Dubai International Academic City (2008). *Why DIAC*. Retrieved December 26, 2008, from www.diacedu.ae.

Fischer, K. (2008, March 14). Despite doubts, 2 prominent universities sign deals with a Saudi university. *Chronicle of Higher Education, 54*(27), A22.

Gioia, D.A., & Thomas, J.B. (1996). Sensemaking during strategic change in academia. In M.C. Brown II (Ed.), *Organization and governance in higher education* (5th ed., pp. 352–378). Boston: Pearson Custom Publishing.

Green, M., Eckel, P., Calderon, L., & Luu, D. (2007). *Venturing abroad: Delivering U.S. degrees through overseas branch campuses* (U.S. Higher Education in a Global Context: Working Paper No. 1). Washington, DC: American Council on Education.

Green, M., Kinser, K., & Eckel, P. (2008). *On the ground overseas: U.S. degree programs and branch campuses abroad* (U.S. Higher Education in a Global Context: Working Paper No. 3). Washington, DC: American Council on Education.

Jaschik, S. (2006, July 27). A divorce in Singapore. *Inside Higher Ed*. Retrieved July 27, 2006, from http://insidehighered.com/news/2006/07/27/singapore.

Knowledge Village (2008). *About TECOM Investments*. Retrieved December 26, 2008, from www.kv-communityguide.com/kv/tecom_investments.

Krieger, Z. (2008, March 28). An economic building boom transforms the Persian Gulf. *Chronicle of Higher Education*. Retrieved January 3, 2009, from http://chronicle.com/weekly/v54/i29/29a02601.htm.

Lewin, T. (2009, March 1). George Mason University, among first with an Emirates branch, is pulling out. *New York Times*, A13.

Lezberg, A.K. (2003). Accreditation in the Gulf: The case of Qatar. *International Higher Education, 30*(Winter), 16–17.

McBurnie, G., & Ziguras, C. (2007a). *The international branch campus*. Retrieved December 28, 2008, from www.iienetwork.org/page/84656.

McBurnie, G., & Ziguras, C. (2007b). *Transnational education: Issues and trends in offshore higher education*. New York: Routledge.

McMurtrie, B. (2000, June 2). Culture and unrealistic expectations challenge American campuses in Japan. *Chronicle of Higher Education*. Retrieved October 7, 2006, from http://chronicle.com/weekly/v46/i39/39a05601.htm.

Magner, D.K. (1990, May 30). "Opportunism" in education ventures between

U.S., Japan. *Chronicle of Higher Education.* Retrieved October 7, 2006, from http://chronicle.com/che-data/articles.dir/articles-36.dir/issue-37. dir/37a00103.htm.

Michigan State University (2007). *MSU expands global presence with Dubai agreement.* Retrieved December 26, 2008, from http://news.msu.edu/story/696.

Ministry of Higher Education and Scientific Research (2007). *Standards for licensure and accreditation.* Retrieved January 31, 2007, from www.caa.ae/caaweb/images/standards2007.pdf.

Neelakantan, S. (2008). In India, limits on foreign universities lead to creative partnerships. *Chronicle of Higher Education, 54*(22), A1.

Ohmori, F. (2004). Japan and transnational higher education. *International Higher Education, 37*(Fall), 13–15.

Organisation for Economic Co-operation and Development: Centre for Educational Research and Innovation (2004). *Internationalization and trade in higher education: Opportunities and challenges.* Paris: Organisation for Economic Co-operation and Development.

Oxford Business Group (2008). *Qatar—Country profile.* Retrieved January 31, 2008, from www.oxfordbusinessgroup.com/country.asp?country=29.

Qatar Foundation (2008a). *Students.* Retrieved December 26, 2008, from www.qf.org.qa/output/page299.asp.

Qatar Foundation (2008b). *Who we are: Vision and mission.* Retrieved December 26, 2008, from www.qf.edu.qa/output/page77.asp.

Qatar National Conference Centre (2009). Retrieved January 31, 2008, from www.qatarconvention.com.

Qatar Science and Technology Park (2008). Retrieved December 26, 2008, from www.qstp.org.qa/output/page559.asp.

Qatar University (2008). *Accreditation.* Retrieved December 28, 2008, from www.qu.edu.qa/offices/vpcao/accreditation.php.

Rodenbeck, M. (2008). Buying the world. *Economist Special Edition: The World in 2009,* 58.

Rubin, A.M. (1996, March 22). U.S. universities close campuses in Japan amid fiscal woes. *Chronicle of Higher Education.* Retrieved October 7, 2006, from http://chronicle.com/che-data/articles.dir/art-42.dir/issue-28.dir/28a04105.htm.

UAE Interact (2008). *Expat growth widens UAE demographic gap.* Retrieved December 26, 2008, from http://uaeinteract.com/docs/Expat_growth_widens_UAE_demographic_gap__/32128.htm.

University of Southern Queensland (2004). *Annual report.* Retrieved December 28, 2008, from www.usq.edu.au/resources/1intro04.pdf.

University of Wollongong in Dubai (2009). Retrieved January 27, 2009, from www.uowdubai.ac.ae/ps/details.php?sec=1,1.

Wende, M.C. van der (2003). Globalization and access to higher education. *Journal of Studies in International Education, 7*(2), 193–206.

World Bank (2008). *The road not traveled: Education reform in the Middle East and North Africa.* Washington DC: World Bank.

Zemsky, R., Wegner, G., & Massy, W. (2005). *Remaking the American university: Market-smart and mission-centered.* New Brunswick, NJ: Rutgers University Press.

4

JOINT VENTURES IN CROSS-BORDER HIGHER EDUCATION
International Branch Campuses in Malaysia

JASON E. LANE

As previously established, the movement of higher education across borders is not a new phenomenon. Students, faculty, curriculum, and research have long traversed geopolitical boundaries; most recently facilitated by intergovernmental agreements such as the Bologna Process in the European Union and its Asian equivalent sponsored by the Association of Southeast Asian Nations. One of the more interesting components of the growing global higher education marketplace is the rapid emergence of International Branch Campuses (IBCs). These are higher education institutions operating in one nation and owned, at least in part, by a university in another nation.

Whether by government requirement or just basic necessity operating in a cross-border environment, many of these IBCs have resulted in various forms of governance arrangements not widely explored in the scholarly literature. In all cases, at least two sovereign governments are involved and many cases involve the development of multinational corporate partnerships. Both of these situations raise concerns not confronted by other types of governance arrangements.

This chapter uses two examples of IBCs from Malaysia to explore the nature of governmental relations and joint ventures in cross-border higher education. These examples were selected because of their similarity. Both have a home campus in Australia; both participated in the opening of an IBC in Malaysia during the late 1990s; both entered into a joint venture to operate the IBC. However, the differences in how they structured the operating agreement and governance process provide the opportunity for comparison. The chapter is divided into three main parts. Part one reviews the development of IBCs, the role of intersectoral interfaces, and an overview of the different structural arrangements for creating an IBC. Part two describes the Southeast Asia context, explains the roles of the governments of Australia and Malaysia, and provides an overview of two IBCs created by a joint venture agreement. Part three explores how joint venture agreements potentially affect the governance of IBCs. It concludes with a discussion of practical implications.

THE GROWTH OF IBCS AND THEORETICAL FOUNDATIONS

IBCs have been operating in Southeast Asia for approximately two decades but such entities have existed elsewhere since at least the 1950s (Verbik & Merkley 2006). Yet, even though such entities have been in operation for more than a half century, there exists no exhaustive list of IBCs, no globally agreed upon definition of what constitutes an IBC, and very little scholarship beyond idiosyncratic case studies and policy reports. This section provides the reader with an overview about what is currently known of the origins, purposes, and growth of IBCs.

Current Status of IBCs

The two most common definitions of IBCs come from a report from the Observatory of Borderless Higher Education (Verbik & Merkley 2006) and McBurnie and Ziguris's (2007) book *Transnational Education: Issues and Trends in Offshore Higher Education*. Both agree that an IBC is an entity that operates in a nation other than the one in which the home campus is located; has a physical presence in the host country; is at least partly owned by the home institution; and from which students can earn a degree from the home campus. McBurnie and Ziguris (2007) further suggest that instruction should occur face-to-face and students should receive similar support services as those provided on the home campus.

In part because of the lack of an agreed upon definition, the total number of IBCs currently operating around the world is not known; but evidence from two recent studies suggests that IBCs are widespread and growing. Using their definition above, Verbik and Merkley (2006) identified 82 IBCs in operation worldwide, only 14 of which were in operation prior to 1995. Those 82 IBCs were extensions of institutions in 16 different countries and were distributed throughout more than 35 different countries. More recently, Lane and Kinser (in press), using information from accreditation agencies and the U.S. Department of Education, found that U.S.-based institutions are offering courses and degrees in more than 130 physical locations outside of the U.S. (whether all locations meet the definitions provided above is not yet clear).

Moreover, important differences exist between many of the modern IBCs and their predecessors. The earliest IBCs were mostly located in developed nations and designed to provide study abroad opportunities for students from the home campus or military personnel stationed abroad (Verbik & Merkley 2006). These entities often operated below the regulatory radar of the host country, largely as they did not compete directly with domestic institutions. This is not the case with the recent wave of IBCs. The entities discussed in this chapter and most of their peer institutions are located in developing nations, intended to serve the local and regional population as well as certain needs of local government (Lane in press a; McBurnie & Ziguris 2007).

Purposes of IBCs

The roles fulfilled by IBCs differ from those of other types of private higher education. With the exception of the United States, private higher education institutions developed mostly as semi-elite, non-secular; identity-based (often religious); or demand-absorbing organizations (Levy 2008). Broadly, private higher education developed as a way to provide something superior or different from what currently existed or to provide expanded educational access to the demand that exceeded the system's existing capacity (Levy 1986). While there can be some overlap, private higher education institutions usually have a primary role of either providing something superior, different, or more mass based.

Using the framework developed by Levy (1986a) to study the expansion of private higher education, Lane (in press) found that IBCs in Malaysia and Dubai fill the roles identified by Levy and more. By design of the government, many IBCs provide something superior (at least in terms of regional reputation) than what is available from the domestic higher education system. Second, they provide something different from what currently exists in the system. Typically, "something different" is used to describe the advent of religious education, which is not provided by the government (Levy 2008). In the case of IBCs, the government may seek out such institutions to provide access to those historically not served by the public system due to legal restriction or provide academic programs not otherwise available. In the case of Malaysia, part of the role of IBCs is to serve the ethnic-Chinese Malays, whose participation in the public system has been limited due to government-imposed ethnic quotas and have often sought educational opportunities abroad (Lee 2001). Third, just by providing new capacity within the system, they fulfill the role of demand absorption as these institutions mostly open in nations that do not have the capacity to meet the increasing demand for higher education. Fourth, and in example of how IBCs are actively engaging in a role not previously observed in private higher education sectors, these institutions not only absorb demand, but also generate demand. The governments in many nations, including Malaysia, have clearly stated that part of the reason to import IBCs is the hope of becoming a regional hub for higher education, attracting new foreign students to their nation.

Intersectoral Interfaces: Government Relations

Readers have likely already begun to note the interesting intersectoral dynamics arising from this form of cross-border higher education. As Lane (in press a), noted in his study, IBCs are regulated by the host government as private institutions, "even though … the [host] governments clearly intend, for better or for worse, for these institutions to serve government needs." As higher education institutions evolve into multinational entities, with locations in multiple countries, the role of the government and division between public and private institutions becomes increasingly blurred.

Indeed, intersectoral interfaces are not new. It is not unusual for a government to be a part of the development of a private higher education sector. Levy (2008) observes that in many nations the government has been involved in the creation of a private higher education sector. This is certainly the case with IBCs in Malaysia as the government has been actively involved in the recruitment of the foreign institutions operating within its borders and have listed IBCs as part of its long-term plan to raise the nation's competitiveness in the global economy (Malaysia Economic Planning Unit 2002).

A primary difference with previous intersectoral interfaces is the fact that in the case of IBCs, there are examples of the host government recruiting (and sometimes supporting) the agents of the home government to set up shop as a private entity and compete with the host government's domestic higher education public and private sectors. With the exception of Dublin Business School, the IBCs in Malaysia all are extensions of public institutions. Thus, these cross-border entities are viewed as public by the home country, but regulated as private institutions in the host country. Such duality raises concerns about quality assurance, governance, and broader intergovernmental relationships (see Lane & Kinser 2008, for a discussion of the issues associated with this public–private duality).

Intersectoral Interfaces: The Academic Corporation

Beyond the intersectoral interfaces between institution and government, many of the legal arrangements pursued to create IBCs involve interfaces between academic and non-academic corporations. The academic corporation is one of the oldest legal entities known to mankind and the legal precedent for its existence can be traced back to developments in Roman law during the first centuries of this millennium (Duryea 2000). Since that time almost all governments have come to perceive universities as corporate entities, institutions that are "an invisible unity of members living by corporate constitution and operating as an ideal person capable of holding property of its own, and distinct from all other persons including its own member" (Karp 1971: 76). However, the creation of campuses in multiple countries provides opportunities for partnerships and arrangements that may not have previously been available to many institutions.

In a *joint venture* two or more partners create a new legal entity to pursue a joint objective (Boyle 1968). For example, the partners retain their separate legal status and share ownership of the IBC, including splitting the financial risk and rewards. Such entities are a common occurrence in inter-firm collaboration, particularly in the international setting (Reuer & Koza 2000). While the parents retain ownership and control of the progeny, the new organization can "incur debt, sign contracts, or undertake other activities in its own name, and without consequence to the financial or legal position of the parents, except to the extent of their investment in the joint venture" (Pfeffer & Nowak 2001: 387). Further, joint ventures are often characterized by equity interest and management control; the two do not have to mirror each other (Choi & Beamish 2004). While equity interests are discussed below, critical focus is placed on management control issues.

In some cases, such as with the Royal Melbourne Institute of Technology's Vietnam campus and Monash University's South Africa campus, a university will build and operate an IBC without entering into a legal partnership with other entities. In a *wholly owned* IBC, the home campus owns the physical presence and assumes full responsibility for all academic and fiduciary aspects of the enterprise. The institution retains exclusive control over the operations of the campus, but also assumes all financial risk.

A *strategic alliance* falls between a joint venture and a wholly owned enterprise. As Scott (2003) notes, strategic alliances are an "increasingly popular way to obtain the benefits of larger scale and differentiation without the costs of investing in and maintaining facilities and personnel" (206). A strategic alliance occurs when two or more partners enter into an agreement to collaborate in the pursuit of joint objectives, but partners remain legally separate entities. Such a model is most common in the Middle East, where the Dubai International Academic City (DIAC) and Qatar Education City (QEC) provide the physical infrastructure for IBCs. The home campus retains complete ownership over the academic institution, typically renting the space from the alliance partner. It is very likely that strategic alliances will also begin to occur in Malaysia. The government is in the process of eliminating the law requiring the creation of a joint venture and the Sarawak government created a foundation to encourage IBCs to locate in that state (S. Morshidi, personal communication, February 9, 2009).

GEOGRAPHIC LOCUS, GOVERNMENT CONTEXT, AND INSTITUTIONAL ARRANGEMENTS

This section provides readers with an overview of the context and the structure of the two joint ventures used for illustrative purposes in this chapter. The first section provides an overview of the growth of private higher education in Southeast Asia. The second section describes the nature of the government relationship with the example institutions. The third section reviews how the governance of the two joint venture examples is structured.

Private Higher Education in Southeast Asia

The most populous and rapidly developing region of the world, Southeast Asia has great diversity in the type, size, and history of private higher education sectors. A combination of underfunding and rapid democratization of public higher education currently propels the development of private higher education (Lee & Healy 2006). Regardless of the amount of national wealth, an increasing number of people in all nations in this region now recognize higher education as a key means for social mobility. The resultant demand for higher education is putting significant strain on existing higher education systems, leading many governments to foster expansion of their public and private higher education sectors.

In terms of the public systems, governments in this region have responded in two primary ways to the increasing demand: democratizing the public system or leaving the system underfunded. Both paths result in pushing students to pursue educational opportunities in the private sector. Democratization has required governments to spend large amounts of money to expand services to move their elite systems (largely influenced by their colonial heritage) to a semi-elite or mass system, opening the system to lower socio-economic groups and historically excluded minority groups. Such a change results in a perception (sometimes based on reality and sometimes not) in a reduction of quality. Similarly, the underfunding of a system results in "under-qualified academic staff and poorly planned curricula, thus poorly taught students" (Lee & Healy 2006: 2). Both paths have led the more affluent classes to seek out different, more exclusive, and, they hope, better quality opportunities. In both cases, the government cannot afford to build enough capacity to meet all of the demand. The result is the private sector grows to meet the various unmet demands of the people of the region, with the government often playing an active role in that sector's development (Levy 2008).

Massification (college participation rates of over 15%) plays one of the most significant roles in the development of higher education in any nation (Trow 1973, 1999). In nations such as Singapore, Thailand, and the Philippines, cohort participation rates exceed 30%. With the exception of the developing nations of Myanmar, Cambodia, and Lao PDR, all nations in the region have growing participation rates that already exceed 10% (Lee & Healy 2006; Program for Research on Private Higher Education [PROPHE] 2008). A large proportion of this growth has occurred in the private sector, but the private proportion of enrollments continues to vary significantly in the region. In Indonesia and the Philippines, more than 70% of enrollment is in the private sector and in Malaysia and India private sector enrollment now exceeds 30% of all college-going students. However, in nations such as Cambodia, China, Thailand, and Vietnam, private participation rates fall below 15% (PROPHE 2008).

The massification of the region resulted in a significant diversification of educational opportunities. Nations once dominated by an elite system of university education, now regulate an array of research universities, teaching colleges, polytechnics, vocational institutes, community colleges, some online institutions; they include public and private, profit and non-profit, and domestic and foreign. One of the most significant areas of growth is in cross-border higher education. Southeast Asia, with Malaysia among the nations leading the way, has rapidly emerged as one of the fastest-growing importers of higher education. For example, the United Kingdom expects demand for U.K.-based educational opportunities in Malaysia and Singapore to grow from 67,000 students in 2003 to 271,000 by 2020 (British Council 2005).

Many cross-border partnerships started with twinning arrangements and have since evolved into fully operational IBCs. As of 2006, China, Malaysia, Singapore, Thailand, and Vietnam had imported IBCs (Verbik & Merkley 2006). Moreover, Malaysia, Thailand, and Singapore all have national goals of becoming regional hubs for higher education, importing education from foreign universities and, in turn, using IBCs to attract students from around the region (Lee & Healy 2006; McBurnie & Ziguris 2007).

Government Context: Australia and Malaysia

Governments are important actors in almost all organizational studies. The government is the primary sovereign of the modern world, responsible for most legal and regulatory frameworks (Scott 2003). Lindbolm (1977) acknowledges the special character of government as the one organization that can "exercise authority over other organizations" (22). In the work here, the government is especially important as IBCs must deal with at least two governments; those of the home and host countries. Thus, they must cope with at least two sets of legal and regulatory frameworks, including the quality assurance parameters.

In each nation there are myriad agencies at both the local and national levels that can affect IBC development. Both the Australian and the Malaysian governments acknowledged a potential benefit for Australian universities to open branch campuses in Malaysia. It falls primarily to the Malaysian government to ensure that their citizens are not unduly harmed by the services provided or the competition with other providers. Similarly, the Australian government sees its role as ensuring that the foreign endeavors do not negatively affect the home campus or the reputation of Australian higher education. While both have roles of national protection, they do not operate mutually exclusive of each other.

For more than a decade, Australia and Malaysia have worked collaboratively in the development of educational opportunities for Malaysian students. In 1996, the Australian Department of Education, Science, and Training and the Malaysian Ministry of Education signed a *Memorandum of Understanding on Co-operation in Education*. By signing the agreement the two nations agreed to the following:

- facilitation of the exchange of academic staff and students for programs of mutual benefit, including exchanges of Malay and English language teachers;
- mutual assistance in the area of technical and vocational training;
- provision of scholarship schemes for study at higher education institutions;
- study of the possibility of credit transfer and split programs between higher education institutions; and
- development of twinning programs for the mutual benefit of both parties and facilitation of the exchange of educational information and teaching materials.

This agreement was made possible when the Malaysian government adopted legislation in 1996 allowing for foreign institutions to engage in cross-border delivery of degree programs by operating branch campuses on Malaysian soil.

In Malaysia, the government is constitutionally required to provide higher education, although demand has long exceeded supply. The 1969 Essential (Higher Education Institution) Regulation legally prevented the domestic private institutions from granting degrees and foreign institutions from establishing campuses. Starting in the 1970s, private institutions were allowed to offer pre-university courses. Then, in the early 1980s, private institutions became involved with foreign providers via twinning and franchise arrangements to provide courses leading to a certificate, diploma, or professional credential. In 1996, passage of the Education Act, Private Higher Education Act, and the National Accreditation Board Act paved the way for the creation of IBCs (Morshidi 2005).

The education sector in Malaysia remains one of the most highly regulated of the nation's service import arenas (McBurnie & Ziguris 2007). As such, the government retains tight controls over the types of institutions that may enter its borders as well as the nature of how those organizations operate. For example, Monash was only able to move into the Malaysian market because the government of Malaysia extended an official invitation. In addition to having to receive an invitation, the Malaysian government requires foreign providers to partner with a domestic entity (Morshidi 2005). As such, even though Monash was able to offer their degree programs in Malaysia, the Malaysian government was able to retain control over the campus because it was owned by a Malaysian company.

The Australian government plays a similar role in the oversight and regulation of this operation in that it has established a set of rules that Australian universities must follow in order to operate abroad. These rules mandate that the main campus/central administration must adhere to a set of quality assurance procedures, including: (1) quality and standards comparable to those on other campus(es) of the institution; (2) teaching by staff qualified at a level comparable to those on other campuses of the institution; (3) resources and facilities adequate for the delivery of the course; and (4) adequate measures to protect the welfare of students (National Protocols for Higher Education Approval Processes 2000: 11). The role of the government is to protect the interests of the government and its people. In this case, the Australian government was working to ensure that new adventures in the international marketplace do not negatively impact the reputation of the institution or the quality of education and other services provided by the university to the people of Australia.

It is important to note that while the Monash campus in Malaysia has been developed to be self-supporting and operate as a separate corporate enterprise, the government of Australia continues to view the organization as an extension of the main campus. Thus, it is invested in ensuring the financial integrity of the new operation for fear that that its failure will negatively impact the exporting campus and the citizens of Australia. As such, in addition to the governance structure described below, the Australian government has provided for its own oversight of these international branch campuses:

> Where an Australian university or other self accrediting institution operates in a distant location and issues an award under its own name the Council or governing body of the university or other institutions is responsible for quality assurance and will be subject to audit by the Australian Universities Quality Agency (AUQA). For overseas campuses the institution will be expected to maintain standards at least equivalent to those provided in Australia regardless of specific governments.
>
> (Griffith University 2004: 1)

Joint Venture One: Monash University Sunway Campus Malaysia (MUSCM)

Monash University was one of the first institutions invited to establish an IBC in Malaysia and partnered, in 1998, with its long-time Malaysian collaborator Sunway Corporation. For 10 years preceding the agreement, Monash had worked with Sunway in a twinning arrangement in which Malaysian students began their education in Malaysia at Sunway College (another tertiary entity operated by Sunway) and would complete their degree in Australia at a Monash campus. Following the passage of the new legislation, Sunway and Monash entered into an agreement that called for the establishment of a Monash branch campus in Bandar, Malaysia near its twinning partner, Sunway College. MUSCM has been developed as a semi-independent, self-funding joint venture. For its part, Monash contributed A$503,000 to the initial start up; and as of 2002, the new campus contributed A$1.4 million per year back to the main Monash University budget. As of this writing, MUSCM continues to operate.

MUSCM is a joint venture in which the two partners are the Sunway Group and Monash University. Sunway retains 76% of the equity interest and is responsible for providing physical infrastructure, including student accommodations. Monash, which holds the other 24% of the equity, provides the intellectual capital to teach the students and awards the degrees. Responsibility for the operation of the campus is shared by both partners. In fact, the governance structure suggests that even though Sunway retains a majority equity interest, management control is split between functional areas, but governed cooperatively.

There are three primary facets of the governance structure worth noting here. First, the Board of Directors of MUSCM is controlled by Sunway. The membership comprises five Sunway members and three Monash University members. Governance of the entity is shared and thus partners share operational and financial knowledge of the venture. Second, a separate planning group coordinates the operations of the corporation. That group has membership from both partners, with Monash having the majority of members. There are two members from Sunway and three members from Monash, one of which chairs the board. Finally, all academic aspects of the organization are controlled by Monash University's normal academic governance structure. Thus, issues like course requirements, course content, and degree conference are controlled by Monash.

Figure 4.1 provides an overview of the operating arrangement between Sunway and Monash. This figure lays out the responsibilities of the partners and illustrates the operation of the IBC.

Joint Venture Two: Royal Melbourne Institute of Technology's (RMIT) Adorna Institute of Technology, Malaysia

The Adorna Institute of Technology (AIT) was a joint venture between RMIT University and the property developer Adorna in Australia and the Malaysian-based Fatimah Binti Abdullah and Yayasan Bumiputra Pulau Pinang Berhad (companies). AIT opened in rural Malaysia in 1996 and concluded its operations in 1999; 302 students attended the institution at its peak in 1998. AIT was run by a legally established joint venture between the four companies mentioned above, each of which was registered in Malaysia. The two indigenous Malaysian companies each held a 10% equity interest in the company. Though their involvement in the parent company was very limited, they fulfilled the requirement that foreign companies operating in Malaysia have some indigenous partners.

Compared to the structure used in the governance of MUSCM, the AIT structure (Figure 4.2) looks like two silos between RMIT and Adorna (again, the indigenous investors had limited involvement) with each having separate management responsibilities.

The interaction that did occur seems advisory at best. Under the operating arrangement, Adorna was almost entirely responsible for the

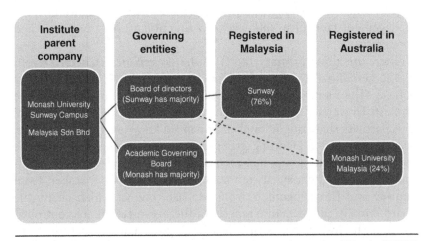

Figure 4.1 Business Structure of Monash University Sunway Corporation Malaysia (MUSCM) (Source: Adapted from Auditor General of Victoria 2002).

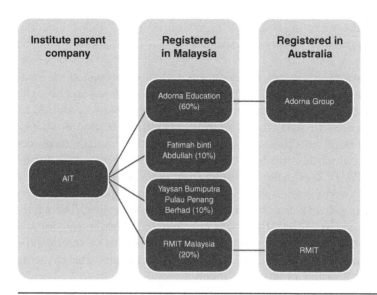

Figure 4.2 AIT Joint Venture Ownership.

financial and non-academic operating aspects of the endeavor, including building the campus and covering any operating losses. All joint venture partners, except RMIT, were responsible for ensuring AIT had sufficient funds to operate. RMIT's 20% equity stake was based on their infusion of intellectual capital. RMIT's responsibilities included providing all educational services, such as designing courses, ensuring the courses were comparable with those offered on the main RMIT campus, providing faculty as needed, and licensing the RMIT brand name to AIT.

Rather than creating collaborative governance arrangements under the joint venture, the partners operated almost entirely autonomously from each other. In fact, a service agreement was reached in which RMIT would invoice AIT for the services provided by RMIT, over and above their 20% share of any operating profits. Thus, even though they were legal partners, RMIT's role was more like that of a contracted consultant. But, even before the joint agreement was reached, many concerns were raised about the endeavor. For example, Adorna had no experience with the education sector, the proposed location was 50 km from a major metropolitan area, and Adorna's previous construction work was perceived by some as sub-par based on local standards (particularly in comparison with potential nearby competitors). Further, it was recognized by the partners that AIT would be successful only in the medium to long term. In the short term, there were likely to be significant operating losses. Adorna assured RMIT that they could cover the potential financial shortfall and that the campus would be competitive.

Four years after it began, the endeavor ended. As predicted the location of the campus made it difficult to attract students in the early years; however, unlike promised, Adorna was not able to cover AIT's operating costs. In part, the economic crisis that affected Southeast Asia in the late 1990s took a significant toll on the financial resources of Adorna, which had invested heavily in Malaysia real estate during that time. RMIT eventually withdrew from the joint venture. Not only did the institution not see any revenue from its 20% equity stake, it also had to write off A$2.3 million for unreimbursed services. The agreement was written so that RMIT was not financially responsible for any part of the operating losses; however, there is no way to account for the potential negative reputational or other repercussions due to being associated with such an unsuccessful endeavor.

DISCUSSION AND IMPLICATIONS

The extent to which higher education institutions use joint ventures either domestically or internationally is not known (see Eckel, Affolter-Caine, & Green 2003 for a review of curricular joint ventures). Such an arrangement is one of many possible inter-organizational arrangements available to an institution looking to develop an IBC. But, why would a university choose to enter into a joint venture? The examples here cannot provide us with a straightforward answer. Malaysia required such an arrangement; thus, if the university wanted to open an IBC in that nation it had to use the joint venture. Yet, the literature suggests possible incentives and the examples illustrate some of the positive and negative aspects of an academic joint venture.

When entering a joint venture, institutions sacrifice some autonomy and control in exchange for increased protection from risk. In a wholly owned enterprise, the institution retains control of the entire endeavor able to make all of the decisions, but also having to assume the financial risks. In both of the examples, the institutions agreed to partner with another entity, giving up some control of the branch campus; but also significantly reducing their financial risk. In the case of AIT, even though the joint venture failed, RMIT was protected from the full extent of the financial loss (even though some services went unreimbursed). However, they also sacrificed a great deal of management control, allowing Adorna to have almost exclusive control over the operations and financial decisions.

Kogut (1988) suggests three explanations for the engagement of a joint venture: transaction costs, strategic behavior, and the acquisition of organizational knowledge. Evidence of each of these behaviors can be found in the examples. First, transaction costs are the costs associated with economic exchange; this includes more than simply a "price" paid for a service or product. Transaction costs can include bargaining costs, oversight and enforcement costs, and information costs. Joint ventures are often employed when there is a high degree of uncertainty in the environment and in how to measure and monitor performance:

> Because a joint venture straddles the border of two firms, it differs from a contract insofar as the cooperation is administered within an organizational hierarchy. It differs from a vertically integrated activity insofar as two firms claim ownership to the residual value and control rights over the use of the assets.
>
> (Kogut 1988: 320)

An organization will pursue a joint venture if the internal production costs or the external acquisition costs are determined to be higher than those associated with entering a joint venture. In a wholly owned endeavor, the academic institution has greater control over the IBC and can more easily monitor IBC performance as it is integrated into the existing systems of the institution. However, it must also cover the cost of the physical infrastructure; spend time learning and negotiating local policies, regulations, and culture; and engage in activities (e.g., construction and property management; supervising employees in a different culture) that it may not have the time or knowledge to be able to do effectively. The creation of MUSCM likely represented a low transaction cost model for both partners. There was an existing working relationship between the two entities, thus there was no need to learn each other's organizational culture. Sunway is a large Malaysian firm with extensive experience in property management. Monash is a reputable academic institution, with well-regarded academic programs, and processes already in place to offer academic degrees. While there is a forced degree of interdependence, the low transaction costs made a joint venture a reasonable endeavor.

Second, strategic management assumes that "firms transact by the mode which maximizes profits through improving a firm's competitive position vis-à-vis rivals" (Kogut 1988: 322). There is overlap between transaction cost explanations and strategic management explanations as the transaction cost approach can be used to assess the value of a joint venture even if the decision to engage in the joint venture is strategic. Opening a campus in Malaysia with a local partner already engaged in the private education sector had the potential to provide Monash with a strategic advantage over other institutions seeking to serve Malaysian students. Also, Vernon (1983) sees joint ventures as a way to strategically hedge against uncertainty in the environment. In fact, the most common joint venture agreement in nations with emerging economies is to have the large multinational organization provide the technology and a local partner provide knowledge of the local environment (Beamish 1993; Inkpen & Beamish 1997).

With the case of RMIT, a great deal of uncertainty existed. Concerns were raised about the location of the campus and the short-term viability of the endeavor. The agreement reached with Adorna allowed RMIT to achieve, in theory, profitability even though the enterprise was forecasted to lose money during its first years of operation; thus, buffering against uncertainty. RMIT was not required to invest any money upfront. It received a 20% equity stake in return for its participation in the process. Finally, it was to receive direct payment for the services it provided to AIT. Thus, even though Adorna was likely to lose money during the first few years, RMIT, with no financial stake, was to be paid for their services. In return, however, RMIT's potential fortunes were based on an entity of which it had almost no direct control.

Third, studies have reported organizations enter into joint ventures to acquire organizational knowledge (Hamel 1991), organizational skills (Beamish 1988), and knowledge about the local economy (Casson 1993). The need for new knowledge may explain, in part, why a property management firm and university would engage in a joint venture. Universities retain what Polanyi (1967) refers to as "tacit knowledge," knowledge that is organizationally embedded. This does not refer to the knowledge of faculty and staff, which may be hired away, likely at high transaction costs. It refers to what Nelson and Winter (1982) call skills and routines. The university is a complex array of decision-making processes and much of the value of an institution's degree is wrapped up in the processes that a student goes through to achieve the degree and the processes used to decide the requirements for the degree. A property management firm could replicate those processes, but it would essentially have to reinvent the academic institution. Further, even if the firm were able to reasonably replicate the processes, there is no guarantee the degree would be valued in the same way. As such, it may simply be simpler and cheaper to partner with the institution that already has the necessary skills and routines. In both examples, each academic institution retained nearly absolute authority over the academic aspects of the enterprise, being responsible for everything from course content to degree conference.

Conflict in Joint Venture Governance

A fundamental component of the joint venture is the existence of at least two principal owners governing a single agent. In the case of MUSCM, Monash and Sunway shared governance of the enterprise. With AIT, four partners owned the venture, although the primary actors were RMIT and Adorna. The preceding section discussed some of the advantages of a joint venture; the following section reviews some of the problems using agency theory. Agency problems arise in relationships where one entity (the principal) enters into a relationship with another entity (the agent) in order to have the agent carry out the goals of the principal. It is assumed that the agent will shirk its duties (i.e., pursue its goals in lieu of the principal's goals) unless compelled by carrot or stick to do otherwise. Agency relationships are ubiquitous in higher education (Lane & Kivisto 2008; Lane in press b). In these examples, the parent organizations are the principals and the progeny is the agent. This section focuses on issues pertaining to the existence of multiple principals.

Multiple principals exist when two or more principals have separate contracts with an agent. Such relationships contain systemic dilemmas for the agent as the multiple agents could potentially desire the agent to pursue contrary goals (although they could also seek pursuit of complementary goals). Competitive, multiple principals are a part of many organizational dynamics in higher education (Lane & Kivisto 2008; Lane in press b) and in governments (Moe 1984). When multiple principals exist, it is often that the agent (in this case the joint venture) is not under complete control of any one entity and it is possible for there to be a lack of understanding of how authority is legitimately divided among the competing principals.

In the example with AIT, the two indigenous principals have almost no role in the governance of the institution, participating mostly as investors. The primary actors are Adorna and RMIT, which entered into an agreement that limited interaction between the two principals, each retaining control over their areas of responsibility. RMIT provided the academic services, in a relationship that more closely resembles a contractual consultant rather than a set of partners engaged in a joint venture. Adorna retained majority control of the organization and assumed responsibility for most aspects of AIT. While such a relationship was financially favorable toward RMIT, it precluded RMIT from being involved in much of the decision making. Eventually, when it looked as if Adorna was no longer able to financially support AIT, RMIT merely withdrew from the partnership. The lack of collaboration and joint control creates a potentially dangerous scenario wherein one partner is subject to the fate and fancy of the other partner.

In the MUSCM example, Monash University and Sunway Corporation serve as multiple principals. Somewhat similar to AIT, the two partners are responsible for the areas that fall within their expertise. Sunway handles property management; Monash is responsible for academic affairs; both share responsibility for the campus. Moreover, they use a form of co-optation to create a governance structure that ensures that information flows between the two principals and that each principal has say in decision making.

As seen in Figure 4.1, two boards are used to control the primary functions of the enterprise. First, there is the board of directors, which provides the primary oversight of all aspects of the IBC. Sunway controls the majority of the directors, but Monash is able to appoint members to the board as well. There is also an academic board, which provides oversight of the academic components of the campus. This board is controlled by Monash, but Sunway has representation. As traditionally used in the organizational studies literature, co-optation refers to the incorporation of representatives of external organizations in the decision-making processes of the organization (Scott 2003). A board can use co-optation to bring specialized expertise and to augment the skills of the management (Mizruchi 1996). Even though the boards are populated by the principals involved in the creation and governance of the agent, a determination was clearly made to avoid the silos that seem to have been the nature of the AIT structure. With both boards, retaining majority membership allows both principals to retain managerial control over their areas of expertise. However, involving membership from the other principal reduces information asymmetry and makes it easier to coordinate the efforts between the two groups.

The existence of two different boards could create a scenario wherein there are competing demands on MUSCM. If competing demands arrive from the two boards, MUSCM has two alternatives: flip-flop based on the most recent contract change or make a choice based on the relative power between the two principals (Lyne & Tierney 2003). In the latter option, the agent must in some way reconcile the difference in demands with the contractual terms with each principal.

When competing contractual demands exist, agent behavior may become erratic or incoherent. Further, a variety of factors involved in the political dynamics further complicates outcomes. Administrative priorities and organizational leaders within the principals change. The contractual expectations of the principal(s) may be unclear as actors, policy preferences, or profit motivations evolve. The agent may not fully understand the power dynamics between/among the principals. In sum, there is no simple solution to the problem of multiple principals with competing expectations; but it is important to note the existence of the potential problems that arise with the use of multiple principals.

Operating in an environment of multiple, complex principals creates a series of dilemmas for researchers focusing on governance structures and institutional explanations for policy outcomes. Rational expectations of actor behavior suggest that when and where possible, agents engage in shirking. Shirking is avoided in an environment when the agent's utility from working is higher than that received from shirking (Frey 1993). This forms the basis of common agency problems: how does one assess the existence of shirking and evaluate principals' efforts to dissuade agents from engaging in such activity?

Answering such questions becomes increasingly difficult as the complexity of principal structures increases. In a single principal relationship, the agent must assess and pursue the goals of only one principal. As such, assessment by the researcher of the existence of shirking (so long as the principal's goals are transparent) is fairly straightforward. Further, the principal alone establishes the contractual obligations of the principal and is solely responsible for ensuring contract compliance. Complexity of agency problems increases with the development of multiple principals. The Board of Directors and the Academic Board are examples of multiple principals in that both are "principals to [an] agent. Yet, neither ... requires the consent of the other ... to monitor, reward, or sanction that agent" (Lyne & Tierney 2003: 6; see also Calvert, McCubbins, & Weingast 1989; and Hammond & Knott 1996). Determination of shirking becomes difficult due to each principal having conflicting goals for the agent.

The existence of multiple principals also increases the agent's ability to engage in shirking behavior, particularly if the agent is able to play the principals against each other. In this case, the principals may become so concerned about each other that they fail to monitor agent behavior. In addition to the potential for competing contracts with the agent, free agency problems may arise for the principals as certain principals may benefit from agent actions while other principals may cover the costs of contract enforcement.

Practical Implications

The movement of higher education across international borders is fraught with much uncertainty: cultures differ, student markets can be volatile, and governments change. The creation of IBCs make such uncertainty even more tenuous as the creation of a physical presence in another country increases the difficulty of extracting from a cross-border endeavor should it prove unsuccessful. Further, unlike their early predecessors, host governments are very active in the recruiting, development, and regulation of IBCs; in some cases signaling that IBCs are part of the government's public policy initiatives (Lane in press b; McBurnie & Ziguris 2007). Such arrangements can be welcoming when the government is supportive; but governments change and so do their policies. One option for mitigating some of the uncertainty is to create a joint venture, which can align organizations with different expertise and knowledge as well as protect the academic institution from some of the financial risk.

As discussed above, there are a number of reasons for organizations to engage in joint ventures. First, such partnerships can reduce the transaction costs associated with opening an IBC, particularly if the academic organization partners with an organization knowledgeable of local customs and regulations. Second, joint ventures can be strategically superior to other options. For example, aligning partners with different levels of expertise can increase the competitiveness of the new venture. Third, the tacit knowledge and processes embedded in the academic organization may not be replicable by other organizations. This is particularly true of reputable academic organizations, whose value is embedded in its processes, knowledge, and decades of producing quality graduates.

The shared ownership inherent in joint ventures does, however, present some potential problems. The existence of two or more principals leads to potential disagreement among partners and confusion for the agent. Gong, Shenkar, Luo, and Nyaw (2007) suggest that the two primary means for reducing the problems associated with multiple principals is through "*ex ante* setup (e.g., contract completeness) and *ex post* management (e.g., partner cooperation)" (1022). Having an explicit contract is important to delineate the roles and responsibilities of the partners and to help mitigate any agency problems that might arise. In entering a joint venture it is important to have an agreement that covers the structure and objectives of the joint venture, the financial contributions to be contributed, ownership of any intellectual property created by the joint venture, how liabilities, profits, and losses are shared, and how disputes will be resolved, and how an organization can exit the venture.

While an explicit contract will help reduce disagreement and confusion fostered by the existence of multiple principals, it is important that the partners cooperate in the management of the agent and that there is a mechanism in place for disagreements to be resolved. Moreover, Gong et al. (2007) suggest that the more partners that are involved in the joint venture the more critical the *ex post* management becomes. Structures such as those used in the MUSCM are important for ensuring cooperation among partners. In fact, partnering with an organization with which one already has a healthy working relationship can prove critical for overcoming strains that will surely arise in the joint venture.

REFERENCES

Auditor General of Victoria (2002, June). *Report on public sector agencies.* Retrieved February 15, 2005, from www.audit.vic.gov.au/reports_mp_psa/psa0202.html.

Beamish, P.W. (1988). *Multinational joint ventures in developing countries.* Routledge: London.

Beamish, P.W. (1993). The characteristics of joint ventures in developed and developing countries. *Columbia Journal of World Business, 20*(3), 13–19.

Boyle, S.E. (1968). An estimate of the number and size distribution of domestic joint subsidiaries. *Antitrust Law and Economics Review, 1*: 81–92.

British Council (2005). *Vision 2020: Forecasting international student mobility: A UK perspective.* London: British Council Publications.

Calvert, R., McCubbins, M., & Weingast, B. (1989). A theory of political control and agency discretion. *American Journal of Political Science, 33*(3): 588–611.

Casson, M. (1993). Contractual arrangements for technology transfer: New evidence from business history. In G. Jones (Ed.), *Coalitions and collaboration in international business* (pp. 18–50). Aldershot, UK: Edward Elgar Publishing.

Choi, C., & Beamish, P.W. (2004). Split management control and international joint venture performance. *Journal of International Business Studies, 38,* 201–215.

Duryea, E.D. (2000). *The academic corporation: A history of college and university governing boards.* New York: Falmer Press.

Eckel, P., Affolter-Caine, B., & Green, M. (2003). *New times, new strategies: Curricular joint ventures.* Washington, DC: American Council on Education.

Frey, B.S. (1993). Does monitoring increase work effort? The rivalry with trust and loyalty. *Economic Inquiry, 31*(4), 663–670.

Gong, Y., Shenkar, O., Luo, Y., & Nyaw, M. (2007). Do multiple principals help or hinder international joint venture performance? The mediating roles of contract completeness and partner cooperation. *Strategic Management Journal, 28*(10), 1021–1034.

Griffith University (2004). *Higher education from non higher ed providers.* Retrieved November 30, 2009, from www.griffith.edu.au/_data/assets/pdf_file/0003/384781/national_protocols.pdf.

Hamel, G. (1991). Competition for competence and inter-partner learning within international strategic alliances. *Strategic Management Journal, 12*(Summer), 83–103.

Hammond, T.H., & Knott, J.H. (1996). Who controls the bureaucracy? Presidential power, congressional dominance, legal constraints and bureaucratic autonomy in a model of multi-institutional policy-making. *Journal of Law, Economics and Organization, 12*(1), 119–166.

Inkpen, A.C., & Beamish, P.W. (1997). Knowledge, bargaining power, and the instability of international joint ventures. *Academy of Management Review, 22*(1), 177–202.

Karp, A. (1971). Roman law and corporations. Unpublished manuscript, New York: Teachers College, Columbia University.

Kogut, B. (1988). Joint ventures: Theoretical and empirical perspectives. *Strategic Management Journal, 9*(4), 319–332.

Lane, J.E. (in press a). Importing private higher education: International branch campuses. *Journal of Comparative Policy Analysis.*

Lane, J.E. (in press b). Studying individual and institutional interests: The role of principal–agent theory in studying higher education organizations. In M. Bastedo (Ed.), *New approaches to studying higher education organizations.* Baltimore: Johns Hopkins University Press.

Lane, J.E., & Kinser, K. (2008). The private nature of cross-border higher education. *International Higher Education, 53*, 11–13.

Lane, J.E., & Kinser, K. (in press). *Review of American universities with international branch campuses.* PROPHE Working Paper.

Lane, J.E., & Kivisto, J.A. (2008). Interests, information, and incentives in higher education: A review of principal–agent theory in higher education governance. In J.C. Smart (Ed.), *Higher education: Handbook of theory and research, Vol. 23* (pp. 141–180). New York: Springer.

Lee, M. (2001, June 20–22). Private higher education in Malaysia: Expansion, diversification and consolidation. Paper presented at the UNESCO PROAP and SEAMEO RIHED Second Regional Seminar on Private Higher Education: Its Role in Human Resource Development in a Globalized Knowledge Society, Bangkok, Thailand.

Lee, M.N.N., & Healy, S. (2006). Higher education in Southeast Asia: An overview. In S. Shaeffer and S.Yavaprabhas (Eds.), *Higher Education in Southeast Asia* (pp. 1–12). Bangkok: UNESCO.

Levy, D.C. (1986). *Higher education and the state in Latin America: Private challenges to public dominance.* Chicago: University of Chicago Press.

Levy, D.C. (2006). The unanticipated explosion: Private higher education's global surge. *Comparative Education Review, 50*(2), 217–240.

Levy, D.C. (2008). The enlarged expanse of higher education. *Die Hochscule* (2), 19–35.

Lindbolm, C.E. (1977). *Politics and markets.* New York: Basic Books.

Lyne, M., & Tierney, M. (2003). The politics of common agency: Unitary, multiple and collective principals. Paper presented at the annual meeting of the American Political Science Association, Philadelphia, PA.

McBurnie, G., & Ziguris, C. (2007). *Transnational education: Issues and trends in offshore higher education.* London: Routledge.

Malaysia Economic Planning Unit (2002). *Knowledge based economy master plan.* Kuala Lumpur: Malaysia Economic Planning Unit. Retrieved October 15, 2008, from www.epu.gov.my/New%20Folder/publication/knoweco.htm.

Mizruchi, M. (1996). What do interlocks do? An analysis, critique, and assessment of research or interlocking directorates. *Annual Review of Sociology, 22,* 271–298.

Moe, T.M. (1984). The new economics of organization. *American Political Science Review, 28*(4), 739–777.

Morshidi, S. (2005). *Transnational higher education in Malaysia: Balancing benefits and concerns through regulations.* National Higher Education Research Institute (Malaysia) Working Paper. Retrieved September 15, 2008, from www.usm.my/ipptn/fileup/TNHE_Malaysia.pdf.

National Protocols for Higher Education Approval Processes (2000). Retrieved November 30, 2009, from www.mceetya.edu.au/verve/_resources/protocols_file.pdf.

Nelson, R., & Winter, S. (1982). *An evolutionary theory of economic change.* Cambridge, MA: Harvard University Press.

Pfeffer, J., & Nowak, P. (2001). Joint ventures and interorganizational interdependence. In P.J. Buckly & J. Michie (Eds.), *Firms, organizations, and contracts* (pp. 385–409). Oxford: Oxford University Press.

Polanyi, M. (1967). *The tacit dimension.* New York: Doubleday.

Program for Research on Private Higher Education (2008, January). *Country data summary.* Retrieved October 24, 2009, from www.albany.edu/dept/eaps/prophe/data/international.html.

Reuer, J.J., & Koza, M.P. (2000). Asymmetric information and joint venture performance and international joint ventures: Theory and evidence for domestic and international joint ventures. *Strategic Management Journal, 21*(1), 81–88.

Scott, W.R. (2003). *Organizations: Rational, natural, and open systems.* Upper Saddle River, NJ: Prentice Hall.

Trow, M. (1973). *Problems in the transition from elite to mass higher education.* Berkeley, CA: Carnegie Commission on Higher Education.

Trow, M. (1999). From mass higher education to universal access: The American advantage. *Minerva, 37*(4), 303–328.

Verbik, L., & Merkley, C. (2006). *The international branch campus: Models and trends.* London: Observatory for Higher Education.

Vernon, R. (1983). Organizational and institutional responses to international risk. In R. Herring (Ed.), *Managing international risk* (pp. 191–210). New York: Cambridge University Press.

Part III
Partnerships beyond the Classroom

5

CROSS-BORDER HIGHER EDUCATION AND THE INTERNATIONALIZATION OF ACADEMIC RESEARCH

STÉPHAN VINCENT-LANCRIN[1]

The dynamics of cross-border higher education—that is, all that entails the international mobility of students and teachers, educational programs, or institutions of higher learning—has changed profoundly since the 1990s. Twenty years ago the primary motivations were academic, political, geostrategic, cultural, and development aid related. At the time, countries took a favorable view of mobility of students and academics as an opening to the world, in the hope of creating international networks of elites. Universities received foreign students and academics, though making no special effort to recruit them. Today, even though these motivations remain valid, cross-border education is becoming increasingly driven by economic considerations.

Governments see it as a fulcrum of economic development and as a means of improving the quality of their higher education. Tertiary education institutions see it as an element of prestige (and sometimes a source of income) that gives a competitive edge. Individuals see it as a further boost to their career both in their country and on the international job market, or even as an aid for emigration purposes.

This trend results from a range of different though not mutually exclusive factors: greater mobility of skilled individuals and workers in a globalized economy; the falling cost of transport and communication; the desire of countries to encourage university and cultural exchanges and attract highly qualified personnel; the wish on the part of tertiary institutions to generate additional income or increase their prestige and raise their profile both nationally and internationally; or the need for a better educated workforce in emerging economies where local capabilities are often quantitatively and qualitatively insufficient.

Cross-border higher education has evolved differently across countries and regions. In very general terms, student mobility has been induced by political action in Europe and by strong demand in the Asia-Pacific region. North America for its part has been a magnet for foreign students, and only in recent years did the United States adopt a policy of more active recruitment. South America and Africa receive relatively few foreign students, mostly from the same regions, but student mobility is also increasing in those continents (OECD 2004a; UNESCO 2009).

The growth and diversification of cross-border education raises a number of questions for governments and higher education institutions. They have given rise to many books, studies, and initiatives in recent years. This chapter looks more particularly at the research dimension of cross-border higher education: how the international mobility of people, programs, and institutions relate to academic research; how academic research has become more internationalized, to some extent as a result of the growth of cross-border higher education; and why governments are supporting cross-border higher education to maintain or develop the capacity of their domestic research.

CROSS-BORDER HIGHER EDUCATION: EVIDENCE OF CONTRIBUTION TO RESEARCH

A growing number of people are going abroad to study, enrolling in foreign programs or establishments present in their country, or simply turning to the Internet to follow courses being run from other countries by universities or other institutions of higher learning.

Student Mobility: The Relative Predominance of Doctoral Student Mobility

Student mobility is the major form of cross-border higher education. It is also the best documented as countries have long collected statistics about it (OECD 2009a).[2] The number of foreign students in the world has increased threefold between 1975 and 2007, to three million international or foreign students (Figure 5.1). OECD countries receive around 85% of the world's foreign students, two-thirds of whom come from out of the Organisation for Economic Co-operation and Development (OECD) area.

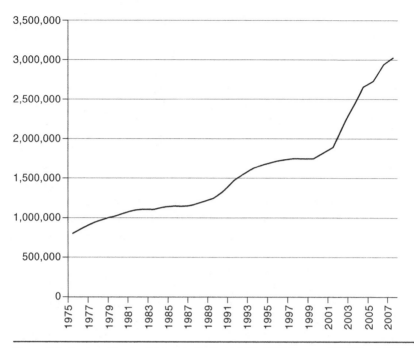

Figure 5.1 Number of Foreign Students in the World, 1975–2007 (Sources: UNESCO and OECD).

Three-quarters of all foreign students are concentrated in just eight countries—Russia (2%) and South Africa (2%) being the only two non-OECD countries. In 2007, the United States accounted for 24% of foreign enrollments; the United Kingdom 14%; Germany 10%; France 10%; Australia 8%; and Japan 5%. The four leading English-speaking countries alone (the United States, the United Kingdom, Australia, and Canada) account for more than half (51%) of all international or foreign students in the OECD area. France receives 40% of all African international students in the world. Student mobility has become more dispersed and somewhat less geographically concentrated over the past decades: the five top destinations host a smaller share of all foreign students in the world, notably because of a relative loss of large receivers such as the United States and France.

Europe is the largest receiving region among OECD countries with 1.3 million foreign students in 2007, but many of these students are moving from one European country to another. About half (45%) of foreign students in Europe are European. North America receives fewer students in absolute terms (with 760,000 foreign students in the United States, Canada, and Mexico), but ranks first in terms of openness to other regions for inward mobility, with Asian students representing almost two-thirds (64%) of all foreign students in North America.

In terms of outward mobility, Asia heads the list of regions sending students abroad, accounting for almost half (49%) of all international tertiary-level students in the OECD area in 2007. Europe ranks second, accounting for 28%, followed by Africa (11%), South America (6%), North America (4%), and Oceania (1%). About 67% of all foreign students studying in OECD countries were from outside the OECD area in 2007, about the same as in 1998.

Student mobility matters for academic research because doctoral students make up a significant share of international students. International students are thus actively contributing to the research capacity of their host and home country (and may continue to contribute to it after their studies abroad). In 2007, 30% of all foreign students were enrolled at the doctoral level (in countries for which information at that level is available). While cross-border students are matriculated mainly in undergraduate courses, by comparison with nationals a proportionally greater number are registered in postgraduate courses. In 2007, an OECD country would enroll on average 9% of its international or foreign students in an advanced research program (doctorate level,

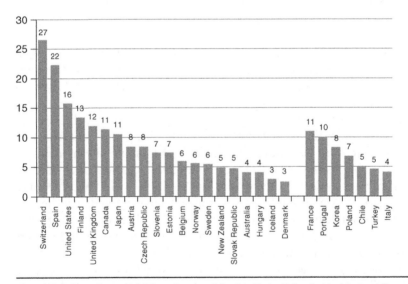

Figure 5.2 Percentage of all International and Foreign Students Enrolled in Advanced Research Programs (2007) (Source: OECD).

Note: For France, Portugal, Korea, Poland, Chile, Turkey, and Italy, foreign students defined on the basis of citizenship; in other countries, international students are defined on the basis of residence or of country of prior studies.

International Standard Classification of Education, Level 6)—against 3% of all its (foreign and domestic) students. Irrespective of their overall international or foreign student numbers, some countries enroll a larger share of their international and foreign students at the doctoral level than others (Figure 5.2).

More significantly, in 2007 the share of international and foreign students in total doctoral enrollments accounted an average 16% and 20%, respectively, in OECD countries for which information was available, that is twice as much as the share of international and foreign students in total enrollments. This share was remarkably high in Switzerland, the United Kingdom, New Zealand, the United States, Australia, Canada, Belgium, and France (Figure 5.3a and 5.3b).

Even in Japan, where migration is relatively low and where international and foreign students represented only about 3% of all tertiary level enrollments, they represented about 16.5% of all doctoral students. The data can vary significantly across countries depending on the definition used for mobile students and the domestic regulation about residency and the access to citizenship for foreign people: in any case, it is noteworthy that the proportion of foreign people enrolled at doctoral level is so significantly larger than the percentage of foreign citizens in the population in so many countries.

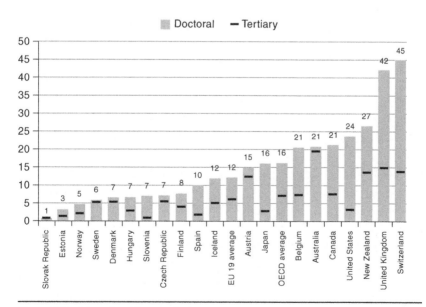

Figure 5.3a International Doctoral Students as a Percentage of all Doctoral Enrollment (2007) (Source: OECD).

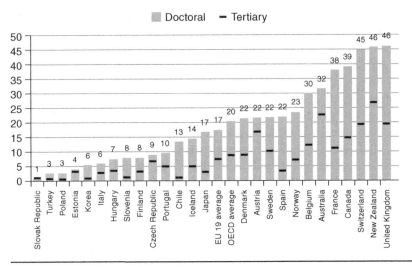

Figure 5.3b Foreign Doctoral Students as a Percentage of all Doctoral Enrollment (2007) (Source: OECD).

As a result, international students can represent a significant proportion of awarded doctorates in some countries. Although this varies (again) significantly across countries, in 2005 international (or foreign) students accounted for a significant percentage of graduates from advanced research (or doctoral) programs in Switzerland, the United

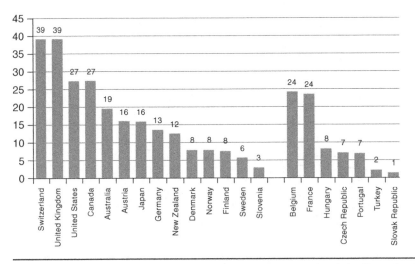

Figure 5.4 Percentage of all Advanced Research Degrees (Doctorates) Awarded to International and Foreign Students (2005) (Source: OECD).

Kingdom, Canada, the United States, Belgium, France, and Australia (Figure 5.4).

In these countries, international students already represent a genuine contribution to the country's scientific output (as well as, possibly, its subsequent output of scientists). As mentioned above, this may also become the case in the near future in other countries such as Japan.

The Mobility of Faculty

The growing international mobility of academics also highlights the importance of cross-border higher education for academic research, and, more specifically, its internationalization. The international mobility of faculty is not as well monitored as student mobility, but extant evidence shows that it has also increased significantly over the past decades. Another indicator is the share of foreign faculty in total academic staff as this partly relates to the share of doctorates awarded to international or foreign students who subsequently stay in their host country (or are hired there at one point of their academic career).

Flows of international academics into the United States increased by 77% between 1994 and 2007, to reach about 106,000 persons in 2007 (Institute for International Education 2008). Similarly, the number of science and engineering postdocs with temporary visas at U.S. universities has tripled from approximately 8,900 in 1985 to 27,000 in 2005, while those with U.S. citizenship and permanent residency increased by a more modest 60%, from approximately 13,500 in 1985 to 21,700 in 2005. The percentage of foreign temporary visa holders increased from 40 to 55% of science and engineering postdocs over this period. Although it is difficult to demonstrate a link with these flows, the share of foreign-born full-time doctoral faculty in U.S. research institutions has increased from 22 to 29% between 1992 and 2003—and from 38 to 47% in the physical sciences, mathematics, computer sciences, and engineering (National Science Board 2008).

In Korea and Japan, a similar rise in numbers of international researchers and/or foreign faculty could also be observed—but from a much smaller starting point. The number of international visiting scholars has almost tripled between 1993 and 2005, from 13,000 to 35,000. The number of foreign academic staff has more than doubled between 1992 and 2008, from 7,200 to 17,500 (with full-time foreign academics increasing from 2 to 3.5% of full-time academic staff over the same period).[3] Similarly, the number of foreign academic staff has doubled in Korea between 2000 and 2008, from 1,300 to 3,200 people and from 2.3 to 4.8% of all academic staff.

While covering only a small part of academic flows in Europe, the intra-European mobility of academics under the Socrates program of the European Commission more than tripled between 1997 and 2007, to 28,500 persons. In the United Kingdom, many teacher-researchers are recruited from graduates who though they do not have British nationality obtained their doctorate in the United Kingdom or the United States. Thus, in anthropology, economics, and linguistics, under 7% of teaching staff were of British nationality in 2004. In economics, only 35% of teachers aged under 35 were British, with 32% of them European Union foreign citizens (Mills et al. 2007). While the United Kingdom hosts the largest proportion of foreign faculty in Europe, this is a trend that is documented for other European countries as well (Enders & Musselin 2008; OECD 2008c).

The same pattern can be observed for postdoctoral positions (OECD 2008a). In the United States, the number of foreign (non-resident) postdocs has tripled between 1985 and 2005, to 27,000, and the share of foreigners in all postdocs at U.S. institutions has increased from 40 to 55%. At the German Max Planck Institutes, 55% of junior and guest researchers were *not* German (National Science Board 2008).

It is noteworthy that national academic markets differ significantly in how they value this mobility. In larger countries, it is often less important than in smaller countries (Enders & Musselin 2008).

The Mobility of Educational Programs and Institutions

The international mobility of programs and establishments has increased over the past decade, especially toward Asia and the Middle East—but also takes new forms within the OECD area. There is less evidence of a significant contribution of these new forms of cross-border higher education to research in their host (or home) country, but there are clear signs of growing interest in cross-border doctoral and research programs.

The mobility of educational programs is the second most common form of cross-border higher education after international student mobility. A growing number of students are taking advantage of the new possibility of following higher or postsecondary education offered by a foreign university without leaving their own country. Although it encompasses distance learning, it mostly takes the form of traditional face-to-face learning, made possible through a partner establishment abroad. Relations between foreign and local establishments have given rise to a variety of contractual arrangements, ranging from development aid to commercial contracts.

It is difficult to put a number on cross-border educational programs or students registered in foreign programs offered in their country. The two countries most active in this field—the United Kingdom and Australia—have some 300,000 students registered in their cross-border programs, mainly in Asia (McBurnie & Ziguras 2007). The number of students following Australian programs from their countries represented 30% of all international students registered in Australian establishments in 2007, a 6% point increase since 1996. While cross-border educational programs can be delivered under franchise arrangements, "twinning" programs have become prominent: students pursue studies with a foreign provider and follow a foreign program; they undergo some of their training in their country of origin and complete it in the country of origin of the foreign establishment, generally under 2 + 1 or 1 + 2 arrangements. This type of cross-border education usually involves mobility of both students and programs. These programs typically offer undergraduate rather than postgraduate or doctoral studies. However, their students can of course subsequently pursue their studies at doctoral level, either in the home campus of their foreign institution or in another institution in their home country.

The international mobility of institutions is still limited, but has nonetheless also become a significant dimension of cross-border higher education. It corresponds to foreign direct investments made by tertiary education institutions or educational enterprises. The most typical form of such mobility is the opening of campuses abroad by universities, and of training centers by other educational service providers.

According to the Observatory on Borderless Higher Education, there were about 100 of these worldwide in 2006, most of which opened during the past 15 years, in fact often after 2000 (Verbik & Merkley 2006).[4] We may cite the examples of Nottingham University (UK), which has campuses in China and Malaysia; Liverpool University (UK), which created an affiliated institution in China with Chinese and U.S. partners; and Monash University (Australia), which has opened campuses in Malaysia and South Africa. Australia's Royal Melbourne Institute of Technology (RMIT) University too has a campus in Vietnam. New York University had 10 campuses abroad as of 2009.

Mobility of establishments also includes creating entirely new educational establishments (not affiliated to any establishment of origin), as well as the partial or total acquisition of an establishment abroad. This latter form, for example, is preferred by the stock-listed U.S. group Laureate International Universities, which owned about 40 universities in 18 countries in America, Europe, and the Asia-Pacific region in 2009.

According to Verbik and Merkley (2006), only about 5% of foreign branch campuses offered doctoral programs. Their contribution to academic research in their host countries is thus arguably limited.

However, it is noteworthy that a growing number of institutions start offering doctoral programs in their foreign branches or programs, generally at the request of governments or partners in the host country. This is for example the case of the Nottingham or Liverpool campuses in China. But this can also be the case with program mobility, as shown by the recent "Partnership for the Future" initiative in Portugal. Singapore and Malaysia also try to attract foreign research universities on their soil, hoping that they would contribute to their domestic research capacity development in some fields (McBurnie & Ziguras 2009; Olds 2007).

Increasingly, foreign programs and institutions explicitly become part of innovation strategies. These foreign institutions and programs are for example grouped in clusters encompassing businesses as part of regional innovation clusters (and strategies): the Knowledge Village in Dubai, the Education City in Qatar, or the Kuala Lumpur Education City in Malaysia are examples of these new innovation clusters. It is, however, too early to know what impact these clusters will have, especially as some of them are still mere plans.

The relationship between these new forms of cross-border higher education and physical mobility of students and faculty, whether immediate or subsequent, is ambivalent. It is conceivable that apart from their potentially beneficial developmental spin-offs for their host countries (Vincent-Lancrin 2007), these new forms are limiting the exodus of skills that could possibly result from student mobility. For another, these forms sometimes entail brief stays abroad and often though not invariably lead to degrees and qualifications recognized in the country of the foreign partner university. Moreover, they do generally entail faculty mobility between the home and foreign campuses, and also of faculty from the partner institutions (if any).

THE INTERNATIONALIZATION OF RESEARCH

Another way to look at the importance of cross-border flows for research lies in the output of research. As cross-border higher education was growing, a major trend in academic research lay in growing international collaboration, international visibility and citation, and international funding. While it is difficult to provide evidence of a link with the cross-border mobility of people, programs, and institutions depicted in the previous section, it is likely that such a link exists.

In academic research, international collaboration has grown significantly over the past decades. This is one of the major trends in academic research worldwide (Vincent-Lancrin 2009). This trend is reflected in the growth of internationally co-authored (or collaborative) scientific articles, that is, articles with at least one international co-author (in terms of institutional affiliation). Between 1988 and 2005, the total number of international articles more than doubled, increasing from 8 to 18% of all scientific articles. Apart from Turkey, all countries have increased their national share of internationally co-authored articles. In an OECD country, the average share of internationally co-authored articles in the domestic scientific article output has increased from 26 to 46% between 1988 and 2005 (Table 5.1).

This growing international collaboration in research output is partly associated to doctoral student mobility: the U.S. National Science Foundation indeed notes a moderate correlation between the number of U.S. PhDs awarded by country to foreign-born students in 1992–1996 and the volume of papers co-authored by the United States and those countries in 1997–2001 (NSB 2004).

Moreover, the breadth of countries with which each country collaborates for scientific research has increased. Between 1996 and 2003, all countries (for which information is available) have raised the number of countries with which they have jointly authored articles: for an OECD country, the average number of collaborating countries in scientific activities has risen from 96 to 117 countries (Table 5.1).

Citation of foreign scientific articles provides an index of accessibility, visibility, and acknowledged influence of scientific literature across borders, but also a measure of the insertion of a country's researchers in international networks of scientists and academics. Foreign scientific articles are increasingly cited in the scientific literature worldwide: in 1992, foreign articles accounted for 55% of all citations, against 62% in 2001 (NSB 2004). The number of cited articles is highly correlated with the country's output of scientific articles and financial input in research. The United States produced 29% of the world output of scientific articles in 2005, and its scientific literature accounted for 41% of citations in the world scientific literature.[5] United States articles remain the most cited, but the share of U.S. scientific output in world citations has declined over time, including in the top 1% most cited articles. Other countries and regions, notably in Asia, have developed their research capacity and are becoming important centers of science. They have expanded their scientific output and their worldwide visibility in terms of citation and "relative prominence" over the last decade.[6]

Table 5.1 Share and Breadth of International Scientific Collaboration Over Time, by Country/Economy

	Share of International Collaboration in National Output (%)			Number of Collaborating Countries	
	1988	1996	2005	1996	2003
Australia	18	27	41	101	114
Austria	29	45	57	78	101
Belgium	32	46	58	111	121
Canada	20	31	43	110	130
Czech Republic	m	48	52	65	72
Denmark	27	44	54	89	112
Finland	23	36	48	m	m
France	23	35	49	126	146
Germany	22	34	47	123	136
Greece	30	38	40	68	82
Hungary	34	51	56	71	77
Iceland	47	52	65	m	m
Ireland	30	42	52	53	77
Italy	24	34	43	110	126
Japan	9	15	23	97	128
Korea	27	27	28	54	91
Mexico	30	41	46	77	98
Netherlands	22	36	49	110	131
New Zealand	21	33	48	55	66
Norway	27	40	52	64	87
Poland	26	46	47	70	90
Portugal	37	52	54	51	86
Spain	21	32	42	88	115
Slovak Republic	m	42	60	51	54
Sweden	25	39	50	100	116
Switzerland	37	48	59	112	116

Turkey	22	23	19	94
United Kingdom	18	29	44	158
United States	10	18	27	172
Country mean	**26**	**37**	**46**	**117**
EU-15	**17**	**27**	**36**	**143**
Brazil	30	42	35	106
Chile	30	47	55	78
China	22	28	25	102
India	10	16	22	107
Indonesia	76	82	85	60
Israel	29	38	44	91
Russia	2	27	43	94
Singapore	24	31	41	64
South Africa	14	30	49	76
Slovenia	m	46	49	m
Estonia	m	58	54	47

Source: Calculations based on NSB 2006 and 2008.

Notes

For the share of national scientific output with international co-authors, 2003 instead of 2005 was used for Iceland, Slovak Republic, EU-15, Chile, Indonesia, Slovenia, and Estonia; in 1988, former USSR was used instead of Russia. For the number of countries, 1994 and 2001 instead of 1996 and 2003 was used for Czech Republic, Greece, New Zealand, Norway, Portugal, Slovak Republic, Switzerland, Indonesia, and Estonia (italicized numbers, excluded in the mean calculation). Calculations are based on data from the Institute for Scientific Information, Science Citation Index and Social Sciences Citation Index; CHI Research, Incorporated; and National Science Foundation, Division of Science Resources Statistics, special tabulations. m: missing data.

Here again, the internationalization of these knowledge networks is most likely to some extent related to the growth in the international mobility of students and academics: this mobility allows them to know about projects and research findings that they would not necessarily be aware of if they had not been mobile. Program and institution mobility also favors this exposure and opening of students and researchers to new literatures.

The growing international nature of research can also be observed through the rise of foreign funding of academic research. Data are rather patchy for the early 1980s. However, the fact that data have become more systematically collected is in itself a piece of evidence of the increasing importance of funding coming from abroad for the performance of academic research. On average, in the 15 countries for which data are available for both years, the share of funding coming from abroad for the performance of academic research has tripled over the past two decades, representing 6% in 2006 versus 2% in 1981 (OECD Main Science and Technology Indicators database).

This can partly be traced back to the strategies and policies of several countries to promote and fund international collaboration in science. The European Union has funded ambitious programs geared toward intra-European collaborative research, such as its "Framework Programs." In the United States, federal agencies such as the National Science Foundation, the U.S. Department of Energy, and the National Institutes of Health, have (or had) programs helping fund internationally collaborative research. However, while probably still insignificant, part of the cross-border funding of research may increasingly include the funding of academic research carried out by foreign campuses in a host country.

The internationalization of academic research is certainly facilitated by the cross-border mobility of doctoral students and researchers: doctoral studies create links between doctoral students and their host university for future international collaborative research (if these students or faculty go back to their country). Moreover, the research topics addressed or the methods used while studying abroad will influence doctoral students who become active researchers or faculty themselves. The personal links created while abroad will likely be reinforced by scientific links as they establish research programs in their country of origin (if they return). Cross-border teaching programs also help create links between academics for non-teaching activities. In short, cross-border higher education creates personal and scientific relations that will typically continue to materialize in international research collaborations.

DEVELOPING RESEARCH CAPACITY THROUGH CROSS-BORDER HIGHER EDUCATION

Why is academic research an essential component of cross-border higher education? And, more generally, why has research become more internationalized? The brief answer is that it has become easier for institutions and governments to use cross-border higher education, and, more generally, foreign people and knowledge, to develop their domestic research capacity.

Beyond any institutional or governmental strategy or will, the internationalization of higher education, including its research mission, occurred because it has become cheaper and easier to travel and communicate worldwide. Staying, working, traveling abroad have become more affordable and desirable to all people, and because of its (usual) timing in a person's life, higher education is a favorable time for international mobility. Three main drivers can explain this trend: first, the fall in the cost of (air) transportation; second, the fall in the cost of communication, thanks to the rise of information and communication technology, the diffusion of English as a lingua franca, and the new possibilities offered by the enhanced capabilities of computers; finally, a political and mediatic environment that has made (some parts of) the world visible and desirable to most people in the world. The subjective cost and meaning of mobility and even migration have been dramatically changed in a few decades (Marginson & van der Wende 2009).

Institutional and governmental policies and strategies have been important drivers too, but they have benefited from this enabling environment. Institutions support cross-border higher education for research capacity development, but also for prestige and excellence in a more competitive global research environment (or at least perceived as such). The 2005 Global Survey on internationalization of higher education carried out by the International Association of Universities shows that overall the two main institutional rationales for internationalization at institutional level were to "increase student and faculty international knowledge capacity and production" and to "strengthen research and knowledge capacity and production"; creating an "international profile and reputation" and contributing to academic quality were coming next. The internationalization of staff and students, the enhancement of academic quality, and the strengthening of research were perceived as the three most important benefits (Knight 2006).

Governments have many rationales to support cross-border higher education (OECD 2009b), but research capacity development is an essential one, especially in economies increasingly relying on innovation for growth.

From a government perspective, the traditional rationale to encourage cross-border higher education lies in mutual understanding and their long-term political, cultural, and economic benefits: governments have long left their doors open to foreign students, subsidized small exchange programs for domestic and foreign students and faculty, and hoped this would contribute to the creation of international networks of elites that would positively affect their country in the long run, be it through trade, diplomacy, scientific exchanges, or better cultural and political understanding. In recent years, additional drivers of internationalization policies have become more economic, or at least have targeted more short-term returns. One rationale that has been emphasized and discussed over the past decades lies in export revenue generation through international students and the building of a higher education industry (OECD 2004a, 2004b, 2008c, 2009b; OECD/World Bank 2007). While countries can have different market positioning, academic research can play an important role in this strategy in terms of quality signaling: as international rankings show, research still plays a predominant role in the reputation of a higher education institution (and, more generally, of its country of origin).

The main rationale for governments to encourage cross-border higher education for research purposes lies in capacity development, from both a quantitative and qualitative standpoint. Countries that already have a developed higher education system, with reasonable quality, want to draw on the global pool of talents to continue to stay at the scientific knowledge frontier and also to encourage communication between researchers of different horizons. Researchers can thus be exposed to other ways of working and thinking that could help them be more innovative or contribute to effective technology transfers (OECD 2008a). Being part of international networks of knowledge is crucial because it offers institutions, academics, and countries quality benchmarks for their research, and also quicker access to new knowledge and new research practices. Here, inward mobility of foreign talents and circulation of domestic ones are key instruments: access to codified knowledge (e.g., a scientific article) is not really the objective, as this could be done from home; what they are really interested in is tacit knowledge that can only be gained through interpersonal relations and co-location (OECD 2008a; Vincent-Lancrin 2008).

Staying at the knowledge frontier becomes a more important goal as economies in richer countries rely more intensively on research and innovation in order to compete with emerging economies with lower labor costs. Well-trained graduates and researchers become a very important asset, wherever they come from, especially in the context of aging populations and relative disinterest in science by domestic people. Countries such as Germany, Japan, Korea, the United Kingdom, Denmark, or the United States have an interest in attracting international talents to their country to contribute to their academic research and higher education sector, be they students or confirmed academics. In the United States and the United Kingdom, for example, the declining interest shown by domestic students in science and engineering is offset by the high enrollment of foreign students in these fields. Given their demographic prospects, countries such as Germany and Japan may have to rely more on foreign talents if they want to keep a good qualitative and quantitative research output (OECD 2008b).

Countries with less developed research and higher education systems follow similar objectives for capacity development purposes. Except possibly in some fields, they are further away from the knowledge frontier, and developing their research capacity by themselves would be slow. Therefore, cross-border higher education and international mobility appears as a good catch-up strategy. Given that their domestic institutions have less to offer to foreign institutions and scholars, they generally tend to emphasize the outbound mobility of their postgraduate students, staff, and researchers, and the inbound mobility of foreign institutions and programs. The idea is to send students and staff abroad to the best universities and research institutions so that they learn the most up-to-date research methods and become sustainably inserted in international networks of knowledge. When enough of these students and faculty come back to academia in their home country, they can contribute to their domestic scientific life and give quality training to their doctoral students. Institutions themselves have similar interests as prestigious international collaborations can be a way to improve their prestige in the national arena—and their chances to be ranked or improve their rank in international rankings.

Although it has become an important scientific producer, Korea still follows this approach and strongly values doctorates earned abroad, especially in the United States. Singapore is another example: the government has invited many prestigious institutions to open branch campuses or offer international programs on its soil, with the aim to improve the research capacity of the country. Malaysia has also explicitly used cross-border higher education to develop its higher education capacity. While its initial emphasis has been on undergraduate courses, it has recently tried to move away from the import of foreign educational programs through franchising. It is now trying to attract foreign research institutions and gave them access to domestic research funding as incentive. Similar moves can also be observed within the OECD area. Following an invitation (and some financial contribution) by the Portuguese government, MIT, Carnegie Mellon University, and University of Texas at Austin offer master's and doctoral programs in Portugal, in partnership with Portuguese institutions. The goal is to develop capacity in doctoral programs and research in some fields, notably in science and engineering. In 2008, Portugal has established a similar partnership with the German Fraunhofer society.

CONCLUDING REMARKS

Academics and research students undertake cross-border studies and collaborate more internationally than they used to. As shown in this chapter, research students and academics make up a significant share of people's cross-border mobility in higher education. This people mobility is often accompanied by institutional partnerships. In fact, "outgoing mobility opportunities for students," "international research collaboration," "outgoing opportunities for faculty/staff," "visiting international scholars" ranked second to fifth in the most common elements of internationalization strategies in the International Association of Universities survey on internationalization ("international institutional agreements/networks" ranked first) (Knight 2006). While research remains a minor activity of program and institution mobility, there is a growing interest in encouraging foreign institutions and programs to carry out some research where they operate. Simultaneously, academic research has become more internationalized, with more international collaboration and the emergence of some international funding. While only partial, there is most likely a link between the two phenomena—the rise of the Internet being another important driver.

As long as it remains relatively moderate, balanced, and reciprocal, this cross-border mobility of research people, programs, institutions, and funding should not be seen as an issue. It is a driver of knowledge creation, preservation, and circulation, and can benefit all. Most countries can see it in a positive light.

However, there is a tension between two important drivers of the trends: competition and collaboration, or self- and collective interests. These two dimensions generally go hand in hand. Competitors tend to collaborate: even though they do not share their most important trade secrets, they do collaborate on many fronts. In fact, all stakeholders may consider collaboration as a means to become more competitive.

However, should this cross-border mobility and internationalization reach very high levels, the internationalization of higher education and academic research could lead to a reshaping of systems that are generally organized under the assumption that they are a domestic investment in the (domestic) future. Tensions may arise from what is perceived as brain drain if people flows are too imbalanced and some countries benefit too heavily from the public investments in education of some other countries, with little visible (though generally actual) benefits. Where it still exists, the traditional model of public funding of tertiary education could also be challenged (Gérard 2007). Tensions may also arise if cross-border funding becomes significant and institutions have a strong interest to gain an international visibility, not just for prestige, but to get research contracts and students: the worldwide competition for funding would further transform all systems. This may lead governments to change the way they support publicly higher education and research.

While the inclusion of education services under the General Agreement on Trade in Services (GATS) in the World Trade Organization has received much attention (Knight 2002, 2003; OECD 2004a, 2004b; OECD/World Bank 2007), the inclusion of research services in the GATS has been relatively little discussed, although research represents a significant part of academic activities. The inclusion of research and development in the GATS as part of the business services sector provides a framework for international trade in academic research, should governments be willing to see it become more privatized.[7] While institutions are encouraged to patent or commercialize the results of their research findings, these activities are still very small, including in the United States where they are arguably the largest. The privatization of academic research is thus unlikely in the short run, but the existence of some private research companies shows that it is not impossible.

A condition of possibility for further internationalization of academic research lies in the openness of science and research findings—and thus in a certain geopolitical atmosphere. In the United States, the events of September 11 have led to some worries about a too heavy reliance on international staff and students for the performance of research and also to a rise of (non-open) military research (Vincent-Lancrin 2009). While foreign students and faculty help improve the quality (and sometimes maintain the quantity) of academic research, whether governments and the public opinion see it in a positive light depends on political circumstances and cannot be taken for granted.

As long as it is the case, there are nevertheless many reasons to believe that the growing cross-border mobility and collaboration in research and higher education will continue in the medium run.

Decreased travel costs, and easier access to global information and multiplied means of communication will remain important drivers. But cross-border higher education will also remain a good strategy for receiving countries to develop capacity in domestic research, for sending countries to continue to improve the quality of their research and to remain at the forefront of knowledge—and, in some cases, a way to be close to new pools of scientists in the global competition for talent, or, more generally, to new markets and political powers.

NOTES

1. The author is a Senior Analyst at the Centre for Educational Research and Innovation (CERI), a division of the Directorate for Education of the Organisation for Economic Co-operation and Development (OECD) (Stephan.Vincent-Lancrin@oecd.org). The analyses given and the opinions expressed in this chapter are those of the author and do not necessarily reflect the views of the OECD and of its members.
2. All data on student mobility come from the OECD education database or from OECD (2009a).
3. Full-time foreign academic staff rose from 2,700 to 5,900 over the period.
4. The report lists 82 campuses abroad, defined as a unit operated by the foreign institution or by a local partner on behalf of a foreign institution, and delivering degrees of the foreign institution. It thus excludes a certain number of other forms of campuses abroad and mainly covers the English-speaking world—thus underestimating the actual number of campuses abroad.
5. Relative to its population, the United States ranked thirteenth in terms of article production in 2003: see indicator D.5 in OECD (2007).
6. One calculates a "relative citation index" for a country or a region by adjusting the frequency of citation of its scientific literature for its world share of scientific articles (NSB 2006).
7. In the GATS services sectoral classification list, "research and development services" are included in the business services, with three sub-categories: R&D services on natural sciences; R&D services on social sciences and humanities; inter-disciplinary R&D services.

REFERENCES

Enders, J., & Musselin, C. (2008). Back to the future? The academic professions in the 21st Century. In OECD, *Higher Education to 2030. Volume 1: Demography* (pp. 125–150). Paris: OECD Publishing.

Gérard, M. (2007). Financing Bologna: Which country will pay for foreign students? *Education Economics, 15*(4), 441–454.

Institute for International Education (IIE) (2008). *Open Doors 2008. Report on International Educational Exchange.* Sewickley, PA: Institute for International Education.

Knight, J. (2002). *Trade in higher education services: The implications of GATS.* London: Observatory on Borderless Higher Education.

Knight, J. (2003, May). *GATS, trade and higher education. Perspective 2003: Where are we?* Observatory on Borderless Higher Education Report. Retrieved February 16, 2010, from www.obhe.ac.uk/documents/view_details?id=698.

Knight, J. (2006). *Internationalisation of higher education: New directions, new challenges* (2005 IAU Global Survey Report). Paris: International Association of Universities.

McBurnie, G., & Ziguras, C. (2007). *Transnational education: Issues and trends in offshore education.* London: Routledge Falmer.

McBurnie, G., & Ziguras, C. (2009). Trends and future scenarios in program and institution mobility across borders. In OECD, *Higher Education to 2030, Volume 2: Globalization.* Paris: OECD Publishing.

Marginson, S. & van der Wende, M. (2009). The new global landscape of nations and institutions. In OECD, *Higher Education to 2030, Volume 2: Globalization.* Paris: OECD Publishing.

Mills, D., Jepson, A., Coxon, T., Easterby-Smith, M., Hawkins, P., & Spencer, J. (2007). *Demographic review of the UK social sciences.* Swindon, UK: Economic and Social Research Council.

National Science Board (NSB) (2004). *Science and Engineering Indicators 2004.* Arlington, VA: National Science Foundation. Retrieved November 7, 2009, from www.nsf.gov/statistics/seind04/pdfstart.htm.

National Science Board (2006). *Science and Engineering Indicators 2006.* Arlington, VA: National Science Foundation. Retrieved November 7, 2009, from www.nsf.gov/statistics/seind06/toc.htm.

National Science Board (2008). *Science and Engineering Indicators 2008.* Arlington, VA: National Science Foundation. Retrieved November 7, 2009, from www.nsf.gov/statistics/seind08/toc.htm.

Organisation for Economic Co-operation and Development (2004a). *Internationalisation and trade in higher education: Opportunities and challenges.* Paris: OECD Publishing.

Organisation for Economic Co-operation and Development (2004b). *Quality and recognition in higher education: The cross-border challenge.* Paris: OECD Publishing.

Organisation for Economic Co-operation and Development (2007). *OECD science, technology and industry scoreboard.* Paris: OECD Publishing.

Organisation for Economic Co-operation and Development (2008a). *The global competition for talent.* Paris: OECD Publishing.

Organisation for Economic Co-operation and Development (2008b). *Higher Education to 2030, Volume 1: Demography.* Paris: OECD Publishing.

Organisation for Economic Co-operation and Development (2008c). *Tertiary education for the knowledge society*. Paris: OECD Publishing.

Organisation for Economic Co-operation and Development (2009a). *Education at a glance*. Paris: OECD Publishing.

Organisation for Economic Co-operation and Development (2009b). *Higher education to 2030, Volume 2: Globalization*. Paris: OECD Publishing.

OECD/World Bank (2007). *Cross-border tertiary education: A way towards development*. Paris: OECD Publishing.

Olds, K. (2007). Global assemblage: Singapore, foreign universities, and the construction of a "global education hub." *World Development, 35*(6), 959–975.

UNESCO (2009). *Global education digest 2009: Comparing education statistics across the world*. Paris: UNESCO.

Verbik, L., & Merkley, C. (2006). *The international branch campus: Models and trends*. London: Observatory on Borderless Higher Education.

Vincent-Lancrin, S. (2007). Developing capacity through cross-border tertiary education. In OECD/World Bank, *Cross-border tertiary education: A way towards development*. Paris: OECD Publishing.

Vincent-Lancrin, S. (2008). Student mobility, internationalisation of higher education and skilled migration. In International Organization for Migrations, *World Migration 2008: Managing labor mobility in the evolving global economy*. Geneva: International Organization for Migrations.

Vincent-Lancrin, S. (2009). What is changing in academic research? Trends and prospects. In OECD, *Higher Education to 2030, Volume 2: Globalization*, Paris: OECD Publishing.

6

FOSTERING ORGANIZATIONAL CHANGE AND INDIVIDUAL LEARNING THROUGH "GROUND-UP" INTER-INSTITUTIONAL CROSS-BORDER COLLABORATION

ANN E. AUSTIN AND CHERYL FOXCROFT

This chapter describes an innovative "ground-up" inter-institutional collaboration aimed at fostering organizational change and providing mutual benefits for all involved. Specifically, the chapter describes a decade-long collaborative process involving Nelson Mandela Metropolitan University (NMMU) in South Africa and Michigan State University (MSU) in the United States. The collaboration began with one faculty member from the U.S. who spent a year in South Africa as a Fulbright Scholar collaborating with colleagues on projects pertaining to the institution's teaching and learning culture, policies, and practices. Building on that initial work, the collaboration has expanded to include teams of faculty members, administrators, and graduate students from the two universities working together on organizational change projects to enhance the learning and teaching environment at NMMU and the knowledge and expertise in change management of the individuals involved in the teams.

The chapter begins with context and background for each of the partner universities, followed by a narrative description of the partnership, its goals, and the stages through which it has evolved over almost a dozen years. The authors then analyze the benefits and outcomes for each of the institutional partners and examine the factors that have contributed to what is widely regarded by those involved at both institutions as a successful and productive collaboration. This is followed by a discussion of the challenges that have arisen and required attention over the years. The chapter concludes with consideration of a theoretical perspective—negotiated order theory—which provides a lens through which to consider this institutional partnership as a case from which lessons emerge that are potentially useful in analyzing or planning other cross-border collaborations in higher education. The authors of this chapter are each from one of the partner institutions and have served as the institutional leaders for the partnership. Thus, the chapter reflects both their understanding of the history of the institutions and their perspectives concerning the views of the wide array of institutional members who have participated in aspects of the ongoing partnership.

CONTEXT

Each of the university partners has a distinctive history and institutional context that relates to the nature and success of this collaboration. The cross-national institutional collaboration initially involved the University of Port Elizabeth (UPE) in South Africa and MSU in the United States. During the course of the collaboration, the UPE became part of a merged institution that is now called Nelson Mandela Metropolitan University.

The collaboration has occurred in the context of the new, postapartheid South Africa. The UPE, situated along the Indian Ocean in the Eastern Cape, was an historically advantaged university. In the late 1980s, several years before the collapse of apartheid in 1994, under the leadership of a Vice Chancellor committed to creating a university that would reflect the diversity of the country and respond to the needs of the region, UPE began the process of admitting a student body more fully reflective of the region's population. By 1998, about one-quarter of the student body included students of color. With students coming from a diversity of previous educational experiences, the academic staff needed to develop teaching strategies that would enhance student success. The traditional teaching approach had emphasized didactic learning, in which academic staff primarily taught through lectures followed by examinations to test student retention. As the student body became more diverse, and as government policy emphasized outcomes-based learning, university leaders encouraged the development of more engaged learning approaches. Overall, during the early postapartheid period, the university faced the challenge of grappling with recreating itself into a higher education institution that could respond effectively to the needs of the region and contribute to the national agenda to rebuild the country after many years of conflict.

Over the past several years, the higher education landscape in South Africa has undergone a radical change through a process of institutional mergers designed to achieve greater efficiency and equity, resulting in a reduction in the number of higher education institutions from 36 to 23. In January, 2005, UPE merged with the Port Elizabeth Technikon and the Port Elizabeth campus of Vista University (two other higher education institutions in the region) to form Nelson Mandela Metropolitan University (NMMU). NMMU is a medium-sized university with a headcount enrollment of about 24,000 students, spread across seven faculties and six campuses. It is one of four comprehensive universities in South Africa offering both general and professionally oriented programs as well as technologically and career-oriented programs, from the entrance level (certificates, diplomas, and degrees) through to the doctoral research level. While the merger is widely considered to be one of the most successful across South Africa, not surprisingly, it has involved many challenges. The collaboration with MSU has been structured to address some of these challenges and support NMMU in the process of organizational development. An additional note is that NMMU has made a strong institutional commitment over the past decade to develop international partnerships and welcome faculty and student visitors to campus. Even back in the 1980s, UPE had partnered closely with colleagues from an American university to develop a specific learning intervention, Supplemental Instruction, used to strengthen student learning. Thus, the collaboration with MSU, described in this chapter, has developed and matured in an environment in which the university has been very open to mutual learning through interaction with colleagues from other countries.

The other partner, Michigan State University, is a large research-oriented university in the United States, with more than 40,000 students. The university has a decades-long history of international involvement, including extensive student study abroad programs and research relationships in many countries. The African Studies Center (one of several such units within the university focused on specific regions of the world) has more than 200 faculty affiliates who research and teach in many different fields about issues related to Africa, and who host and collaborate with colleagues from African universities. In addition to the many international partnerships and collaborations in which MSU faculty members are engaged, the university is also a leader in the U.S. in providing opportunities for students to study in other countries. Thus, the collaboration described in this chapter involves both partners building on a strong commitment to interacting with higher education colleagues and institutions in other countries around teaching, research, and development projects. Also of note is that the partners at MSU include faculty members and students from the graduate program in Higher, Adult, and Lifelong Education, a program offering master's and doctoral degrees that prepare graduates for administration, teaching, and policy work in higher education. The program has long attracted graduate students from many countries, and, in recent years, has worked to integrate more attention to international issues into its curriculum.

STAGES OF THE COLLABORATION

The NMMU–MSU cross-border collaboration has involved three stages to date. During each of these stages, the partnership has expanded in each of three areas: personnel involved, focus of the work, and scope of the collaborative work. That is, over the past 11 years, the collaboration has developed to include more people (particularly an expansion of MSU personnel), more topical areas, and greater impact on each institution.

Stage One: Fulbright Year

The collaboration began when the former University of Port Elizabeth requested a U.S. Fulbright Scholar with expertise in higher education, organizational change, academic staff development, and teaching and learning issues. Seeking an opportunity to work and gain professional experience in another country, and offering knowledge and skills directly responsive to those requested by UPE, a faculty member in the Higher, Adult, and Lifelong Education Program at MSU applied and was accepted to spend the 1998 year as a Fulbright Scholar at UPE. Her appointment was located in the Office of Organizational and Academic Development, which was led by a senior-level university administrator. The initial work focused specifically on academic staff development (faculty development), including co-leading an induction course for new academic staff and providing frequent seminars on teaching and learning issues for interested academic staff from across the institution. Her overall approach and philosophy was to couple a willingness to respond to requests for programs with an eagerness to listen carefully in order to learn about the experiences, challenges, and interests of the academic staff. This approach opened the way for invitations to talk with departments about the issues they were confronting with their students and for many informal conversations with a great number of academic staff, department chairs, and senior administrators about the changing environment at the institution and the related staff develop-ment and organizational development needs. Among the various con-nections that developed, the American Fulbright Scholar had occasions to interact with and develop a professional relationship with a South African who was, at the time, a faculty leader within the Department of Psychology and an emerging institutional leader recognized for the quality and strength of her ideas concerning institutional change and priorities.

During the 1998 year, the national policy for education was pre-sented in the form of the National Qualifications Framework, which emphasized outcomes-based education and required universities to prepare new curricular plans in a relatively short time frame. In response to the concerns in institutional departments about the cross-unit collaborations necessary to create new programs and the overall uncertainty of academics about the process of systematic curricular design, the American began working closely with a number of depart-ments to help support their work in this area. She also was invited by a number of departments to offer seminars designed to help them address specific teaching and learning needs, and, thus, through these activities, came to know a large number of the academic staff across the university.

In addition to working with department chairs and academic staff, the American Fulbrighter interacted regularly with the senior-level administration, including the Vice Chancellor. These conversations usually focused on the nature of the organizational change that UPE was undertaking, including efforts to broaden the student base to reflect the diversity within the region, to encourage academic staff to develop new, more student-focused, interactive teaching and learning approaches, and to envision and enact a deeper commitment to univer-sity engagement with the community. As she came to know the univer-sity better and to interact with senior administrators, she was invited to speak to the University Council, attend some of the Senate meetings, and to participate in the management group's annual planning retreat.

Stage Two: Continuing and Expanding Work (1999–2007)

Following the year of on-site work, the collaboration continued, with the focus on strengthening UPE's institutional capacity for organ-izational change. The partnership involved visits of representatives from each institution to the other university. The director of an inter-institutional consortium whose president was located at UPE led a team of senior higher education leaders to the United States for a study tour. The visit was hosted by the American Fulbrighter, now back at MSU, and involved participation of the team in the national conference of an American higher education association and several days of meetings with senior institutional leaders at the MSU campus to discuss issues of higher education management and organizational change processes.

During this stage of the collaboration, the American also visited UPE several times. At the request of the Vice Chancellor, she devoted one of the visits to conducting an extensive qualitative interview-based study on the process of organizational change at UPE, the impact of change strategies, and the nature of the changing culture. This report was presented to the senior leadership and governing body of the university. During each visit, she also was involved in consultations with senior management at UPE concerning various aspects of the organizational change process, including strategies for supporting the professional growth of the academic staff, and she led workshops and seminars for academic staff from throughout the institution on research skills and effective teaching strategies. The two-week visit in 2007 was focused primarily on working with the psychology professor mentioned earlier, who had become a senior institutional leader in the now-merged NMMU, as well as with other institutional administrators, on plans for enhancing a culture of learning and teaching excellence and discussions about institutional policies concerning faculty appointment patterns, evaluation, and professional growth opportunities.

By the later years of this stage of the collaboration, the two institutional leaders were engaged in ongoing planning to ensure that each visit was used in a strategic and purposeful way. Recognizing that the work in which they were engaged was linking theoretical and research-based knowledge with practical and important institutional issues, they began to envision ways to include a larger team from MSU—and particularly to include faculty members and graduate students studying higher education issues who had both theoretical and professional experience related to organizational change and other issues in higher education. The emerging plan would enable a team from MSU to work with corresponding colleagues at NMMU on institutional issues in ways that would advance NMMU's agenda for change as well as the commitment of the Higher, Adult, and Lifelong Education Program at MSU to provide hands-on experience for its graduate students.

Stage Three: Broadening the Collaborative Partners and the Collaboration Focus (2008–)

One of the merger-related challenges experienced at NMMU is that the three pre-merger institutions brought with them similarities and differences in approaches to teaching and learning. Some of the differences stem from the more applied, career-focused context in which "technikon-type" programs were delivered, as opposed to the more theoretically oriented "university-type" programs. Some of the similarities are associated with the fact that the three merging institutions enrolled a substantial percentage of students who were not well prepared for higher education studies. Thus, the teaching and learning methods needed to combine a strong developmental focus with commitment to producing well-qualified graduates. In the new university, there is great potential for cross-pollination among differing approaches to teaching and learning. However, it is difficult in a merged institution to develop a distinctively new approach that is not simply a "potluck" of approaches used in the previous institutions. It is in this context that renewed emphasis has been placed on collaboration with MSU. MSU faculty members and doctoral and master's students who have expertise in facilitating faculty and organizational development with respect to teaching and learning have been invited to present workshops to NMMU faculty and to engage in strategic conversations with the senior leadership of NMMU. As a result, these collegial voices have significantly shaped thinking at NMMU around teaching and learning and faculty development. Furthermore, the opportunity to collaborate with an institution that is internationally recognized for its expertise in higher education, adult, and lifelong education, has enabled NMMU to start benchmarking the practices and methods it adopts with those at MSU.

Collegial conversations led by MSU faculty on holistic student development, key principles of good practice in undergraduate education, and seamless learning fueled interest at NMMU to reconceptualize institutional approaches to support student development and success. In the process, collaboration with MSU has expanded to include Student Affairs staff. In 2008, the first team of MSU faculty, administrative staff, and senior students visited NMMU to present a series of workshops. This was followed by a visit of NMMU staff from Student Affairs and Higher Education Access and Development Services to MSU to learn about living–learning communities and residence hall programs at MSU. The collaborative work on enhancing the learning environment at NMMU continued in the summer of

2009, when a team of MSU faculty and graduate students visited the university for 2 weeks of collaborative work. One group worked with institutional leaders and academic staff on policies and practices to encourage research on teaching and learning issues and a second group collaborated with NMMU colleagues on issues concerning student life.

CONTEXTUAL FACTORS AND PROCESSES CONTRIBUTING TO SUCCESS

The NMMU–MSU collaboration has developed in a ground-up fashion, based on ongoing work between institutional leaders and faculty members at both institutions. Those involved consider it successful and can point to specific, tangible, and important ways in which the partnership has made a difference in the teaching, research, and professional work of those involved, and in institutional matters (e.g., the curriculum) at both NMMU and MSU. In the following section we analyze the factors that have contributed to the success of the collaboration and the resultant impact on each university involved.

Opportunities for Mutual Learning

A critical factor in the success of the partnership is that the work has brought benefits to both institutions. Mutual learning has characterized the relationship, although the learning outcomes have differed for each institution. For NMMU, the partnership has opened conversations to its faculty about innovative approaches to teaching and learning, stages of student development, and strategies for enhancing the relationship between in-class and out-of-class learning. The partnership has brought to NMMU new ideas about faculty development, scholarly work, and approaches to faculty professional development. From MSU's perspective, collaborating with a university situated in a national context of rapid and major change, and one with a very diverse student and staff body, has provided faculty members, administrators, and graduate students with unusual opportunities to apply and adapt theories and to conduct research.

The stark contrasts that exist between the collaborating institutions enhance the opportunities for learning and collaboration. MSU is large and residential, while NMMU is a medium-sized non-residential university. MSU has a long history and recognized reputation in the U.S. as well as internationally, while NMMU, as a recently merged institution, is striving to re-establish itself in the higher education sector in

South Africa and internationally. Why would these stark contrasts be a critical factor in the success of the collaboration? From NMMU's perspective, exposure to practices at an internationally recognized institution provides greater opportunities for benchmarking and for developing organizational aspirations than would have been the case if the exposure had been to an institution in the "same league." For example, through its collaboration with MSU, which has an extensive, well-established residence hall system, NMMU has initiated planning related to the design of new residences, management and staffing structures, student work opportunities in residence halls, and the establishment of living–learning communities and residence hall programs. From the MSU perspective, the differences in the contexts between the two institutions enable MSU faculty and graduate students to step back and consider the relevance of the theories that guide their work in an array of contextual settings.

A Committed "Driver" at Each Institution

Another critical success factor has been having at least one person at each institution committed to "driving" the collaboration. In the early years, when the collaboration was based on the invitation from NMMU to have a Fulbright Scholar, the main players were several institutional leaders at NMMU (the director of the Office of Organizational Development and the Vice Chancellor, and the higher education scholar, who was the Fulbright visitor from MSU). Over the past six years or so, the psychology professor the American Fulbright scholar had come to know in her first year moved into a role as a senior-level institutional leader and assumed the responsibility of facilitating the collaboration on behalf of NMMU, working closely with the Vice Chancellor (several changes have occurred over the years among those who serve in this position) and other senior administrators to discuss the areas of emphasis for each visit, and ensuring that the schedules for visits are organized to produce maximum collaboration, benefit, and impact on the institution. At MSU, the original Fulbright scholar, now a senior-level faculty member and director of a higher education institute focused on global issues, manages the collaboration, which has involved identifying other MSU faculty and institutional leaders to bring into the partnership and cultivating their interest. Each of the drivers also has needed to assume the responsibility to seek institutional funding to support the collaboration and has helped institutional leaders perceive the strategic benefits to each university in investing in and continuing the partnership.

Those serving as drivers invest time, focus, and commitment into the partnership. They have regular discussions about the specific topics for inter-institutional collaboration, the strategic dimensions of scheduling visits, where to secure funding for visits and projects, the research topics to emphasize, and so on. Such planning discussions make it possible for the collaboration to be dynamic and in step with the needs and aspirations of the two institutions. Without drivers to undertake ongoing planning, the collaborative venture would probably fizzle out over time.

Support from Senior Administrators

Another critically important factor has been the buy-in and strong support of the senior leadership at NMMU and a key department chairperson at MSU. As noted, the collaboration started when NMMU's senior management extended an invitation for a U.S. scholar to spend a year at the South African university. Consequently, the MSU faculty member was briefed about the university leaders' concerns and needs around teaching and learning matters, which provided her with a platform to initiate discussions with faculty and administrative staff. Furthermore, she was able to share common themes that emerged in these conversations with senior management to sharpen their understanding of faculty development needs and teaching and learning issues. This set the trend for the ongoing collaboration between the institutions, including the involvement of senior-level administrators. All visits to either campus involve scheduled time for conversations with some of the senior academic leadership. Furthermore, after the NMMU staff team visited MSU in 2008 to explore living–learning communities and the management of residence halls, the insights gained were shared at an NMMU institutional workshop attended by senior academic leaders and a report was submitted to the senior management of the university. In this way the senior leadership is kept closely informed about the collaborative efforts of the two institutions.

Commitment to Flexibility and Dynamism

Willingness by those involved at both institutions for the collaboration to evolve and change over time has been an important factor in its longevity and impact. Over the 11 years of the partnership, the drivers at each institution have framed and reframed the conceptualization and presentation of the partnership in order to shift it away from a relationship between a few individuals to, instead, a partnership between the two institutions. While the willingness of the two drivers to take a leadership role in coordinating and directing the partnership has been critically important, equally important has been the interest by all involved to welcome new levels of partnership and new topics of focus. In recent years, as more people from MSU have become involved, for example, colleagues at NMMU have welcomed them and integrated them into projects.

Collaborative Approach

Willingness of MSU and NMMU staff to familiarize themselves with the educational contexts in the country of the partners has been another critical factor contributing to the success of the collaboration. As a result, the ideas offered during visits are based on sensitivity to the local context while still being linked to international and research-based best practices. As the collaboration has evolved, an important part of the preparation for visits has been to ensure that those involved have comparative information on the educational contexts in the United States and South Africa. This preparation process has broadened the knowledge base of participants, and helped them translate ideas and suggestions into forms relevant to the new context.

Success Breeds Success

The "slow but steady," ground-up progress of this partnership has built a base of mutual trust among those involved. The leaders involved at each institution trust each other and look forward to learning together. The collaboration started with modest projects and goals. As those worked well, new goals and more extensive projects emerged. At the start of the collaboration, the U.S. scholar tried to learn about the NMMU context prior to offering suggestions and did not assume that the South African colleagues would necessarily want to arrange their professional development programs or curricula in ways similar to U.S. practices. Now, with years of interaction, those leading the collaboration at each institution know and respect each other well and trust their colleagues' intents. Their mutual commitment to a long, sustained relationship, rather than only short-term goals and interactions, deepens the trust and opens the way to new possibilities for the collaboration.

OUTCOMES AND BENEFITS

The partnership has produced outcomes widely recognized as useful. At NMMU, outcomes include faculty members whose interest in teaching has been renewed, a thoughtfully conceptualized faculty development program, deeper understanding about the curriculum design process, and emerging plans to enhance the learning environment outside the classroom. Additionally, the collaboration has provided the senior management of the university with information about how other universities worldwide organize policies pertaining to faculty work, reward systems, and career paths, as well as strategies used elsewhere to support teaching excellence. The partnership has also opened up new research areas for NMMU academic and administrative staff, particularly concerning student development.

For MSU, the collaboration has contributed to the institution's decades-long commitment to engage with colleagues in the international context to improve education and other key elements of national infrastructures. MSU was an international leader in calling for and encouraging the end of the apartheid period. Involvement in a long-term relationship with NMMU builds on, honors, and extends these aspects of institutional history and pride and commitment to a more just future. The research opportunities that are developing within the partnership also offer MSU faculty and graduate students opportunities for involvement in collaborative, cross-border research projects. While the partnership has not been designed as an undergraduate learning opportunity, it does have the added value, beyond the benefits already mentioned, for providing unusual professional growth opportunities for graduate students in the field of Higher, Adult, and Lifelong Education, and, thus, for enhancing the quality of the graduate program at MSU in higher education.

Not only do the two partnering institutions benefit; so too do the individual faculty members, institutional leaders, and graduate students involved. Participants in the partnership, from both institutions, have expanded their knowledge of higher education systems, issues, and processes. For some, their horizons and aspirations have expanded, partly due to the opportunities to learn about another institution and national context and become engaged in cross-border research. Participants have noted that their views of what we "know" and believe have been challenged, opening the door for entertaining new ideas and possibilities about their own and their institution's work. Heightened confidence and new friendships are other outcomes, harder to measure but of considerable importance as those involved in the partnership talk about its impact and meaning in their lives.

CHALLENGES

All those involved over the years in the NMMU–MSU cross-border partnership seem to consider it a successful relationship and expect and hope the institutions will continue to work together. Unexpected negative or problematic outcomes have not emerged, possibly because of the care of those involved to develop the relationships slowly and to respect the interests of each institution. However, while the partnership is widely considered by leaders and participants at both institutions to be successful, several challenges are evident and require the attention of institutional leaders. Inadequate attention to, or lack of resolution of these challenges, could seriously challenge the extent, quality, and benefits accrued through the partnership.

Resistance to Change

As discussed, the partnership has resulted in outcomes widely recognized as useful. Nevertheless, an ongoing challenge as the leaders from each institution assess what has been accomplished through the collaboration and discuss appropriate next steps to enhance the academic workplace and strengthen the learning environment at NMMU, is underlying resistance on the part of some staff at NMMU. The motivation for resistance is the notion that individuals from another country, especially the United States, could not understand the African context. The expression of this kind of resistance is subtle and infrequent, mentioned quietly only in behind-the-scenes comments. While this kind of resistance has not been explicitly apparent during the years of the collaboration, it must be taken seriously.

The U.S. partners strive to remain alert to the importance of presenting themselves as colleagues who are interested in mutual learning, rather than as experts trying to impose ways of working or thinking on others. Expressions of genuine humility, respect, and eagerness to learn as well as to share are necessary ingredients in this kind of collaboration. From the NMMU side, senior leaders involved in the collaboration have been thoughtful and strategic about the partnership. This thoughtful approach has involved making strategic decisions about how to highlight the ideas and suggestions brought by the MSU team, what topics to invite the MSU team to facilitate, who to include in meetings, and what timelines to follow in implementing policies and programs. The senior leader at NMMU facilitating the collaboration has been especially strategic about when and how to involve the institution's Vice Chancellor in making decisions or participating in activities pertaining to the collaboration. While this collaboration has seemed to encounter little explicit resistance, leaders must be aware that resistance can spring up unexpectedly and, therefore, it is a force that must be acknowledged, recognized, and managed. In claiming the seeming success of this cross-border collaboration, one would be naïve to overlook the power and influence of subtle resistance. Any partnerships that illuminate new approaches to teaching, alternative personnel systems and rewards, and new ways to extend learning beyond the classroom are bound to encounter some colleagues who are hesitant to change the status quo.

Financing

A second challenge pertains to the financing of the collaboration. Beyond the initial Fulbright funding, this partnership has not received external funding support. Thus, each year's exchange of faculty, staff, and students must be negotiated in the context of the economic environment within each institution at the time. Travel funds and ground expenses need to be secured. At MSU, faculty members contribute their time to partnership work, and thus, their participation must occur either in the form of leading a course that travels to South Africa in which MSU students participate or during a holiday or institutional break.

Institutional contributions to the financing of a partnership signal an institution's commitment to the success of the collaboration and recognition of the value of the work offered by the partner. From the start, NMMU has taken great care and pride in its hospitality to the U.S. visitors. As teams from the U.S. have visited NMMU for several weeks, NMMU has been firm in its commitment to provide lodging for the faculty leaders, and to offer supplemental support to the U.S. team (e.g., ground transportation). The South African leader has had to work hard and creatively to find funding within the institution to support the collaboration; nevertheless, she explained a few years ago that NMMU needed to make a financial contribution to the partnership in order for members of the university community to take the endeavor seriously. A partnership that involves commitment of resources by only one partner seems far less likely to succeed for any length of time.

Logistics

Practical issues also present a challenge to a cross-border partnership such as the one forged by MSU and NMMU. For example, NMMU and MSU are in different hemispheres and thus have different academic calendars, making many months of the year unworkable for visits. Careful planning is needed to find weeks that will work for all involved. Another issue pertains to the multiple details that must be handled as teams of people travel to the partner campus. A partnership that involves only a few people traveling would be much easier to manage. For example, arranging for the MSU team to visit one of NMMU's more distant campuses involved renting a large van—and required an MSU faculty member to be willing to take the responsibility of driving a large vehicle filled with colleagues and graduate students for an extended period in unfamiliar terrain. While these are, in a way, small details, they also must be addressed if the partnership is to succeed. Unaddressed, these logistical issues become problems that could deter institutional leaders less committed to making the partnership work.

Expansion of the Collaborative Team

Expanding the participants in the collaborative work to include, in team visits and projects, more colleagues as well as graduate students who study higher education has both enhanced the partnership and posed a challenge. In the early years, the South African facilitator, along with a few other institutional leaders at NMMU, and the original Fulbright scholar from MSU easily determined the nature of work that the collaboration would address. When a small group was involved, the goals of the partnership, the plans for each visit, and the logistics of travel were easy to accomplish. In more recent years, the scope and impact of the partnership has expanded as more people have become involved.

Beyond logistical implications, however, this expansion has meant new roles for the key collaborators. They are now not only working together on institutional projects, but also managing groups of people and logistics at each institution. With more time necessary for logistical management and facilitation, care is required to protect time for substantive collaborative work and discussion. But of even greater import, there is also the need to help new participants understand the spirit of respect, reciprocity, and mutual learning that has both characterized the collaboration, and, arguably, created the basis for its success. As individuals less accustomed to international work and collaboration participate, there is the opportunity for more learning—but also the possibility that frictions or mishaps may occur that would have been less likely with fewer people involved. Those leading and facilitating the collaboration believe the benefits from the expansion of the collaboration outweigh these challenges. However, the changes and challenges that accompany the growth of the collaboration need to be recognized and the institutional leaders need to be attentive to the new dynamics of an expanding network of people involved in the collaboration.

The Importance of Trusting the Process

The process of inter-institutional collaboration requires institutional drivers and thoughtful planning, as we have discussed. It also requires willingness of participants to welcome serendipity and unexpected developments. The facilitators always plan in some detail the agenda for the 10-day team visits for collaborative work. At the same time, they expect that unscheduled meetings and new ideas and projects will emerge from the interactions. Thus, the schedule must include both carefully constructed formal meetings and workshops (to discuss, identify, and frame key issues for collaborative work) and open spaces for fitting in, as the time together unfolds, new meetings for emerging collaborative ideas. Planning and flexibility must be woven together in the collaborative process.

Experience has shown that, as others have joined the collaborative teams, some colleagues favor planning (which has the potential to result in rigidity), while others veer toward flexibility (which has the potential to move toward laxness). For example, graduate students who have worked hard to plan workshops sometimes find it difficult to completely revise the structure of the workshop, based on observations from emerging interactions, the evening before. Helping team members find a balance between planning and flexibility has become one of the important responsibilities of the team leaders. At the same time that they are facilitating the involvement of others in the collaboration, the two leaders have had to find ways to preserve their own opportunities to interact to assess the changing nature of the cross-border collaboration, the next priorities, and the issues that need to be addressed within their institutional teams.

CONCLUDING ANALYTICAL OBSERVATIONS

One purpose of this volume is to explore the ways in which higher education institutions collaborate across national boundaries, particularly to address non-instructional purposes, such as, in this case, faculty development and institutional culture around learning. The partnership discussed in this chapter between Nelson Mandela Metropolitan University and Michigan State University is modest and focused, but is widely perceived by institutional leaders and faculty at each of the partner institutions to have made a significant difference. It began with just one faculty member from MSU spending a year working with colleagues at NMMU. It has expanded to include teams of institutional leaders, faculty members, and graduate students from each institution. Benefits have accrued both at the institutional and individual levels.

The partnership has been successful, with no apparent problems; nonetheless, the institutions and the leaders of the collaboration have had to recognize and handle challenges that, unattended, could have undermined the outcomes or the institutions' commitment to continuing the collaboration. Have unexpected consequences emerged from the collaboration? Perhaps the answer is that the expansion and continuation of the collaboration over the past decade is the unexpected consequence. No one would likely have predicted more than a decade ago that a year-long visit by one American scholar to a university just emerging from the turmoil of the conflict to end apartheid in South Africa would develop, over the subsequent decade, into a vibrant, ongoing, dynamic collaboration involving many institutional leaders, faculty members, and graduate students and addressing major issues concerning academic personnel, teaching quality, and institutional culture.

Negotiated order theory, applied by Gray (1989) to analyses of inter-organizational collaboration, sheds light on the process through which NMMU and MSU have developed their cross-border collaboration. Negotiated order theory offers a conceptualization of collaboration as dynamic and fluid, rather than static and fixed. It emphasizes change and conceptualizes collaboration as a process through which participants engage in ongoing negotiation that guides the collaboration. Relationships, according to this theory, are constantly renegotiated as the partners seek to find ways to satisfy the needs of multiple stakeholders. Additional literature on inter-organizational relationships suggests that factors relevant to the success of such relationships include trust (Koza & Lewin 1998; Kelly, Schaan, & Joncas 2002), communication (Kelly et al. 2002), and leadership (Philpot & Strange 2003). These theoretical perspectives on the process through which effective inter-organizational collaboration occurs resonate with our experiences with the NMMU and MSU cross-border collaboration. This partnership has been and continues to be dynamic, constantly changing, and moving forward as the partner institutions find ways in which the collaboration can serve emerging needs and interests on both sides. Additionally, the trust and communication patterns that have developed over time, and the commitment of key leaders in each institution to the quality and continuation of the partnership, have been key elements in its longevity, impact, and widely perceived overall success.

REFERENCES

Gray, B. (1989). *Collaborating: Finding common ground for multiparty problems*. San Francisco: Jossey-Bass.

Kelly, M.J., Schaan, J., & Joncas, H. (2002). Managing alliance relationships: Key challenges in the early stages of collaboration. *R&D Management, 32*(1), 11–22.

Koza, M.P., & Lewin, A.Y. (1998). The co-evolution of strategic alliances. *Organization Science, 9*(6), 255–264.

Philpot, J.L., & Strange, C. (2003). On the road to Cambridge: A case study of faculty and student affairs in collaboration. *Journal of Higher Education, 74*(1), 77–95.

7

CROSS-BORDER COLLABORATION FOR QUALITY ASSURANCE IN OMAN

Contested Terrain

THUWAYBA AL-BARWANI, HANA AMEEN, AND
DAVID W. CHAPMAN

Countries experiencing rapid growth in higher education enrollments often face a thorny problem. When enrollments grow faster than qualified instructors can be recruited and trained, and faster than administrative and quality assurance systems can be designed and effectively implemented, quality declines. Seeking to protect and assure quality, some countries have turned to international affiliations, pairing local higher education institutions (HEIs) with well-established international counterparts. The affiliated HEI typically has some level of responsibility for assuring the academic integrity of the instruction at the local college or university. This "outsourcing" of quality assurance provides credibility and, often, a mechanism for capacity development.

This chapter focuses on the experience of Oman in using international affiliations in higher education. But the story has a twist. On a per capita basis, the higher education system in Oman is arguably the fastest growing in the world, a growth rate that put considerable pressure on academic quality. A well-conceived and largely successful effort to assure quality of national HEIs through a system of international affiliations ultimately led to unanticipated consequences that slowed the government's eventual effort to introduce its own national accreditation system.

BACKGROUND

Oman is an oil-dependent economy that is running out of oil. The Government of Oman (GoO) expects its oil reserves to be largely depleted within the next 10–15 years (Ministry of Higher Education 2004). Believing that the transition to a post-oil economy will require a highly educated citizenry, GoO has invested heavily in the creation of a public higher education system and strongly encouraged Omanis to pursue postsecondary preparation. Initially this encouragement came through a combination of policies that provided free higher education to Omani citizens who met admissions standards, assurances of public sector employment for graduates, and strong job protections for Oman citizens once they were hired (Chapman, Al-Barwani, & Ameen 2009).

These policies were effective and the public system quickly expanded. Enrollments grew quickly, outstripping the capacity of the public sector to afford such largesse. Moreover, faced with the prospect of declining oil production, GoO also needed to slow the intake of graduates into public sector employment, preferably without antagonizing the citizenry who had come to regard free higher education as a "right." Incentives of the past had grown into entitlements that, in turn, were becoming liabilities for the future (Chapman et al. 2009).

To address these issues, GoO, in 1995, legalized private higher education and promoted its expansion through a generous set of incentives to those willing to invest in and/or operate private colleges and universities. Government provided the land on which to build the private universities, exempted those institutions from taxes for 5 years, provided those institutions with scholarships for students from low-income families, and, further, in 2006, awarded each of the private universities a capital grant of up to RO 20 million (US$52 million). Even though the government heavily subsidized the start-up and ongoing operation of private colleges and universities, the creation of the private higher education system offered two forms of relief to government.

The first was financial. Private HEIs are all operated as profit-seeking enterprises. Each college and university has an owner and some have shareholders who invest in the anticipation of a financial return. Their investment provides important capital to the college. Moreover, private HEIs, unlike their public counterparts, can charge tuition, thereby providing a means of recovering at least some of the cost of education. The capital infusion from shareholders and the tuition revenues have allowed expansion of higher education at a lower cost to GoO. The second form of relief was that graduates of private HEIs have not been given any assurances regarding public sector employment after graduation. Graduates are expected to find their own employment, generally outside the public sector.

Since its beginning in 1995, private higher education has grown rapidly. There are now four private universities and 19 colleges. Enrollment in private higher education went from none in 1995 to 20,353 students in 2007 (Ministry of Higher Education 2007a: 200). Consequently, the private higher education sector has been successful in achieving one of the government's purposes. The growth of private higher education has allowed GoO to quietly slow enrollment growth of public higher education. In particular, the strategy has allowed expanded access to higher education while avoiding the need for the government to change the popular policy of free public higher education.

ASSURING QUALITY IN PRIVATE HIGHER EDUCATION

Recognizing the need to assure quality of these new private HEIs, but lacking a national accreditation system, the government sought a cross-border solution. Specifically, GoO mandated that all private colleges and universities needed to enter into an affiliation with an international counterpart institution. The general arrangement was that the international partner would review the overall curriculum and individual course content, would often be involved in the appointment of teaching staff and administrators, and would oversee the examination process. This intent was to assure that student achievement in the Omani institution was comparable to that of students at the international partner institution (Ameen, Chapman, & Al-Barwani 2010). In return, the international affiliate was paid for their services, either as a fixed fee, a percent of profits, or on a per capita enrollment basis. At times, these fees could be substantial. Some affiliates received over US$100,000–200,000 per year for their oversight services.

Within Oman's international affiliation system, there was room for some extent of variation. Most affiliations developed as franchise agreements, others as validation agreements. In a *franchise system*, the program offered in Oman is supposed to be identical in all important respects to the program offered at the affiliate institution. Hence, in franchise arrangements, courses are developed by the foreign affiliate, instruction is delivered by personnel in Oman, and tests are graded both in Oman and again by staff at the affiliate institution as a double-check on comparability of outcomes. Certificates and/or diplomas are awarded by the affiliate institution. Within this general framework, affiliations differ in the flexibility offered to the Oman institution to adapt the course to local needs. An important aspect of this arrangement is that students are earning an international degree which, in turn yields prestige, employability, and mobility often not attached to locally issued degrees. Consequently, the affiliation is an important element in the ability of a college to recruit students. They can get a European, American, or Australian degree without ever leaving Oman.

In a *validation system*, at least in theory, the international partner institution does not develop the course; they only approve the courses developed and delivered by instructors in the Oman institution as comparable in quality to what would be expected at the affiliate's home institution. More responsibility falls to the Oman college instructors to design their own courses and student assessment procedures. Nonetheless, courses can only be developed and offered in subject areas in which the affiliate institution has a program and, presumably, the capacity to validate the coursework. In practice, affiliate institutions tend to provide considerable support to Oman staff in actual course development. Box 7.1 provides a snapshot of four of the affiliation arrangements as a way of illustrating the diversity in their design and operation.

Within the literature on quality assurance in higher education, Oman's affiliation model of cross-border quality assurance stands as unique. While it has received some international attention, most of that consideration has focused on describing the operation of the system (Martin 2007; Wilkinson & Al Hajry 2007). This chapter goes further in offering a data-based analysis of how well the affiliation system is perceived by Oman educators and public officials to have worked and the issues that arose as Oman tried to move beyond the affiliations as the primary quality assurance mechanism to its own higher education accreditation system.

LINGERING QUESTIONS ABOUT QUALITY IN PRIVATE HIGHER EDUCATION

While the creation of the private sector was successful in reducing financial demands on government, it yielded an unanticipated impact on the college attendance patterns of secondary school graduates. The academically strongest secondary school graduates still preferred to attend public colleges and universities, since those are still free to the students who are admitted. Consequently, public HEIs were able to be highly selective in their admissions. This left the private HEIs to

---

Box 7.1 Snapshots of Affiliation

Affiliate A does not interfere with specific teaching practice at College A. Indeed, Affiliate A is only interested in comparability of outcomes. All modules are approved by Affiliate A.

Affiliate B helps College B develop courses uniquely for Oman. These courses are not courses developed for use at the affiliate's campus. They are not run or controlled by Affiliate B. However, Affiliate B validates the equivalence of courses when they are developed and validates subsequent student performance in those courses.

Affiliate C: College C, working with Affiliate C has developed its local capacity to the point where it is now approved to offer courses certified by the accrediting organization of the affiliate's country. The certificates it offers are designed by and the diplomas are offered by the accrediting authority of the affiliate's country. Affiliate C and College C sit for exactly the same examination on the same day in both locations. Examinations are double-marked locally and a representative sample is then sent to Affiliate C to undergo an independent marking.

Affiliate D: College D determines the courses that it offers, but it can only offer programs that are also offered on the home campus of Affiliate D. The College D team visits College D annually to talk to students and instructors, examine sample examinations, and assess the comparability of student outcomes.

Source: Based on interviews conducted by the authors with the deans of four colleges.

---

compete for those mostly academically weaker secondary graduates unable to gain admission to the public sector but willing to pay tuition.

The net result was a two-tier system with respect to both cost and academic quality of entering students. This has created a financial bind for the institution. On one hand, students with weaker academic abilities are expensive to educate as they often need additional academic remediation and ongoing support. On the other hand, colleges need to provide a return on investment to their shareholders. While colleges could presumably generate more income to allow them to better address both pressures by charging higher tuition, tuition levels are effectively capped by the ability of parents to pay. The concern of some in government, the private sector, and the colleges themselves is that, caught in this financial bind, private colleges are allowing quality to suffer (Chapman et al. 2009).

Recent research has indicated that many national leaders, in both the public and private sectors, believe that the quality of higher education in Oman is low and needs to be raised (Ameen et al. 2010). However, there is little consensus about whether the lower quality is centered in public or private institutions. These observers believe that quality varies widely from institution to institution; differences among private institutions are seen as greater than the differences between public and private institutions. However, a recent study of 252 college and university instructors in Oman, those closer to the operation of the country's colleges and universities, found that a majority of them consider the quality of most private HEIs to be lower than the quality of public HEIs (Chapman et al. 2009). Moreover, most of the respondents (66%) thought that private colleges and universities have the least sufficient procedures for ensuring quality.

FROM AFFILIATION TO ACCREDITATION: CONTESTED TERRAIN

By the early 2000s, the Ministry of Higher Education (MoHE) was concerned about the adequacy of the affiliation system as a mechanism for quality assurance. In some institutions the affiliation system worked well. The international partner was involved, attentive, and committed to quality assurance and improvement. Other affiliates took a more relaxed approach to the arrangement and quality assurance was weak (Ameen et al. 2010). This unevenness caused some both in the government and the private sector to question the effectiveness of the affiliation system.

Then, too, the system had grown to a size and complexity that Oman wanted a more country-centered quality assurance system. Omani HEIs had affiliated with a wide range of international partners, as indicated in Table 7.1, often with different curricula, instructional philosophies, and assessment schemes.

One consequence was that curricula across the private colleges and universities variously took on some of the features of Australian, British, Canadian, English, Jordanian, German, Lebanese, Scottish, and U.S. universities (among others). Students frequently found it difficult to transfer across institutions without losing the credit they had already earned. The government found it difficult to judge the equivalence of programs. The MoHE wanted to bring some greater level of coherence to what had become a hodgepodge of curricula and operating procedures.

In 2001 a Royal Decree was issued establishing the Oman Accreditation Council (OAC) (see www.oac.gov.om) as an autonomous organization which reports to the Council on Higher Education. However, the Decree stated that the Directorate General of Private Universities and Colleges in the Ministry of Higher Education would assume the tasks of the Technical Secretariat of the Accreditation Board. This created the impression in the minds of some that OAC was part of the MoHE and led to occasional confusion about the boundaries between MoHE and OAC with respect to operational issues.

The new OAC concentrated on developing a national classification system, national standards, and processes for program and institutional accreditation. However, between 2000 and 2005 only two institutional reviews were completed. These reviews did not go well. The two colleges had no experience conducting internal self-studies and OAC did not provide them with adequate support or guidance on how to do this. External team members for the review were drawn from multiple countries and were oriented toward quite different higher education systems. The team members did not share a common understanding of the standards they were expected to apply and OAC did not provide training for the teams that might have addressed these issues. The college personnel and review team lacked a shared understanding of appropriate standards or procedures at the institutional level and, in retrospect, the standards they applied were unrealistically high for the stage of development of Omani private higher education.

The MoHE realized that the accreditation system was not working as anticipated. Institutions were not getting accredited and college leaders were afraid of the system. Consequently, in 2006 the MoHE and the OAC adopted a new approach (see Oman Quality Network 2008; Oman Accreditation Council 2008; Carroll 2006). Staffing was increased to a current level of eight professional staff. The quality-audit approach, which compared institutional practice against international standards, gave way to a standards-based quality assessment, in which the emphasis was on feedback and support to the institution rather than a summative pass/fail judgment. The revised approach is less summative in nature and provides guidance to the college on how to improve standards. While the plan is to eventually shift back to a more summative type of review, OAC recognizes the need to support institutional development as well as assess standards.

Table 7.1 International Affiliation and Annual Tuition Costs of Private Higher Education Institutions in Oman

University/College Name	Tuition[1]	International Affiliation
Oman–German University of Technology	12,740***	RWTH Aachen University, Germany
Oman Dental College	10,335**	A.B. Shetty Memorial Institute of Dental Sciences, India
International Maritime College Oman	9,100	Shipping and Transport College (STC) Group, the Netherlands
Oman Medical College	9,100***	West Virginia University, USA
Caledonian College of Engineering	7,540	Glasgow Caledonian University, UK; VIT University, India
International College of Engineering and Management	7,800	University of Central Lancashire, UK
Nizwa University	7,020***	Jordanian University, Jordan; Oregon State University, USA; Leipzig University, Germany; University of Exeter, UK; University of Reading, UK; University of Algarve, Portugal; University of Porto, Portugal; University of Sunderland, UK; University of Wisconsin, USA; Institute of Environmental and Process Engineering UMTEC, University of Applied Sciences at Rapperswill HSR, Switzerland; University of Jordan, Jordan
Modern College of Business and Science	7,020***	University of Missouri-St. Louis, USA
Majan College	4,225	University of Bedfordshire, UK; University of Leeds, UK
Sohar University	5,200**	University of Queensland, Australia; Mutah University, Jordan
Dhofar University	5,460***	American University of Beirut, Lebanon
Scientific College of Design	5,850***	Lebanese American University, Lebanon; Arab Community College, Jordan
Gulf College	5,850	Staffordshire University, UK; University of Hull, UK; University of Reading, UK
Muscat College	6,381.96**	Scottish Qualifications Authority, UK; University of Sterling, UK
Al-Bayan College	5,460***	Purdue University Calumet, USA
Middle East College of Information Technology	5,200	Coventry University, UK
Al-Buraimi College	5,070***	California State University, Northridge, USA
Sur University College	4,680	Bond University, Australia
Al-Zahra College for Women	4,836 ***	Al-Ahlia University, Jordan

Oman College of Management and Technology	4,290***	Yarmouk University, Jordan
Mazoon College	4,680***	Missouri University of Science and Technology, USA; Banathali–Vidyapiyh–Rajasthan, India
Waljat Colleges of Applied Sciences	5,200**	Birla Institute of Technology, India
Arab Open University Oman Branch	3,016	Open University, UK
Oman Tourism College*	1,040	International Institute of Tourism and Management (ITM), Austria; University of Applied Management Sciences, Austria

Source: Adapted from Ministry of Higher Education 2007b.

Notes
1 Fee per two semesters (BA program) US dollars.
* Diploma 2-year program only is offered.
** Fees increase or change in subsequent years of study.
*** Actual cost is dependent upon program and/or number of credit hours taken.

As the Accrediting Council sought to develop a common metric for assessing institutional quality and establish course credit transfer procedures for students wanting to transfer to a different college, it became clear that some private HEIs would likely have to change aspects of their curriculum and operating procedures to accommodate a more unified national system. It was not that some institutions' procedures were better than others, only that they were different. This resistance to change was largely responsible for the slow progress of the Accreditation Council in establishing an Omani accreditation system (Ameen et al. 2010). Further, the early missteps by OAC gave private HEIs both a legitimate reason for concern and an opening for some directors and deans to mount resistance to further intrusion in areas of institutional operation they wanted to protect.

THE STUDY

This study investigated the extent that leaders of private colleges and universities in Oman supported the move away from the international affiliation system and toward a national accreditation system. The study employed a mixed method design in which data were collected through a survey of 26 college administrators, semi-structured interviews with four senior level college administrators and two staff members of the OAC, and a document review. The survey instrument was sent to the senior administrator in each of the 43 private colleges and universities in Oman. A total of 27 completed questionnaires were returned from administrators at 17 of the 23 HEIs, as summarized in Table 7.2.

Upon return of the surveys, interviews were conducted with deans of four private colleges in the Muscat area and two permanent staff members of the OAC. The interview protocol collected respondents' views regarding the nature of their affiliation agreement, the effectiveness of their international affiliation arrangement, and their views of the emerging accreditation process in Oman.

FINDINGS

Success of the Affiliation System

Most respondents (84%) believed that the international affiliation system had been successful in ensuring that the program in their own institution met acceptable international standards (Table 7.3).

However, only 67% thought the system worked well across all the private colleges. While a majority was positive, these findings indicate

Table 7.2 Selected Personal and Institutional Characteristics of Survey Respondents

	Number	Percent
Professional Position		
Chancellor	1	3.7
Vice Chancellor	2	7.4
Dean	15	55.6
Head of Department	1	3.7
Director	1	3.7
Associate Dean	1	3.7
Quality Assurance Officer	1	3.7
Lecturer	1	3.7
Not reported	4	14.8
Total	27	100.0
Professional Qualification		
PhD	17	63.0
MA	3	11.1
Professor	1	3.7
Not reported	6	22.2
Total	27	100.0
Country of Affiliated Institution		
Lebanon	7	25.9
USA	6	22.2
United Kingdom	4	14.8
Jordan	2	7.4
Australia	1	3.7
India	1	3.7
Not reported	6	22.2
Total	27	100.0

doubt among fully one-third of the college leaders about the overall effectiveness of the affiliation system in some of the other colleges. Presumably, this doubt reflected concern with how some international affiliates undertook their oversight role. This finding is consistent with the interview results discussed later.

A big concern with the affiliation system was its cost, with nearly 40% questioning whether the financial burden posed by the affiliation was worth the cost. Over half thought the cost of maintaining an international affiliation outweighed the benefit. Still, respondents were evenly divided about whether any savings gained by ending the affiliation system would necessarily be reinvested in strengthening the quality of the private colleges. Table 7.4 provides a summary of the comparative advantages of each approach to accreditation, at least as viewed from the vantage point of college deans in Oman.

Table 7.3 Quality Assurance through International Institutional Affiliations

	N	Strongly Agree	Agree	Somewhat Agree	Do Not Agree
1. The affiliation with International HEIs is a successful strategy for assuring quality of private higher education institutions in Oman.	26	46.4	25.0	21.4	7.1
2. The affiliation of my institution with foreign HEIs ensures that our programs meet an acceptable international standard.	25	44.4	40.7	11.1	3.7
3. The financial burden of my institution's international affiliation process is worth its cost.	26	25.0	32.1	35.7	7.1
4. The affiliation with foreign HEIs is necessary to assure quality only for the first 5 years of the HEIs.	27	17.2	27.6	31.0	24.1
5. The financial cost of maintaining an international affiliation is more than it is worth.	25	18.5	33.3	29.6	18.5
6. After 5 years, the financial savings of the international affiliation process can be reinvested to strengthen HEIs' quality.	25	18.5	37.0	25.9	18.5
7. The licensing and accreditation requirements by the OAC checks that the programs offered in private HEIs meet national needs and accept international standards.	26	32.1	53.6	3.6	10.7
8. The OAC licensing and accreditation requirements will have a negative impact on the affiliation strategy.	26	0	0	25.0	75.0
9. Implementation of the OAC licensing and accreditation plan may lead to dramatic change in the following processes:					
curriculum development	27	13.8	37.9	27.6	20.7
assessment	27	13.8	41.1	24.1	20.7
teaching and learning.	26	14.3	46.4	21.4	17.9
10. The imported programs are already accredited by their HE provider and there is no need for them to be accredited by OAC.	27	6.9	10.3	24.1	58.6
11. The application of the program licensing and accreditation plan needs a lot of:					
work	27	48.3	41.4	6.9	3.4
time	27	41.4	48.3	6.9	3.4
funds.	27	31.0	55.2	10.3	3.4
12. Overall, *administrators* at my institution would prefer to continue using an international affiliation system to help ensure quality.	26	17.9	28.6	14.3	39.3
13. Overall, *instructional staff* at my institution would prefer to continue using an international affiliation system to help ensure quality.	25	18.5	25.9	25.9	29.6
14. Overall, I believe that the OAC system should replace the international affiliation system as a means to ensure the quality of higher education in Oman.	27	27.6	27.6	10.3	34.5
15. I believe that SQU can act as a National Affiliate for most of the programs offered in HEIs.	25	29.6	7.4	22.2	40.7

Source: Authors.

Table 7.4 Comparison of Advantages and Disadvantages of Affiliation and Accreditation Arrangements as they Currently Operate in Oman

Affiliation	Accreditation
Focused at the program level	Focused (currently) at the institutional level
Focus is on outcomes	Focus currently is mainly on process
Affiliation is viewed as a private relationship	Accreditation is a government relationship
Quality is established through a comparison with another institution	Quality is established through a comparison with an ideal target level of performance
Operating procedures, instructional practices, and educational outcomes can vary widely across colleges as long as they align with the different international affiliate institutions	Tends to bring more consistency and conformity across Oman colleges with respect to operating procedures, instructional practices, and educational outcomes
Focused on learning outcomes; gives little attention to operational procedures	Interested in inputs, processes, and procedures; not yet focused on learning outcomes
Provides (often) considerable technical assistance and ongoing support to institution in course development and delivery	Provides limited technical assistance to help institution address problems that are identified
Compares institution only with international partner institution	Seeks common benchmarks across Omani higher education institutions
Provides colleges with more help in upgrading instructional practices	Identifies weaknesses but offers only limited help in addressing those weaknesses
Focuses on teaching and learning	Focuses on institutional procedures and operations
Narrows the difference between affiliate–Oman college pairs	Narrows the difference among Omani institutions
Provides credibility that is important in attracting students	Quality standards not yet sufficiently recognized by parents, employers, or international marketplace to provide the credibility to attract admissions

Source: Authors

Transition to Accreditation

Responses indicted widespread (though not universal) support for the introduction of an accreditation system. Most respondents (82%) believed there was a role for national accreditation within Oman even if the programs they were offering had also been "accredited" by their international partner institution. At the same time, they recognized there would be problems in making the transition and harbored significant doubt about the readiness of the OAC to actually undertake reviews. Indeed, nearly all senior HEI leaders questioned the readiness of the OAC to implement its accreditation plan. Around 90% thought that applying the OAC plan needs more time, a lot of work, and more funding.

About half the respondents thought that the implementation of national accreditation would hold fairly substantial consequences for the workload within their institution. In particular, about half believed that implementing the accreditation system would lead to fairly dramatic changes in curriculum development, teaching and learning, and assessment strategies. As interviews later confirmed, they worried about the cost of these changes. At the same time, respondents generally did not expect that implementing a national accrediting system would have a negative impact on the international affiliations now in place, though some suggested (in the interviews) that the nature of the present affiliations may need to change. The systems could co-exist.

One further alternative tested in the survey was the possibility that private colleges might look inside Oman for the help with quality assurance that they now get from their international affiliates. Specifically, could an affiliation with Sultan Qaboos University, the premier public university, provide an acceptable substitute for international affiliation? There was sharp disagreement though; for the most part, respondents did not see this as an acceptable option.

Looking Ahead

Overall, the picture painted by the survey results is one of thoughtful ambivalence. Views were divided as to whether administrators and instruction staff at their institutions would prefer to continue an international affiliation system to help ensure quality. While about two-thirds thought that the OAC system eventually should replace the international affiliation system as a means to ensure the quality of higher education in Oman, there was an overwhelming belief among college administrators that implementation of the national accrediting strategy will require considerably more time and money.

INDICATORS OF QUALITY: CONTESTED TERRAIN

Interviews with selected deans and OAC staff provided elaboration of findings from the survey. One of the central dimensions of controversy around the shift from affiliation to accreditation concerns what indicators will be used to judge institutional quality. Within the affiliation system, quality was defined in terms of comparability of curriculum coverage, instructional approach, and learning outcomes between the college and the affiliate institution. For the most part, international affiliations have focused only on the comparability of learning outcomes. They have been reluctant to get into the operational details of their Oman partner institution. Such intrusion was not cost effective and went beyond what many affiliates thought was an affiliate's proper role in quality assurance. Even when the affiliate provided expatriate staff or administrators, they typically left internal administration to those on the ground in Oman.

The OAC takes a broader view. While attending to learning outcomes, the OAC process also examines the adequacy of institutional procedures and policies. For example, the accreditation process looks at the presence of such things as written policies and procedures, formal job descriptions, transparency in budget management, the extent that key committees keep minutes of their meetings, and the availability of those minutes. This more intrusive approach has been prompted by the concern of OAC leadership that there is considerable variability in the attentiveness and rigor with which international affiliates perform their oversight responsibilities and that some give limited or no attention to internal management issues of the colleges. Questions have been raised about the financial and operational management of some colleges. OAC recognizes that many affiliation arrangements are working well but they are concerned that other affiliation partners may be more interested in the financial returns from the arrangement, to the point that they give too little attention to quality control.

Survey and interview data suggest their observations have foundation. In a few of the institutions internal management and administration appears to be conducted in a top-down and often casual manner. Operating procedures are not always well defined, job descriptions are not always available, rules are sometimes made up as needed, financial transparency is weak or non-existent, and decision making is often closely held by directors and deans. It was these abuses that led the

OAC to take more intrusive actions than might otherwise have been the case.

Overall, private higher education leaders raise five main concerns about the move toward accreditation. *First*, in the interviews deans acknowledged the importance of accreditation, the value of having a more common metric of institutional quality, and the need to do something about weak affiliations. At the same time, they believed their institutions have been subjected to too many audits and self-studies. The redundancy is viewed as time consuming, expensive, and not worth their cost. In short, while differing in their level of support for the emerging accreditation process, deans were uniformly critical of the manner in which it was being implemented. It seems to be clearer to the deans what they are giving up than what they might gain when they make the transition to a national accreditation system.

Second, some deans view OAC attention to internal procedures as intrusive and inappropriate, particularly since they operate as private enterprises. Those deans argue that, in the move to accreditation, quality should continue to be judged only in terms of learning outcomes. College policies and specific internal operating procedures should not be the subject of government oversight as long as the desired levels of student learning are achieved.

The management structure within some Omani HEIs has characteristics of what the management literature describes as a "steep hierarchy" (Savage 1990; Chapman et al. 2009), in which power tends to be concentrated at the senior levels of the organization. The accreditation process tended to interfere with this orientation. Some deans viewed the accreditation process as a potential threat to their own administrative prerogatives. They found the attention to clarity and to the effectiveness of institutional processes and operating procedures to be intrusive and unwelcome.

Third, deans' financial concerns go beyond just the cost of preparing for an accreditation review. One of the most salient advantages of their existing affiliation system is the crucial role it plays in student recruitment. Hence, deans worried that any weakening of the affiliation system threatens the financial solvency of their college. Students want the international certificate or degree. Without them, deans fear that students would seek admission elsewhere. National accreditation and the provision of an Oman-based diploma do not have the same attraction to would-be students.

Fourth, some of the concern, however, was grounded in a worry that the accreditation process could become overly bureaucratic. On this point, some deans seemed to blur the distinction between the OAC and the MoHE, even though the OAC is an autonomous organization. They expressed dismay at the bureaucratic and occasionally intrusive practices of the MoHE and worried that the accreditation process could take on those characteristics. If accreditation were to take on such characteristics, deans feared the process would be oppressive.

Other deans believed that the affiliation process and the accreditation process could quite comfortably co-exist. The general view was that, over time, Omani colleges would take more responsibility for design, development, and quality control of their own instructional programs and the current franchise arrangements would evolve into looser international collaborations. Again, deans differed on how they thought this would affect them financially. Some colleges saw a financial advantage in this, as they would no longer pay an affiliation fee. Some fear that without the credibility of the international affiliate, recruiting students would be more problematic.

CONCLUSION

Cross-border affiliations of Omani HEIs with more established international colleges and universities were undertaken as a mechanism to assure quality at a time when no national system was available. For the most part it worked well, but over time concerns emerged both among government leaders and educators about the effectiveness of some of the affiliations in actually ensuring quality. Despite weaknesses with the affiliation system, GoO efforts to establish a national accreditation system encountered considerable resistance. This resistance emerged not only from HEIs involved in weak affiliations wishing to protect their prerogatives, but from HEIs involved in strong affiliations who (accurately) thought their existing system was working fine.

In the end, the transition from affiliation to accreditation is marked by distrust on both sides. The OAC does not fully trust all the international affiliates to provide diligent oversight and quality control. College leaders do not fully trust the MoHE and OAC to implement an oversight system that is efficient, has international credibility, is free of political pressure and influence, and could attract high student enrollments. As the Oman experience demonstrates, quality assurance can be quite political, as stakeholders try to favor aspects of quality on which they excel or thwart efforts that might change management strategies that currently work in their favor. It is likely that only as institutions engage in the new accreditation system will these issues be resolved. Nonetheless, virtually all the stakeholders viewed the move to a national accreditation system as inevitable.

REFERENCES

Ameen, H., Chapman, D.W., & Al-Barwani, T. (2010). The tension between profit and quality: Private higher education in Oman. In L. Portnoi, V.D. Rust, & S. Bagley (Eds.), *Higher education, policy and the global competition phenomenon* (pp. 87–100). New York: Palgrave Macmillan.

Carroll, M. (2006). *Strategic and operations plans for an Omani higher education quality management system.* Muscat, Oman: Ministry of Higher Education and the Oman Accreditation Board.

Chapman, D.W., Al-Barwani, T., & Ameen, H. (2009). Expanding post-secondary access in Oman, and paying for it. In J. Knight (Ed.), *Financing higher education: Access and equity.* Rotterdam, the Netherlands: SENSE Publishing.

Martin, M. (2007). The cross-border challenge of higher education: Comparing experiences. In M. Martin (Ed.), *Cross-border higher education: Regulation, quality assurance and impact* (Vol. 1, pp. 11–57). Paris: International Institute for Educational Planning.

Ministry of Higher Education (2004). *The strategy for education in the Sultanate of Oman, 2006–2020.* Muscat, Oman: Sultanate of Oman.

Ministry of Higher Education (2007a). *The annual statistical book for the higher education, academic year 2006–2007.* Muscat, Oman: Sultanate of Oman.

Ministry of Higher Education (2007b). *Higher education institutions in the Sultanate of Oman.* Muscat, Oman: Sultanate of Oman.

Oman Accreditation Council (2008). *Quality audit manual, institutional accreditation: Stage 1.* Muscat, Oman: Oman Accreditation Council.

Oman Accreditation Council (n.d.). *Requirements for Oman's system of quality assurance in higher education: Oman's system for quality assurance: Part one: Standards.* Muscat, Oman: Oman Accreditation Council.

Oman Quality Network (2008, October 28–29). Oman national quality conference on quality management and enhancement in higher education [Conference Brochure]. Muscat, Oman: Oman Quality Network.

Savage, C. (1990). *Fifth generation management.* Maynard, MA: Digital Press.

Wilkinson, R., & Al Hajry, A. (2007). The global higher education market: The case of Oman. In M. Martin (Ed.), *Cross-border higher education: Regulation, quality assurance and impact: Chile, Oman, Philippines, South Africa, Volume I* (pp. 129–180). Paris: International Institute for Educational Planning.

Part IV
Partnerships in Fields of Practice

8

GLOBAL NURSING
Sustaining Multinational Collaboration Over Time

JANE C. SHIVNAN AND MARTHA N. HILL

Nursing encompasses autonomous and collaborative care of individuals of all ages, families, groups and communities, sick or well
and in all settings. Nursing includes the promotion of health, prevention of illness, and the care of ill, disabled and dying people.
Advocacy, promotion of a safe environment, research, participation in shaping health policy and in patient and health systems
management, and education are also key nursing roles.

(International Council of Nurses 2004: 9)

The nurse's role is critically important to promote health, relieve suf-
fering, and improve quality of life. The International Council of Nurses
(ICN) estimates that there are more than 12 million nurses worldwide,
but it is not enough to meet the current or projected needs of human-
ity (ICN 2004). The majority of developing countries have severe
shortages of nurses, exacerbated by migration to countries with better
working conditions and salaries. Regionally, the number of nurses per
1,000 population varies from 0.8 per 1,000 in Southeast Asia to 7.44
per 1,000 in Europe (World Health Organization 2008). In 2004 the
number of nurses varied from less than 0.1 per 1,000 population in
countries such as the Central African Republic, Liberia, and Uganda
to more than 10 per 1,000 population in Finland and Norway (ICN
2004: 10). In the United States the current undersupply of nurses is
approximately 140,000 and is expected to peak at 800,000 by 2020

(Rosenkoetter & Nardi 2007). Nursing has suffered historically from misperceptions of its contributions to health care and limited recognition of its scientific base. In most societies nurses are predominantly female, with the consequence that nurses are generally less well paid and have worse working conditions than similar professions with more balanced gender representation. Universal issues contributing to the nursing shortage include inadequate workforce planning, uneven distribution of available nurses, insufficient capacity in educational systems, and limited incentives to become—or stay—a nurse (ICN 2004).

Nurses are educated using a wide variety of curricula and models, with most nurses prepared outside university settings. Even in the United States, approximately 60% of nurses in practice do not have a university degree. In the United Kingdom, less than 10% of nurses have a baccalaureate degree at registration (Shields & Watson 2008). There is some evidence to suggest that the level of education of nurses at the bedside has a direct impact on patient morbidity and mortality. Aiken and her colleagues found that the odds of dying within 30 days of admission were 19% lower in hospitals where 60% of the nurses had a baccalaureate or higher degree as compared to hospitals where only 20% had degrees (Aiken, Clarke, Cheung, Sloane, & Silber 2003). Globally, a few countries have established a baccalaureate as entry-level education for the nursing profession, including Canada, Sweden, Portugal, Brazil, Iceland, Korea, Greece, and the Philippines (American Association of Colleges of Nursing 2005). A number of factors make the movement toward university preparation of nurses challenging, including the shortage of qualified faculty at that level.

Doctoral education of nurses is an important mechanism to advance nursing science and prepare nurse leaders in research, education, policy, and clinical practice. In particular, the development of doctorally prepared nurses is seen as critically important to provide qualified faculty for baccalaureate and master's programs in schools of nursing. In 2005 the International Network for Doctoral Education in Nursing (INDEN) identified over 230 nursing doctoral programs, of which over 170 (75%) were in just four countries—the United States, United Kingdom, Canada, and Australia. At the INDEN 2007 biennial meeting addressing the challenges of doctoral education, several themes were identified: a growing crisis in the health workforce shortage, requirement for rigorous research training in doctoral education, and engaging nurses in the health and social policy arena (Redman 2007). Ketefian, Davidson, Daly, Chang, and Srisuphan (2005) highlighted the importance of developing a global perspective in doctoral nursing education, while assuring the development of clear standards and sensitivity to cultural and societal needs. International collaboration and cooperation in nursing research and doctoral nursing education thus becomes a path to solving global health problems.

Establishing sustainable multinational collaboration in nursing education is extremely challenging, but brings significant rewards to all involved. At a fundamental level, such partnerships provide nurses with opportunities to address the pressures of globalization. Allan and Ogilvie (2004) distinguish between internationalization and globalization, defining internationalization as concerned with relationships among and between countries and globalization as concerned with interdependent and interconnected world systems that exist distinct from local and national life. Any discussion of these topics must recognize the inherent tension between a national and global perspective. The dominance of Western values and culture, particularly those of the United States, are widely seen as threatening by many cultures and nations. This dominance is as true in nursing as in any other field, driven in part by the use of English as the standard language for publication. Nevertheless, Allan and Ogilvie argue that nurses are uniquely placed to address such concerns, given our long history of questioning the status quo to protect our patients. The holistic approach of nurses to their work is readily transferred to a holistic view of global relationships, recognizing the complexities of the issues and the need for respectful and reciprocal communication. Nurses have also developed a strong ethical code that protects the individual patient and population and respects the rights of others. The *ICN Code of Ethics* (2006), used by many national nursing bodies as the starting point for their codes of ethics, states:

> Inherent in nursing is respect for human rights, including cultural rights, the right to life and choice, to dignity and to be treated with respect. Nursing care is respectful of and unrestricted by considerations of age, color, creed, culture, disability or illness, gender, sexual orientation, nationality, politics, race or social status.
>
> (1)

Davis (1999) earlier highlighted the importance of awareness of our nursing values and ethics, particularly contrasting those from individualistic cultures predominant in North America and Europe with collectivist cultures found throughout Africa, Asia, and South America. In collectivist cultures, constituting 70% of all cultures, loyalties of the individual to the group can outweigh individual rights. In individualistic cultures the rights of the individual are central, and must be balanced against the common good. Although this draws a simplistic dichotomy, these differences in cultural values inform many of the perceived ethical conflicts faced by nurses working across cultures—informed consent, end-of-life decision making, rights of human subjects in research, health-care rationing. These differences in cultural values also inform the relationships with patients that are at the very center of the nursing process.

Crigger (2008) reflected on the development of global nursing ethics based on a methodology of inclusive decision making, balance between the rights of the community and the individual, the use of reflexivity (i.e., the ability to reflect critically), openness to new approaches to human rights and freedoms, and a realistic view of business and technology. Globalization is described as "a process by which the world is interdependently organized and understood ... the process is discursive and holistic, and will in turn affect people economically, psychologically, spiritually, politically, and culturally" (Crigger 2008: 19). Like Allan and Ogilvie (2004), Crigger argues that nursing is uniquely placed to address health disparities that are often rooted in social and economic disparities.

A theory of mutuality (based on Galtung 1975; Hayhoe 1989; Xu, Xu, Sun, & Zhang 2001) provides a framework for approaching collaboration with sensitivity to the context of differing cultures and value systems. Galtung (1975) suggested that the principles of equity, autonomy, solidarity, and participation could offset the exploitation and dominance characterizing imperialism in international relations. Hayhoe (1989) and Xu et al. (2001) expanded on these ideas, applying them to activities such as knowledge transfer and partnerships to promote education. In partnerships framed by mutuality, processes of agreement on goals and structure are equitable, with interactions symmetrical and horizontal rather than vertical and imbalanced. The principle of autonomy is demonstrated by mutual respect. Solidarity is defined as the networks of interactions that allow participants to critically use and disseminate the results of the partnership. Finally, the theory of mutuality assumes the possibility of full participation of all partners from the beginning. This framework can be used to suggest structures and processes to guard against dominance of one partner and identify strategies for encouraging the partnership's success.

JOHNS HOPKINS: KNOWLEDGE FOR THE WORLD

The Johns Hopkins Hospital and Johns Hopkins University School of Nursing are located in Baltimore, Maryland, on the eastern coast of the United States. The Johns Hopkins Hospital, a world-renowned tertiary hospital, is part of the Johns Hopkins Health System. Among its 8,600 employees are about 2,500 nurses. On the same east Baltimore campus, the Johns Hopkins University School of Nursing joins the Schools of Medicine and Public Health in the university's mission: to educate its students and cultivate their capacity for life-long learning, to foster independent and original research, and to bring the benefits of discovery to the world. The School of Nursing, recognized for its eminence in community health nursing research and its graduate programs, has 68 full-time faculty. It educates nurses at the baccalaureate, master's, post-master's, doctoral, and post-doctoral levels. The mission of the Johns Hopkins University School of Nursing is to improve the health of individuals and diverse communities locally and globally through leadership and excellence in nursing education, research, practice, and service. Many opportunities exist within the school to explore global health issues. The School of Nursing is home to the first Peace Corps Fellows Program in nursing, and has graduated over 300 returned Peace Corps volunteers since 1991. The Minority Global Health Disparities Training Program funded by a grant from the National Center on Minority Health and Health Disparities of the National Institutes of Health, provides students with international health disparity research training opportunities. The School of Nursing participates with the Schools of Public Health and Medicine in the Center for Global Health. On this academic health-care campus, nurses, faculty, and staff from the hospital and university collaborate closely in clinical practice, education, and research.

The Johns Hopkins University has also extended its global reach in recent decades. It has campuses in Bologna, Italy; Singapore; and Nanjing, China. Significant global education and research programs are conducted by many divisions, including the School of Advanced International Studies, the Peabody Conservatory, and the Johns Hopkins Bloomberg School of Public Health. Johns Hopkins Medicine International (JHI) leverages the resources of the Johns Hopkins Health System and the School of Medicine to bring to the world the best of Hopkins in biomedical research, education, and patient care. JHI offers to international health-care institutions a suite of services known as Knowledge Transfer. These services include consulting arrangements and educational programs in Baltimore, abroad, via telemedicine or e-learning. JHI also manages several health-care organizations for international clients. Many of these activities include nurses as consultants, teachers, and practitioners.

Hopkins nurses also have opportunities to work closely with JHPIEGO, an international non-profit health organization affiliated with Johns Hopkins University. Its mission is to build global and local partnerships to enhance the quality of health-care services for women and families through training and support for health-care providers including doctors, nurses, midwives, and health educators. JHPIEGO staff work in limited resource settings throughout Africa, Asia, the Middle East, Latin America and the Caribbean, and Europe.

OFFICE OF GLOBAL NURSING

In the context of these internationally focused activities and recognizing the value of nursing's contributions to global health, the Global Nursing Task Force was appointed in 2004 by the Dean of the Johns Hopkins University School of Nursing and the Vice President of Nursing and Patient Care Services of the Johns Hopkins Hospital. It was charged to provide recommendations for an Office of Global Nursing as an infrastructure for strategic, organized, and effective international initiatives for Hopkins Nursing.

Guided by shared goals, the Dean and Vice President for Nursing applied the principles of the theory of mutuality to approach this collaboration. Although the cultures of the School of Nursing and the hospital Department of Nursing differ, they shared similar values, particularly excellence in scholarship, teaching, research, and patient care, and a commitment to share best practices with external audiences. The School of Nursing's strategic plan for 2004–2009 includes the goal of "positioning Johns Hopkins Nursing as a global leader." The task force used a broad definition of global nursing: the application of nursing theory and practice to the health-care needs both of international communities and immigrant populations within the United States.

Task force members included students, faculty, staff, and hospital nurse leaders from the Johns Hopkins University School of Nursing, Johns Hopkins University, the Johns Hopkins Hospital, and JHPIEGO. They met 11 times over 4 months to gather data, reviewing the results of surveys, focus groups, and the work of the task force's subcommittees. Themes identified from the data were used to develop guiding principles and recommendations for the Office of Global Nursing.

Gathering Information

Online surveys were used to elicit input from School of Nursing faculty, students, and staff. A total of 65% (55 out of 84) of full-time faculty representing all ranks responded to the online faculty survey. Of these, 77% of respondents indicated they had participated in one or more global activities and 43% indicated they had taught students abroad including baccalaureate, master's, post-master's, doctoral, and post-doctoral levels. Faculty reported global experiences in all regions of the world, with most experiences in Western Europe (n = 15) and sub-Saharan Africa (n = 9). Nineteen faculty indicated their experiences were self-funded, with the next highest funding source being government. The greatest interest in global opportunities was for student education (74%), international clinical and research presentations (53%), conduct of research (50%), and hosting international visitors (43%).

Out of 690 full-time students, 115 (17%) representing all program levels responded to the online student survey, with the majority of respondents (78%) from the baccalaureate program. A total of 78% of respondents indicated they had participated in one or more global activities; 79 respondents indicated they had completed coursework abroad, 74 had participated in relief efforts, 57 had conducted research abroad, and 66 had worked abroad. The greatest interest in global opportunities was for coursework (75%), relief effort (71%), work (63%), and research (54%).

Of the School of Nursing staff, 21 members responded (approximate response rate of 25%) to an online survey in which they were asked to provide input and advice on an Office of Global Nursing. Several of the respondents (nine) indicated they had traveled abroad, some having experiences abroad for up to 1 year and a few having proficiency in speaking other languages. When asked about the type of global nursing activities in which Hopkins Nursing should participate, staff members validated the same priorities as students and faculty.

A variety of documents were also reviewed by task force members. Interviews and focus groups were used to further explore issues with thought leaders from the Johns Hopkins community. Data from these activities were analyzed and discussed. The emergent themes suggested that Hopkins Nursing should:

- form collaborative partnerships around global issues,
- develop and disseminate knowledge for the world,
- increase sensitivity/awareness of global issues,
- leverage Johns Hopkins resources for international programs,

- obtain funding to support programs for the Office of Global Nursing, and
- provide logistical support for global activities.

The Global Nursing Task Force completed its work in early 2005 with recommendations for establishing an Office of Global Nursing to support the educational, research, and practice mission of Johns Hopkins Nursing, and support global service projects (Figure 8.1).

The new Office of Global Nursing was established in 2006 within the Institute for Johns Hopkins Nursing (IJHN). This created a natural synergy with IJHN's mission to share the innovations of Hopkins Nursing in practice, education, and research—locally, nationally, and globally.

Implementing Recommendations

The work of the Office of Global Nursing includes providing structured educational programs and individualized observerships for nurses vis-

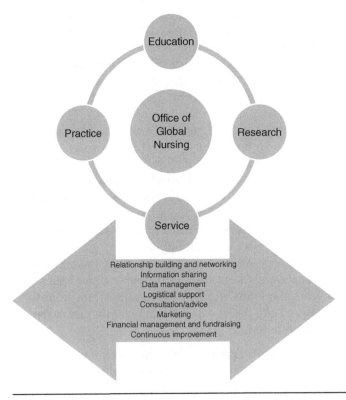

Figure 8.1 Scope and Functions of the Office of Global Nursing.

iting Hopkins. More than 100 individualized visits were arranged between 2006 and 2008 for over 250 visitors from Australia, Austria, Belgium, China, Holland, Hong Kong, Ireland, Japan, Lebanon, the Netherlands, Panama, Portugal, Singapore, South Africa, South Korea, Switzerland, Thailand, Turkey, United Arab Emirates, United Kingdom, United States, and Vietnam. In response to increasing requests for visits, the Office of Global Nursing created a structured week-long program combining presentations with observerships. "Inside Johns Hopkins Nursing: Visitors Week" was offered once in 2007, twice in 2008, and will be offered three times in 2009. Several of IJHN's continuing nursing education programs have also attracted international participants, particularly its leadership development program (Nurse Manager Academy) and the Research Coordinator Training Program.

The Office of Global Nursing also supports the Pan American Health Organization and World Health Organization Collaborating Center in Knowledge, Information Management, and Sharing. This Collaborating Center is the first concentrating specifically on nursing information and communication technologies. Among its activities it hosts the Global Alliance for Nursing and Midwifery to provide collaborative networking and continuing education opportunities to nurses and midwives through a low-bandwidth online community. As of April 2009, 1,850 nurses and midwives in 138 countries are actively participating in this online community of practice.

Johns Hopkins University School of Nursing students and faculty are also providing logistical support by the Office of Global Nursing for their international activities. Examples of assistance include managing the student selection process, making travel arrangements, obtaining visas, and monitoring for potential travel risk. Baccalaureate students have the opportunity to complete a community health practicum in St. Vincent and St. Croix or Haiti. In Haiti, for example, students providing community-oriented primary care learn to respect clients regardless of economic or social status, and learn to be flexible and realistic in their expectations as they approach the challenges of providing care in low resource settings (Sloand & Groves 2005). The final "Transitions" practicum for baccalaureate students includes the option of an international placement, and 10 to 20 students take advantage of this in each graduating class. Since the first student completed this international placement in 2004, 68 students have completed the 240 hour clinical experience with preceptors at hospital sites in China, Lebanon, India, Singapore, South Africa, Tanzania, and the United Arab Emirates.

The Office of Global Nursing is also the "keeper" of the collaborative agreements between the Johns Hopkins University School of Nursing and 15 schools of nursing in 11 countries (Table 8.1).

All agreements are philosophically grounded in the theory of mutuality and expectations and resources were candidly discussed by the deans before any commitments were made. The agreements are individualized to address the interests and needs of both partners, but generally focus on working together to provide faculty and student opportunities in educational and research activities. All partnerships have one or two faculty champions from each school who nurture the relationship and seek funds to support it. The collaborative agreements vary in their impact, but at a minimum include ongoing faculty visits between the partner institutions and sharing of strategies and ideas. These interactions are mutually beneficial and stimulate professional relationships and scholarly productivity, leading to career advancement for faculty. The rewards from these relationships have helped to sustain the collaboration. The most productive partnerships have been supported by philanthropic gifts or grants, allowing for significant investment in collaborative work to create new educational programs, providing for student as well as faculty exchanges, and disseminating new knowledge through presentations and publications. To illustrate the benefits and challenges of sustaining such partnerships, a case study is presented describing the history of the collaboration between

Table 8.1 Johns Hopkins University School of Nursing Formal International Academic Collaborations as of June 30, 2009

Country	Institution
Australia	Flinders University School of Nursing and Midwifery
Australia	University of Technology, Sydney
China	Peking Union Medical College School of Nursing
China	Yanbian University College of Nursing
Lebanon	American University of Beirut School of Nursing
Slovenia	University of Maribor College of Nursing Studies
South Africa	Northwest University School of Nursing
South Africa	University of Kwazulu-Natal School of Nursing
South Africa	University of the Western Cape Department of Nursing
South Korea	Yonsei University College of Nursing
Sweden	Göteborg University Institute of Health and Care Sciences
Switzerland	University of Basel Institute of Nursing Science
Thailand	Chiang Mai University Faculty of Nursing
Turkey	Koç University School of Nursing
United Kingdom	King's College London School of Nursing and Midwifery

Source: Authors.

Peking Union Medical College School of Nursing and the Johns Hopkins University School of Nursing.

Case Study: The First Doctoral Program for Nurses in China

In 2004 the Peking Union Medical College School of Nursing in Beijing, China (PUMC), created the first full-time doctoral program for nurses in China in collaboration with Johns Hopkins University School of Nursing and funded by the China Medical Board. PUMC has had a long history of collaboration in medical and nursing education with Johns Hopkins University. Early in the twentieth century, the Rockefeller Foundation endowed the China Medical Board of New York, Inc. The China Medical Board funded the founding of the PUMC School of Medicine in 1917, the PUMC School of Nursing in 1920, and the PUMC Hospital in 1921. A graduate of the Johns Hopkins Hospital School of Nursing class of 1915, served as PUMC's Superintendent of Nurses from 1919 to 1924. She also established a collegiate nursing education program at PUMC and served as its Dean. During this period Hopkins physicians and nurses trained Chinese practitioners both at Johns Hopkins in Baltimore and at PUMC in China. PUMC remained the only postsecondary nursing program in China until its closure in 1953. Between 1924 and 1950, 238 baccalaureate nurses graduated from PUMC and more than two-thirds of those graduates held leadership positions in administration and nursing education (Xu et al. 2001).

In 1983, a baccalaureate nursing program opened at Tianjin Medical College after a 30 year gap in collegiate nursing education. By 2001 there were 203 higher diploma, 92 baccalaureate, and nine master's degree programs in China. But even in 2004, only six Chinese nurses were reported to have doctoral degrees, three of whom were at PUMC (Nolan, Liu, Li, Lu, & Hill 2010). The PUMC School of Nursing reopened in 1985 with a baccalaureate degree program in nursing, and opened a master's program in 1996.

In June 2001, the Dean and a faculty member of the PUMC School of Nursing met with the interim Dean of the Johns Hopkins University School of Nursing. In this collaboration the theory of mutuality principles guided discussions, which were grounded in a shared tradition of excellence in teaching, research, and patient care. In spite of different national cultures, the shared institutional history and a desire to continue the legacy expedited discussion of activities and shared outcomes to prepare leaders for nursing's future. They agreed to work together with the goal of re-establishing the PUMC and Hopkins nursing education collaboration. In October 2002, the Dean of the Johns Hopkins

University School of Nursing and the Chief Executive Officer of JHPIEGO, visited PUMC to discuss the establishment of the first full-time Chinese doctoral program to enroll nurses at PUMC. Further visits between the two universities continued in 2002–2003 and included representatives from the Chinese Embassy in Washington, the Ministry of Education, and the Chinese Academy of Medical Sciences. In subsequent visits between institutions, administrators and faculty were able to clarify expectation and responsibilities, while upholding high academic standards and a commitment to preeminent leadership of each university.

The goals of the program were mutually developed by the two schools of nursing and described in the grant proposal submitted to the China Medical Board:

1. implement an internationally recognized nursing PhD model at PUMC, the first full-time program in China to prepare doctorally educated nurses,
2. prepare PhD graduates in the tradition of PUMC and Hopkins who would become leaders in nursing research, education, administration, and policy,
3. increase the number of PUMC faculty who were qualified by the PUMC Graduate School to serve as dissertation advisors for future PUMC doctoral students, and
4. plan to obtain support for the continuation of the program after the initial funding ended.

Funding for the first 5 years of the new doctoral program was provided by the China Medical Board (2004–2009).

The first year of intensive planning and collaboration led to the acceptance of five students in the fall of 2005. Quality criteria for doctoral nursing education identified by both INDEN and the American Association of Colleges of Nursing were used to guide the curriculum. The structure of the doctoral program provides for Johns Hopkins University School of Nursing faculty involvement in candidate selection. Faculty from Baltimore also develop and teach courses at PUMC each year. After successful completion of the comprehensive evaluation at the end of the first year, the students spend 6 months of their second year in Baltimore, taking coursework and finalizing and rehearsing presentation of their dissertation proposals. In the third year students conduct their dissertation research in China, guided by a Hopkins advisor and a PUMC advisor. Per PUMC expectations, the student submits one manuscript in Chinese and one in English, and defends the dissertation at PUMC.

Most of the PUMC students had not previously traveled outside China. During their time in Baltimore, PUMC students live together near campus and their adaptation to the new culture is facilitated by staff of the Office of Global Nursing. To date, 15 students have completed their coursework in Baltimore and have returned to Beijing to conduct their research with five more expected to earn their degrees by 2012. The first doctoral degrees for this group were awarded in July 2008. The graduates of the PUMC doctoral program in nursing are prepared to assume leadership positions in education, research, and practice. Their preparation for academic leadership will undoubtedly influence the development of doctoral education for nurses across China.

DISCUSSION AND CONCLUSIONS

Successful partnerships require commitment to a shared and significant goal, mutual respect and trust, a transparent structure for managing the collaborative work, and resources to support the activities. The Johns Hopkins University School of Nursing is one of a number of schools of nursing in North America, Europe, and Australia and New Zealand that are committed to advancing the science and professional status of nursing by partnering to support graduate nursing education worldwide. Working across cultures requires special attention to the expectations of mutual respect and trust. The theory of mutuality described in the introduction to this chapter is an example of a framework for valuing the contributions of each partner and paying attention to perceived imbalances of power that may arise in such relationships. Through the Office of Global Nursing, the Johns Hopkins University School of Nursing provides support and coordination to its collaborative partnerships.

Limited nursing literature exists describing the factors that contribute to the success of partnerships between organizations. Casey (2008) identifies seven areas in her review of the literature: trust and valuing the partner, leadership and managing change, a partnership framework, communication and interaction within the partnership, equity and being involved in decision making, power sharing, and the role of partnership coordinator. These seven areas are congruent with the principles of equity, autonomy (mutual respect), solidarity, and participation in the theory of mutuality. Sustainability also requires consideration of the reality of funding the work of partnerships. Among the partnerships engaged by the Johns Hopkins University School of Nursing, the most productive have added external sources of funding through philanthropic gifts or grants to institutional resources.

International partnerships have significant benefits in their potential to foster cultural awareness and sensitivity, enhance communication, and deepen our understanding of diverse points of view. International partnerships among nursing organizations have the potential to address significant challenges in the nursing profession, and in global health. The world faces an international crisis in health care—a growing workforce shortage at a time when the needs of aging populations in developed countries and fundamental health needs in developing countries are creating increasing demands. The recruitment and retention of nurses has never been more important—or more international in its impact. This crisis drives a sense of urgency and need for action that may place pressure on the partnership timeline and challenge the relationship.

International partnerships may also advance the science of nursing by promoting collaborative nursing research. Most health-care research—including nursing research—is conducted in and benefits wealthier countries. Developing countries receive only 10% of health-care research funding (Rosenkoetter & Nardi 2007). Most nursing research is conducted in theoretical frameworks derived from work in Western countries. Partnerships promoting nursing research, education, and clinical practice may help to balance the predominance of Western, particularly American, funding and intellectual influence on the profession. As nurses listen to each other, they enrich their experiences and understanding of what it means to be a nurse. In listening, they may hear the distinct tones of cultural and social heritage that harmonize the practice of nursing. As Pang et al. (2004) commented in describing their qualitative research study "Towards a Chinese theory of nursing"—listening gives a voice to nurses. Their analysis, grounded in traditional Chinese medicine and concepts such as *qing* (affection, emotion, situation), *li* (truthfulness, responsibility, service), *zhi* (understanding, creativity, knowledge), and *xin* (guard, protect, manage, interact), defines nursing in China as an activity intended "to understand the dynamic health status of a person, to dialectically verify health concerns, and to devise interventions with the goal of assisting the person to master the appropriate health knowledge and skills for the attainment of optimal well-being" (Pang et al. 2004: 661).

International partnerships among nursing organizations provide mechanisms for hearing each other's voice, amplifying the quietest voices among us, and nurturing the new and harmonious melodies we create.

REFERENCES

Aiken, L., Clarke, S., Cheung, R., Sloane, D., & Silber, J. (2003). Educational levels of hospital nurses and surgical patient mobility. *Journal of the American Medical Association, 290*(12), 1617–1623.

Allan, M., & Ogilvie, L. (2004). Internationalization of higher education: Potentials and pitfalls for nursing education. *International Nursing Review, 51*(2), 73–80.

American Association of Colleges of Nursing (2005). *The impact of education on nursing practice.* Retrieved March 9, 2009, from www.aacn.nche.edu/EdImpact/index.htm.

Casey, M. (2008). Partnership: success factors of interorganizational relationships. *Journal of Nursing Management, 16*(1), 72–83.

Crigger, N.J. (2008). Towards a viable and just global nursing ethics. *Nursing Ethics, 15*(1), 17–27.

Davis, A. (1999). Global influence of American nursing: Some ethical issues. *Nursing Ethics, 6*(2), 118–125.

Galtung, J. (1975). Is peaceful research possible? On the methodology of peace research. In J. Galtung (Ed.), *Peace: Research, education, action* (pp. 273–274). Copenhagen, Denmark: Christian Ejlers.

Hayhoe, R. (1989). *China's universities and the open door.* Armonk, NY: M.E. Sharpe.

International Council of Nurses (2004). *The global shortage of registered nurses: An overview of issues and actions.* Geneva, Switzerland: International Council of Nurses. Retrieved February 18, 2009, from www.icn.ch/global/shortage.pdf.

International Council of Nurses (2006). *ICN code of ethics.* Retrieved February 18, 2009, from www.icn.ch/ethics.

Ketefian, S., Davidson, P., Daly, J., Chang, E., & Srisuphan, W. (2005). Issues and challenges in international doctoral education in nursing. *Nursing and Health Sciences, 7*(3), 150–156.

Nolan, M., Liu, H., Li, Z., Lu, C., & Hill, M.N. (2010). Partnering in international doctoral education: The first nursing PhD graduates in China. Manuscript submitted for publication.

Pang, S.M.C., Wong, T.K.S., Wang, C.S., Zhang, Z.J., Chan, H.Y.L., Lam, C.W.Y., & Chan, K.L. (2004). Towards a Chinese theory of nursing. *Journal of Advanced Nursing, 46*(6), 657–670.

Redman, R.W. (2007). Critical challenges in doctoral education: Highlights of the biennial meeting of the International Network for Doctoral Education in Nursing, Tokyo, Japan, 2007. *Japan Journal of Nursing Science, 4*(2), 61–65.

Rosenkoetter, M.M., & Nardi, D.A. (2007). American Academy of Nursing expert panel on global nursing and health: White paper on global nursing and health. *Journal of Transcultural Nursing, 18*(4), 305–315.

Shields, L., & Watson, R. (2008). Where have all the nurses gone? *Australian Journal of Advanced Nursing, 26*(1), 95–101.

Sloand, E., & Groves, S. (2005). A community-oriented primary care nursing model in an international setting that emphasizes partnerships. *Journal of the American Academy of Nurse Practitioners, 17*(2), 47–50.

World Health Organization (2008). *Global atlas of the health workforce.* Retrieved October 12, 2009, from www.who.int/globalatlas/autologin/hrh_login.asp.

Xu, Z., Xu, Y., Sun, J., & Zhang, J. (2001). Globalization of tertiary nursing education in post-Mao China: A preliminary qualitative assessment. *Nursing and Health Sciences, 3*(4), 179–187.

9

MAKING CROSS-BORDER PARTNERSHIPS WORK

The Case of China's Hong Kong System

PETER FONG AND GERARD POSTIGLIONE

One of the most frequent forms of cross-border instructional collaboration between universities has been programs in business, including the Master in Business Administration (MBA). This chapter examines how Hong Kong employs its special attribute as the most globally connected part of China to become an international hub for cross-border collaborations in higher education. In particular it examines the motives, strategies, and issues in the planning and implementation of instructional programs by two or three universities. The chapter begins with an historical background to understand the basis upon which Hong Kong has initiated international collaborations. Hong Kong's status within China and how it made a transition from being a bridge between China and the West to being a logistical center for knowledge transfer (Postiglione 2005) is also discussed.

The chapter illustrates how international collaboration in higher education is encased within the Hong Kong legal system, which provides for a high degree of institutional autonomy, the protection of academic freedom, English as a medium for higher education, bicultural and multilingual capacity, a communications infrastructure, and houses world-class universities. Finally, cross-border programs in business and public administration launched by the University of Hong Kong are introduced. The chapter recounts the design and implementation of these programs, the challenges confronted, the experience gained, and the manner in which such cross-border programs can be successfully sustained.

MAKING GLOBALIZATION WORK FOR CHINA

International collaborations in higher education have increased, especially in the Asia region and particularly in China (Chapman, Cummings, & Postiglione 2010). This chapter focuses on China's most international space—the Special Administrative Region of Hong Kong. It makes for an especially interesting case study due to its separate constitution, high degree of autonomy, expansive global linkages, highly ranked business environment, bilingual Chinese population, common law legal system, highly mobile population, notably efficient civil service, absence of corruption and terrorism, and world-class infrastructure in communications, transport, and banking (Chan & So 2002). These conditions, coupled with its geographical position adjoining the Chinese mainland, would seem to make it an ideal location for cross-border partnerships in higher education. With at least three of its eight universities regularly appearing at the top of international rankings, it has proceeded more slowly in cross-border university collaborations than might be expected (Times Higher Education 2008). Unlike Singapore where international collaboration in higher education is driven by government mandate, Hong Kong's government-funded universities enjoy institutional autonomy under the law and proceed with cross-border collaborations as and when they see fit.

After examining the context and organizational environment of higher education from which collaborations are nested and nurtured, the chapter will focus specifically on collaborations in business and public administration, since Hong Kong's reputation is so closely tied to its capacity in these two areas. The chapter will end by discussing how such collaborations may be affected by global or regional economic crises.

POSITIONING HONG KONG'S UNIVERSITIES FOR CROSS-BORDER COLLABORATION

Each society and university system has a set of characteristics conducive to a particular style of cross-border collaboration, with advantages and obstacles that change over time in relation to external and internal environments. Despite its size and great distance from the

Chinese capital, Hong Kong has long served as China's bridge with the larger world. As early as the mid-nineteenth century it was the place from which Chinese students crossed the Pacific to study in America (Ting & Pan 2003).

These early study abroad activities involved arrangements between the Chinese government and universities abroad. However, these became an integral part of the unprecedented transformation of South China. Strengthened by social capital embedded within the expansive overseas Chinese community's education networks, Hong Kong began an economic integration with the adjoining regions in East Asia that continues to this day, supporting Hong Kong's role in trade and transport, banking and finance, travel and tourism, communication and diplomacy. As changes occurred on the Chinese mainland, Hong Kong continued to adapt itself to these changes. This has been especially true during the last quarter century when over a million Chinese students were sent to study overseas. Hong Kong reaped the benefit of this student mobility, since it was able to recruit large numbers of Chinese scholar returnees to staff Hong Kong's rapidly expanding university system.

University collaborations involving student exchanges added to Hong Kong's remarkable ability to attract human capital. It also contributed significantly toward its unique capacity to operate bilingually and biculturally. Hong Kong continues to have the most highly international academic staff in all of China with 40% of the academic staff of the University of Hong Kong in 2009 hailing from other countries.

As the post-1978 reform era unfolded in China, Hong Kong refined its traditional bridge role to facilitate cross-border collaboration. As overseas universities become able to circumvent Hong Kong's brokerage role and establish contacts directly with mainland universities, Hong Kong came to rely more on its cross-cultural sophistication and easy access to mainland sources to provide Western universities with useful perspectives and reliable advice for planned collaborations with the mainland universities. Such pragmatic adaptations became part of Hong Kong's transition to a knowledge economy, and came to constitute the nucleus of its vision for cross-border collaborations. Hong Kong capitalized on its intimate knowledge of China, international links, communication infrastructure, and cultural affinity with the Chinese mainland. It remains a key center for interpreting China's reform across cultures, and building mutual understanding between China and the rest of the world. In this respect, its universities play a central role. They coordinate academic collaborations within an atmosphere of academic traditions, values, and practices unlike their counterparts on the Chinese mainland. A majority of Hong Kong's academic staff earned doctorates overseas and an increasing number have their roots on the mainland before having gone overseas for advanced study and then joining the professoriate in Hong Kong.

Historical Context

Hong Kong has long been distinguished as an open trading port (Tsang 2004). Through most of its history, it was mainly driven by economic concerns and colonial interests (Chan & Postiglione 1996). One English-medium university carried the colony for over 50 years until mass schooling contributed to the establishment of a Chinese-medium university in 1963. Hong Kong's two universities became training centers for civil servants, professionals, and urban elites in business and commerce. By 1981, only 2% of the relevant age group occupied a university place. This grew to 8% by 1989 when Hong Kong experienced a major outflow of professional talent. University enrollments doubled and the number of universities was increased to eight by 1997 (University Grants Committee 1996). As knowledge economics and massification came to dominate policy discourse, Hong Kong moved away from a sector-based manpower forecasting model of tertiary education.

In 2006, Hong Kong had 12 degree-granting institutions, of which most were publicly funded. The Chief Executive announced in 2000 that 60% of the 17–20 age cohorts would be in higher education by 2010, a doubling of the 2001 figure. This was achieved by 2006, largely though self-financed associate degree programs. It is envisioned that by 2012, the long-standing education structure with 7 years of secondary and 3 years of university education will be converted to a 3 + 3 + 4 structure (3 years of junior and 3 years of senior secondary education, plus a 4-year university system). Although competition for the best students and the most research funds among the eight universities is intense, new incentives have been introduced to speed up cross-institutional collaboration as a way of cutting costs and strengthening areas of teaching and research (Sutherland 2002). However, consolidation of universities has been resisted by individual institutions.

Three main context-embedded drivers determine the direction of higher education: competing within the global market, operating effectively as a system within China, and keeping a lead in the brain race. Market competition has long been a sacred part of Hong Kong's way of life (Lau, Lee, Wan, & Wong 1999). The mainland's transition to a socialist market economy has only emboldened those proponents who see improvements in higher education as inextricably linked to strategies of market competition. As cities like Beijing, Shanghai, and Guangzhou bear down on Hong Kong's position as China's economic powerhouse, the academy is affected through the reforms in higher education.

It is within this context that Hong Kong has imported a more entrepreneurial model of higher education and situated it within a post-colonial society unable to expand university admissions due to an economic crisis that stretched from 1997 to 2005 (Jao 2001). Several forces that go beyond the Asian financial crisis affect Hong Kong's higher education system. These include a transfer of manufacturing to the hinterland in mainland China, a transition to a knowledge-based service economy, and the cultural implications of being a part of greater China. Moreover, the availability of top-notch mainland talent, many returning from overseas study, has led to new policies to attract them to work in Hong Kong's universities. This has been accompanied by a shift from elite to mass higher education, and the aspirations of China to establish several world-class universities (Altbach & Balan 2007).

The Chinese mainland's economic reforms and opening to the outside world mean there is a need to strengthen innovative capacity within the increasingly competitive global economy. It also means there is a need for a shift from the traditional university role of being an academic bridge between China and the West to being an international center/hub for trade in educational services. It is also generally accepted that the success of Hong Kong's higher education system depends heavily upon its internationalism. This is reflected in its staff composition, a large proportion of which come from other countries (mostly English speaking), and a larger proportion of whom have earned their highest degrees overseas. Most university students are graduates of local secondary schools. However, several universities in Hong Kong have set a target of admitting a 20% proportion of non-local students. There is no limit on admission targets for non-local postgraduate research students. Several universities have initiated recruitment of first-year students from top mainland universities, and the number has grown to over 2,000, a feature that is also viewed as a drawing card for attracting international students to their campuses.

Despite the new emphasis on higher education for social and civic development, Hong Kong's future is viewed as depending heavily on its human resources—the skills of its people in such fields as financial management, law, science and technology, tourism, the management of trade and business, and related fields. In a 2006 poll of 11,000 business leaders, almost 20% highlighted an inadequately educated workforce as the most problematic factor for doing business in Hong Kong. In the World Economic Forum's Global Competitiveness Report of 2005–2006, Hong Kong dropped seven places to 28 out of 117. To build and maintain human capital, Hong Kong requires innovative and competitive universities. Singapore, similar to Hong Kong in its size and dependence on brains and innovation, has been rapidly internationalizing its higher education system, actively recruiting scholars and students globally and from mainland China as well. This includes inviting overseas universities to set up shop there, including the University of Pennsylvania and Johns Hopkins University. Moreover, Singapore (along with South Korea and Taiwan) attained a jump on Hong Kong by heavy investment in research and development in science and technology in the 1980s and 1990s. Hong Kong continues to lag behind the pack with a gross domestic product (GDP) expenditure on research and development of 0.7% compared to a 1.9% average in the EU in 2004, 2.26% for OECD countries, 2.59% in the United States, 3.15% in Japan, and 2.25% in Singapore. Even renowned astrophysicist Steven Hawkings on a visit with a Hong Kong chief executive in June 2006 called for the funding of more research and teaching posts at Hong Kong's universities. Hong Kong's quick-profit business community of the 1990s chose to rely more on the approaching reunion with China for keeping the economy charging ahead, rather than following the path of the other three Asian Tigers by investing in high technology.

Hong Kong's universities also play a key role in sustaining the city as a key location for innovation and commerce, both internationally and within the region. However, another widely held perspective is that Hong Kong benefits greatly from robust university growth on the mainland and the proximity to and unique relationship with universities in the Chinese mainland, and that this will become instrumental to enhancing Hong Kong's global competitiveness. As university presidents from around the world visit Beijing, Qinghua, and Fudan universities, they cannot help noticing the massive amount of funding being funneled into expanding and modernizing these campuses. They also witness a series of new measures to raise academic quality. Still, mainland universities need further development in the software that characterizes "an advanced academic culture focused on research, collaborative work, meritocratic advancement, and top-quality teaching and advisement" (Altbach & Postiglione 2006).

It is in the culture of academic management that Hong Kong's universities have important advantages that go beyond their impressive facilities. The University of Hong Kong (HKU) is undergoing a major expansion and renovation of its campus in anticipation of its 100th anniversary. However, it is in the software of academic culture and traditions where Hong Kong's top universities have a competitive advantage. These include transparency and a governance style requiring that personnel decisions and allocation of resources be based on performance-based standards. Academic freedom is sufficiently well entrenched to have withstood several major challenges in the last decade. An international faculty compliments the cosmopolitanism of the local staff and their institutions. Favorable working conditions attract academic staff, even though salaries have declined and are now closer to international norms. The competitiveness of Hong Kong's salaries and working conditions may gradually decline as those on the Chinese mainland improve and as academic salaries in other places like the United States and elsewhere continue to rise. Mainland China's universities continue to struggle at establishing regularized personnel policies, with appropriate expectations and evaluations.

The discourse on knowledge economy means that Hong Kong's key universities need to be supported in their efforts to compete globally. Specific policy initiatives include a closer relationship with universities on the mainland and joint programs of academic cooperation and exchange, internationalization in student recruitment, the continued use of English as the language of higher education, an emphasis on academic and professional fields especially relevant to Hong Kong's competitive future, dedication to intellectual freedom that has been a hallmark of higher education in Hong Kong, attracting Hong Kong overseas scientists to return home, continued reform of the school system, an undergraduate curriculum that builds problem-solving skills, commitment to community building, and a research culture that is supported with bold initiatives to sustain a new intellectual environment of discovery and application.

Cross-system Recruitment and Joint Degrees

A main reason behind the late twentieth century expansion of higher education in many parts of the world was the need to respond to and support the development of a global knowledge economy (Task Force on Higher Education and Society 2000; World Bank 2002; Mok & Welch 2003). This applies to developing countries like China, as well as developed systems like Hong Kong, which spent over 4.1% of its GDP on education in 2000 of which 26.5% was designated to higher education. Hong Kong went from a two-university British Territory in 1990 to an eight-university Special Administrative Region in 2000. In 1981, only 2.2% of the 17–20 year old age cohort could enter local universities. A decision to nearly double the number of students admitted to university first-degree studies from 8 to 16% by 1994 was taken in October of 1989, even as emigration from Hong Kong rose rapidly as a result of events on the mainland. The proportion of the age cohort in first-degree places was nearly 18% in 2001 (Sutherland 2002: 1). If all postsecondary places, including diploma, certificate, and associate degree places are counted, the figure is estimated to be around 25%. Hong Kong aimed to double the number of places in higher education between 2000 and 2010, eventually reaching 60%, and actually achieved this aim by 2006.

For reasons of cost and social stability, Hong Kong and the Chinese mainland kept a tight rein on higher education expansion until the last decade of the twentieth century. As both expanded rapidly, this led to an increase in recruitment of students across the two systems. Until 2002, Hong Kong's universities only recruited graduate students from the Chinese mainland. Hong Kong students also attend mainland universities in greater numbers than before. Although this cross-system student flow is still modest, it will continue to grow as restrictions are removed for mainland graduates working in Hong Kong. The bridge role enters here in that some mainland students who, after attending their first year at a top mainland university, transfer to the University of Hong Kong for 3 years to earn a bachelor's degree, and then enroll in graduate study in the United States.

The rapidly globalizing environment led to changes in higher education, including a credit unit system, staff and management reviews, recurrent funding assessment, teaching and learning quality process reviews, new admission standards, liberal arts/broadening courses, staff re-titling, as well as an increase of students from outside Hong Kong, and a "top-slicing" of department budgets for reallocation by university heads. The mission and functions of universities are a constant topic of debate within Hong Kong. Even though most academics in Hong Kong feel relatively powerless in the running of their institutions, their level of job satisfaction is not low by international standards.

There are fundamental differences in the way that the two Chinese higher education systems of Hong Kong and the mainland perceive and react to globalization. It is in the interest of Hong Kong's universities to be both global and national. Hong Kong still has the only

English-medium universities in China and larger proportions of international staffing. While globalization has led to convergence in some respects, the two university systems are separately encased. This is especially apparent with respect to institutional autonomy.

As the mainland has become more market and globally oriented, central planning has been removed as an obstacle to increased academic openness. Academic exchanges have been stepped up, resulting in more understanding of the culture of higher education in each other's systems, and a more common perspective about the mission and functions of higher education. Both systems are dominated by state-funded universities, which are increasingly being told to be more cost effective and raise more of their own funds. That said, great differences between the systems still exist. The gap between income and qualification of staff between Hong Kong and the rest of China will remain for years to come, as well as some limitations on academic discourse within mainland universities.

COLLABORATIONS AND LEARNING CURVES

The relative newness of cross-border collaboration in higher education means that learning curves are especially important. Assessing prospects, initiating contacts, responding to initiatives, communicating motives, arguing internally for the educational merits of cross-border programs, managing financial and legal dimensions, harmonizing collaborations with system-wide priorities, successfully navigating obstacles, and sustaining long-term collaborations require a knowledge of contextual and system characteristics. What is learned through initial collaborations can be disseminated to other collaborative efforts. However, this is not often the case. There is a dearth both of detailed case studies and of critical analyses of cross-border collaborations involving Hong Kong's colleges and universities.

Cross-border collaborations in higher education appear in a multitude of formats. These include student exchanges, curriculum development, short-term appointments and sabbaticals, service learning arrangements, cyber-based linkages of classroom learning, and most notably joint research projects. Many of these are hardly new. However, the most emergent types of cross-border collaboration in higher education and the types that have the most implications for the internationalization of higher education in the coming decades are those driven by the need for how specialized knowledge fits into other national contexts as economies, organizations, and public administration of societies become more globally interdependent.

These may involve joint degrees or certificates, short- and long-term intensive programs for young students or experienced professionals, or transplantation of managerial strategies to improve the delivery of instruction and capacity building. Hong Kong has three main forms of collaboration: those with universities in mainland China, those with universities abroad, and those that involve partners from both these locations.

COLLABORATION IN BUSINESS ADMINISTRATION

In this section, three instances in which the University of Hong Kong collaborates with overseas institutions in the delivery of academic programs will be introduced. After presenting the basic characteristics of these collaborations, issues and questions that highlight general aspects of cross-border collaborations related to their success or failure will be analyzed.

The collaborating institutions have long histories and are premier institutions internationally as well as in their respective regions. The University of Hong Kong (HKU) is among the earliest established universities in Asia. Approaching its 100th anniversary, it is ranked first in China and 26th in the world by Times Higher Education (2008). Its alumni are among the "Who's Who" in business, education, and government, including 11 of 15 Secretaries of the Hong Kong government. HKU's Faculty of Business and Economics offers a full range of programs including six master's degree programs, a doctoral degree, and a non-degree open enrollment and executive education program for senior executives, namely the Executive MBA-Global Asia, Global Partnership Executive Program.

Remaining true to the spirit of entrepreneurship, the vision of the faculty is to become the leading international center for the study of economics and business in Asia and to serve the development needs of Hong Kong as an international financial center. It positions itself as a provider of high-quality executive education programs that enhance business executives' knowledge development in the context of contemporary international business practice. Its self-financed executive education programs at its Cyberport campus serve senior executives from Hong Kong, mainland China, and the Asia-Pacific region and beyond. The portfolio of new postgraduate degree programs includes an executive MBA (EMBA) program and non-degree executive education programs.

The three examples cited include the EMBA-Global Asia program in which HKU partners with London University's Business School

(LBS) and Columbia University's Business School (CBS), and two non-degree Global Partnership Programs: the Oxford–HKU Senior Executive Program in Corporate Leadership and the Cambridge–HKU Senior Executive Program in Corporate Finance.

Case One: The Executive MBA-Global Asia program

The Executive MBA (EMBA)-Global Asia program offered jointly by London University's Business School and Columbia University's Business School is presently ranked number one in the world. EMBA-Global Asia combines the EMBA-Global programs with the regional prominence of HKU. Classes are held in a unique once-a-month format in Hong Kong, Shanghai, New York, and London. The first intake commenced in May 2009 and its "rising star" executives came from 12 countries mainly in the Asia-Pacific region. Graduates will receive a joint MBA degree and become alumni of all three institutions.

When universities from two or more regions of the world collaborate on an instructional program, one of the first requirements is a thorough market analysis. In this case, the economic growth worldwide (that preceded the global economic downturn in 2008) created an unprecedented demand for executive education. Leading business institutions responded to this demand by offering EMBA programs. The emergence of the Asia-focus in management education and the thriving economies of East Asia further fueled a regional demand, particularly in China, which created a compelling opportunity to serve this high-end market. EMBA and MBA programs carry the same academic rigor and standard, same approval process, and share the same vision of awarding a MBA degree, with the only difference in the level of targeted participants and mode of study. Three comparable joint EMBA programs that place prominently in EMBA rankings include the EMBA-Global Program (offered by Columbia Business School and London Business School; ranked number one globally), the Kellogg-HKUST EMBA Program (offered by the Kellogg School of Management of the Northwestern University and the School of Business and Management of the Hong Kong University of Science and Technology; ranked number two globally), and the TRIUM Global EMBA Program (offered by the Stern School of Business of the New York University, the London School of Economics and Political Science, and the HEC School of Management, Paris; ranked number three globally).

The three universities involved in this cross-border collaboration agreed on the compelling need to develop a joint part-time EMBA program in 2009 to meet the demand in Asia. By combining courses at London University and Columbia University's Business School with HKU's China expertise, the program quickly gained an Asian appeal and a Memorandum of Understanding was signed in January 2008. Targeted participants of the EMBA-Global Asia Program were generally high-performing leaders, top-level global executives, and successful entrepreneurs with international exposure to Hong Kong, mainland China, the Asia-Pacific region, and other parts of the world with at least 10 years of work experience, including 4 years of managerial experience. Participants needed to be sponsored by their firms.

Teaching loads are equally shared amongst faculties from the three partner institutions. Each institution delegates its most experienced professors for corresponding expertise subjects. The academic management of the EMBA-Global Asia Program is consistent with existing MBA program provisions. A set of academic regulations was drawn up and agreed upon by the three partner institutions. Upon satisfying the graduation requirements, participants are given one official transcript of academic results under the names of the three partner institutions. Graduates are conferred a joint degree by the three institutions. Program management and governance is handled by a Program Management Board, comprising three senior members appointed by the deans of the three partner institutions responsible for program oversight. The Board's remit includes making strategic decisions pertinent to the development of the program and its operations. Since program participants have high expectations about management, the EMBA programs usually require skilled staff, high-level service and facilities, and quick response time. A Program Management Team reports to the Program Management Board on a regular basis for the day-to-day execution of program logistics.

Case Two: Oxford–HKU Senior Executive Program in Corporate Leadership

The Oxford–HKU Senior Executive Program in Corporate Leadership is designed and delivered by the two universities. The program draws on cutting-edge theory and practice in the art of corporate leadership by experts worldwide. It is based on the idea that new business models and channels, globalization, technology advancement, higher stakeholder expectations, and the current global economic crisis make sustainable success in competitive markets more and more elusive. It promises to enable strategic leaders to think more effectively and enhance their strategic thinking and leadership capabilities in addressing organizational challenges. Teaching focuses on relating practical aspects of management to organizational operations. However, the themes and case studies are of particular relevance to Asian organizations. These include strategic innovation, creativity and business innovation, and the impact of globalization on China.

Prior to the launch of the program, both Oxford and HKU agreed on a set of primary responsibilities for the collaboration. The Oxford Saïd Business School co-designs the program and its periodic review, delivers half of the program in Hong Kong, pays the speakers from Oxford including honorarium and related expenses, assigns the program director throughout the duration of the program in Hong Kong, includes information about the program on Oxford's website, and issues a certificate of attendance to the participants jointly with HKU.

The HKU Faculty of Business and Economics co-designs the program and its periodic review, delivers half of the program in Hong Kong, pays its speakers' honorarium and related expenses, designs and prints the publicity materials, markets and publicizes the program in Hong Kong and the region, includes information about the program on its website, arranges venues for the program, provides meals for participants, handles enquiries and registration, collects payment from participants before the program commences, conducts the program evaluation, and issues participants a joint certificate of attendance.

Included among the benefits to participants are: exposure to leading-edge thinking on important challenges facing organizations, their implications, and best practices for dealing with these challenges; learning from distinguished professors and experts from the University of Oxford and the University of Hong Kong who have experiences in senior executive development and appreciation of global business issues, as well as a deep understanding of Asia and its particular challenges; integration of the best of East and West in management education, in theory and practice; enhancement of strategic thinking capabilities, the ability to see both the big picture as well as specific organizational implications; gaining knowledge of important global trends and developments, and useful frameworks for analysis; application of concepts and frameworks to participants' own organizations and challenges; networking with other senior executives; membership in an extensive global network by becoming members of Oxford and HKU Alumni; and certification from University of Oxford and the University of Hong Kong.

Among the envisioned benefits to the subscribing organizations are: training leaders with strategic thinking skills and knowledge of best practices, acquiring knowledge of international trends and developments with particular relevance to Asia, and extensive and influential alumni networking with the University of Oxford and the University of Hong Kong.

The format for delivery of the program is an intensive 5-day workshop using interactive lectures, case analysis, discussion, and group work. The program aims to combine the best of East and West in management education with an international magnitude, constantly relating concepts and frameworks to organizational challenges and dilemmas. In terms of the target population to attend the program, it is viewed as suitable for chief executive officers, board directors, senior managers, senior civil servants, and other senior executives with high-level strategic responsibilities.

Case 3: Cambridge–HKU Senior Executive Program: Strategic Issues in Corporate Finance

Similar to its collaboration with the University of Oxford, the Cambridge–HKU Senior Executive Program: Strategic Issues in Corporate Finance in Hong Kong follows very much the same arrangements. As for each collaborator's responsibilities, they are basically similar to that of the Oxford–HKU program. The main difference is that this program focuses on corporate finance instead of leadership. This program is designed to give opportunities for senior executives and officials to examine current strategic issues in corporate finance. It aims to build participants' understanding of the interaction between strategic decisions and corporate finance and provide the tools to ensure maximum alignment between corporate strategy and financial structure, decision-making and value-based management, risk management, the global financial crisis and the future of the international financial system, capital budgeting, and capital structures in the context of modern, global financial markets including China. Renowned professors provide lectures in the program, along with local business experts, and leaders with strategic finance responsibilities to share their vision and strategies.

With respect to the benefit to participants, it is envisioned that through participation in the program, they will be able to: understand the key links between corporate strategy and financial structure that are vital in these turbulent financial times; learn from the research of experts in the field, experience the tools needed to ensure maximum alignment between goals and resources, acquire decision-making strategies and management incentives; get answers to strategy and financing questions in today's global markets, including China; network with other senior executives; participate in a global network by becoming members of Cambridge University's Judge Business School Executive Education Alumni and HKU's Executive Alumni; and be qualified to receive a certificate of attendance from the University of Cambridge and the University of Hong Kong.

The program format is also similar to the Oxford–HKU program, which includes an intensive 5-day workshop using interactive lectures, case analysis, and group discussion. Finally, the program is aimed at and most suitable for chief financial officers, board directors, investors, shareholders, financial controllers, and other high-level executives with finance responsibilities.

CASE ANALYSES: RATIONALE FOR COLLABORATION

Having described the three cases of collaboration, an analysis of some of the issues involved in the cross-border collaboration will be provided. In the final analysis, the extent to which the collaboration design and implementation is driven forward hinged heavily upon the envisioned and realized benefits. These collaborations added strength to each collaborating institution and increased the influence of the programs and their participants.

In all three cases, the institutions wished to tap into new unmet market demand, but they also aimed to generate additional revenues for strengthening the capacity of their research and teaching. There had to be an unquestionable commitment by each participating institution that the collaboration would not only build upon their respective international reputations in the academy but also that it would have to significantly enhance the global branding of their universities in a direct way. Moreover, within the dialogue of collaborative planning and implementation was the consistent expectation that the collaboration would measurably improve the quality of teaching and research, provide a steady stream of new knowledge through technology transfer, and create social and political impact in certain regions.

In the case of the EMBA-Global Asia program, each of the three partnering universities also had its own separate objectives. For London University and Columbia University's Business School, it was a desire to be positioned to serve a larger number of students from Asia. While they were already doing this to some extent on their home campuses, their geographic locations in London and New York place limitations on their capacity to be strategically positioned in the Asia-Pacific region. The collaboration made their programs more attractive by reducing travel time and expenses. Aside from geographical factors, HKU possessed an intimate knowledge of the new and complex dimensions of a rapidly emergent Asia-Pacific region, making HKU an ideal partner for such a program.

Half of the world's population is within 5 hours' flying time of Hong Kong. The partnership of London University, Columbia University's Business School, and HKU can capitalize on the high demand for executive education in the world's fastest growing regions of China and India. It will be more convenient for students to take courses in Hong Kong rather than flying to London or New York. Under this collaboration, each university will benefit significantly. For London University and Columbia University's Business School, it can serve more students in the Asia-Pacific and exert their influences in the region.

The three universities can also generate additional income from the increased student enrollment. For HKU, there are several objectives and benefits to partner with the world number one EMBA program: EMBA-Global. HKU's strength is mainly in the traditional professional fields, such as medicine and engineering. Its Business and Economics Faculty is relatively young. By 2008, it still did not have an EMBA program. In order to be among the top providers in executive education in a short period of time, it is beneficial to join forces with the world's top ranking programs. HKU can learn from the high-quality faculty and curriculum provided by London University and Columbia University's Business School. Therefore, branding and ranking in executive education is the primary driving force for HKU to participate in this cross-border collaboration. If the program is successful, HKU will soon be in the league of top EMBA program providers. This is a much faster way to climb the EMBA ranking ladder than by doing it alone. In short, HKU will gain both monetary and non-monetary benefits.

The short-term executive programs conducted with Oxford University and Cambridge University also provide manifold objectives for collaborating with HKU. Both are top universities and their brands are already well recognized. Their goals are to extend their political and ideological influences on Hong Kong and China in particular. The University of Cambridge also wishes to serve a larger global community, particularly the Asia-Pacific. Through the proactive and global vision of new leadership, the Cambridge–HKU joint program was launched in 2008. The Oxford University joint program with HKU was first launched in 2005. Financial consideration is not the primary concern for either Oxford or Cambridge University as the revenues for these short courses are relatively small. The primary objective for HKU to collaborate with both Oxford and Cambridge

University is brand building. To bring in leading academics from two of the UK's elite universities to teach with the local professors and business leaders is very attractive to executives in the Asia-Pacific region. It helps to develop HKU as a provider of premium executive education in a much shorter time.

CRITICAL SUCCESS FACTORS FOR SUCCESSFUL COLLABORATION

These cross-border collaborations in higher education show similarities with alliances and partnerships in business. They begin with the identification of potential partnership institutions and programs. Collaborations may vary extensively, from the sharing of resources in faculty and student exchanges and offering joint programs, to more simplified activities, such as having symbolic links and occasional co-organization of joint activities. However, the most common form of partnership is the offering of joint programs. HKU chose to adopt this form in the three cases presented earlier.

Although the above collaborations focus on program and instructional partnership, they carry research, faculty development, and accreditation implications regarding:

- Research—networks are formed among instructors from the three institutions who have already expressed interest in joint research.
- Faculty development—joint collaboration in teaching programs results in faculty development by sharing experiences of teaching different types of students who work in several countries.
- Accreditation—benchmarking and international collaborations are required for institutional accreditation by many business schools.

In the case of the EMBA-Global Asia program, each business school initially prepared their program proposals and sought their own institution's internal approval. At the same time, the three schools negotiated the form and terms of collaboration, including the financial arrangements. Finally, all three parties signed an agreement governing the entire operation of the program. Before reaching an agreement, the partners had to work out differences and obstacles to ensure all parties accepted the terms of the contract. Naturally, reaching a final agreement with three parties required sharp but sensitive negotiation skills, mutual understanding, trust, and a willingness to accommodate. The critical success factors included:

Partners

While it was essential that all parties had mutual trust, common goals, and cooperative outlooks in the pursuit of long-term program success, partners differed in the strength of their position due to their past program offerings. Yet, there was a consensus that any indication of one partner nudging toward dictating terms or another partner being relegated to a secondary role was unacceptable. In the EMBA case, London University and Columbia University's Business School had offered the world's number one ranked EMBA-Global program for many years and in this context, HKU was the newcomer. Thus, the former two partners had the potential to dominate in the decision making. Yet, since program operations were based in Hong Kong, and HKU had the regional expertise, it preferred to have more decisions made locally. In the final analysis, however, every effort was made to ensure that decision making for all matters was shared equally.

Cross-border collaborations inevitably involve crossing cultural boundaries. An understanding of the characteristics of each partner's culture and work style was vital to the success of the program. In the case of the EMBA-Global Asia program, the three collaborating institutions are from three continents—Europe, North America, and Asia. Partners select their representatives on the basis of their understanding of the cultures of their partners, whether British, U.S. American, or Chinese.

Programs

It is vital for the program to be in high demand within the cross-border market and a detailed background market analysis is essential. The collaborating parties should have unique contributions that add value to the new program. Risks include the possibility that the local partner may later move on to launch an independent program after acquiring the essential features of the collaborating program, to maximize the financial return. At the same time, the possibility also exists that one partner will decide to seek a more suitable partner for financial or other reasons. The factor that binds the collaboration is the need for each party to make the program successful.

Quality

It is necessary that programs have relevant content and curriculum, high-quality teaching faculty, good supporting services for students, as well as modern venues and facilities. The most important aspect of quality is students' positive feedback. Participants are only willing to pay a much higher fee for a joint program if it provides value that cannot be provided by other programs launched by a single institution in one location. It was often noted in the cases described here that students who were satisfied with the overall performance of the joint program were far more likely to refer other potential students for the program.

Apart from meeting collaborating institutions' own regulations, most joint programs are also regulated by the government. They have to satisfy government requirements in order to continue their offering. Some partner institutions may put more emphasis on quality than others and are willing to invest more resources to maintain high quality. However, another partner may want to increase its net margin on the revenue and spend less. A balance between maximizing financial returns and maintaining high quality and branding has to be worked out between the partners in order to make the collaboration successful.

Models

Sound business and financial models are essential for sustainable instructional operations and to ensure that financial arrangements are fair to all parties. One commonly used principle is based on equal contribution of resources and an equal share of financial risks and returns. What is equal has to be made clear in both the contract and the budget. An objective assessment of inputs, including efforts and resources, should be conducted and agreed upon before the launch of the collaboration. Since most cross-border collaborations involve different political, legal, and administrative systems, as well as accounting procedures and currencies, the application of one or more systems for the governance of the operation also needs to be worked out in the contract agreement. Tuition fees are normally collected by one party and thus how and when the surplus of income should be transferred to other partners also has to be spelled out clearly in the contract in order to avoid any disputes.

CONCLUSIONS

Changes in institutional management and the emergent forms of entrepreneurialism are critical factors responsible for the success of cross-border collaborations. In short, these facets have to be synchronized for the collaboration to succeed. This is especially true for programs dealing with global business. Moreover, in an Asian context, personal factors and relationships are extremely important. For example, the mutual understanding of those involved in the negotiation and operation, the building of trust across cultural contexts, and complementary work style and attitudes, contribute key elements to the success of the collaboration.

Cross-border education is part of the globalization process and in that context Hong Kong has a remarkable ability to attract human capital. It has a significantly unique capacity to operate bilingually and biculturally with the most international academic staff in China. Hence HKU functions competently in coordinating academic collaborations within an atmosphere of academic traditions, values, and practices, unlike HKU's counterpart institutions on the Chinese mainland.

Government also plays a significant part in the development of cross-border collaborations. With government support through a conducive atmosphere of transparency in regulating cross-border enterprises, it is easier to establish and sustain a successful program. Government policies also facilitate collaboration between overseas higher educational institutes and local partners if qualifications awarded by overseas universities are recognized locally. If a local government restricts overseas institutions from operating in its territory, overseas institutions will look elsewhere for collaborative partnerships. Some governments support cross-border collaborations in higher education because they believe prestigious overseas universities that are willing to establish themselves in their territories can help upgrade human resources. The Singapore government is one example of proactively reaching out to bring in the top universities to its territory and facilitate cross-border collaborations.

China has been more cautious in permitting overseas universities to offer programs in its tertiary system. All collaborations require a local host and all degree programs must be reviewed and approved by the Ministry of Education. Few joint degree courses have operated successfully in the mainland thus far. The Hong Kong SAR government is far less restrictive in allowing overseas programs to operate and has declared the aim of making Hong Kong an international education hub. There are over 100 degree programs offered by overseas universities in Hong Kong. Although the Hong Kong government is not proactive in seeking overseas programs, its open policy certainly helps overseas institutes to collaborate with local organizations.

The experience of the University of Hong Kong sheds light on the success of cross-border collaboration in higher education. The above cases provide some lessons for those interested in developing cross-border collaborations in higher education. The initial planning, identification, and selection of potential partners, the identification and development of appropriate programs, the development of sound business and financial models, the negotiation and implementation of agreements, and the eventual operation of the enterprise require careful thought and a great deal of sustained effort.

REFERENCES

Altbach, P.G., & Postiglione, G. (2006). Can Hong Kong keep its lead in the brain race? *International Higher Education, 45*(Fall), 24–26.

Altbach, P.G., & Balan, J. (2007). *World class worldwide: Transforming research universities in Asia and Latin America.* Baltimore: Johns Hopkins University Press.

Chan, M.K., & Postiglione, G. (Eds.) (1996). *The Hong Kong reader: Passage to Chinese sovereignty.* New York: M.E. Sharpe.

Chan, M.K., & So, A.Y. (Eds.) (2002). *Crisis and transformation in China's Hong Kong.* New York: M.E. Sharpe.

Chapman, D.W., Cummings, W.K., & Postiglione, G.A. (Eds.) (2010). *Crossing borders in East Asian higher education.* Hong Kong: Comparative Education Research Centre and New York: Springer Publishing.

Jao, Y.C. (2001). *The Asian financial crisis and the ordeal of Hong Kong.* Hong Kong and London: Quorum Books.

Lau, S., Lee, M.K., Wan, P.S., & Wong, S.L. (1999). *Indicators of social development in Hong Kong.* Hong Kong: Hong Kong Institute of Asia-Pacific Studies.

Mok, K.H., & Welch, A. (Eds.) (2003). *Globalization and educational re-structuring in the Asia Pacific region.* Basingstoke, UK: Palgrave Macmillan.

Postiglione, G.A. (2005). China's Hong Kong bridge. In C. Li (Ed.), *Bridging minds across the Pacific: U.S.–China educational exchanges, 1978–2003* (pp. 201–218). New York: Lexington Books.

Sutherland, S. (2002). *Higher education in Hong Kong.* Hong Kong: Research Grant Council.

Task Force on Higher Education and Society (2000). *Higher education in developing countries.* Washington, DC: World Bank.

Times Higher Education (2008). *World university rankings: The top 200 universities.* Retrieved June 15, 2009, from www.timeshighereducation.co.uk/hybrid.asp?typeCode=243&pubCode=1&navcode=137

Ting, J.S.P., & Pan, Z. (2003). *Boundless learning: Foreign educated students in modern China.* Hong Kong: Hong Kong History Museum.

Tsang, S. (2004). *A modern history of Hong Kong.* Hong Kong: Hong Kong University Press.

University Grants Committee (1996). *Higher education in Hong Kong: A report by the Universities Grants Committee.* Hong Kong: Government Printer.

World Bank (2002). *Constructing knowledge societies: The new challenges for tertiary education.* Washington, DC: World Bank.

10

COLLABORATION FOR INSTRUCTIONAL TECHNOLOGY SYSTEMS IN AGRICULTURE

GAURI MAHARJAN AND ROBIN SAKAMOTO

Universities have long been a base for agricultural extension. This chapter examines a way that universities are now collaborating across national borders to support agriculture at the community level in developing country contexts. This chapter introduces a recent advancement in agricultural modernization that holds vast potential for developing countries like Nepal. The chapter begins by discussing the unique topographical features of Nepal, which have slowed the use of instructional technology in agriculture. The chapter then discusses economic factors and the role of agriculture in Nepal. Finally, the authors introduce research on the use of a web-based system for providing field diagnosis of plant diseases, with a discussion of the benefits of this system for farmers and the larger society.

The system helps build farmers' knowledge of agriculture by assisting in the diagnosis of plant diseases in the field using a camera-equipped mobile phone. When stress or other disorders are found on a plant, the farmer can send an image by mobile phone to the correspondent university. That photo is then analyzed by a computer-based automatic identification system or by university-based experts and the resulting diagnosis returned to the sender. The use of such a system therefore incorporates an environment of learning as farmers will become more familiar with disease diagnosis through direct and easy interaction with the system. It also provides a new development in agricultural extension capable of making quick diagnosis possible. This, in turn, prevents the spread of crop damage, reduces the risk of financial loss for the farmer, and ensures better food safety for the society. In developing countries with only a limited pool of experts, this potential form of cross-border collaboration is not only highly beneficial but an absolute necessity.

STATUS OF THE REGIONAL INFORMATION NETWORK IN NEPAL

An information network is considered one of the most important elements in the development of a country. Information and Communication Technology (ICT) opens new possibilities of development across many sectors and can play a particularly important role in agricultural development. However, implementation of instructional technology-based services in both agriculture and rural environments is still unsatisfactory, a situation that is becoming a strategic concern both for developed and undeveloped countries. Gelb (2008) has reported on constraints in the application of IT in agriculture, such as farmers' IT skills and lack of infrastructure, and offered some needful steps for effective adoption in the future.

As one of the least developed countries, Nepal has faced a number of problems in providing the flow of information and communication services to the regions of the country. While the Nepalese government and private sector organizations seek to utilize information technology and provide possible data transmission services to the regions, serious constraints remain. The most notable of these constraints are a weak economy and political instability. Consequently, establishing a sufficient information network system throughout the remote areas has been a challenging job for government and private investors.

The Nepalese government has tasked the Ministry of Information and Communication and the Ministry of Science and Technology to promote, facilitate, and regulate information and communication technology. Moreover, His Majesty's government has established a separate autonomous body, the Nepal Telecommunication Authority, which is dedicated to creating a favorable environment to expand and operate telecommunication services and facilities in rural and urban regions of the country with the participation of national and foreign private investors. Despite continuous efforts to implement flexible policies and expand information infrastructure, Nepal still faces several problems in the arena of information and communication technology. One of the biggest challenges is extending the information network to wider areas of the country.

Geographical Topography

Nepal is a mountainous country bordering the northern side of India. Elevation ranges from 70 meters to the highest peak of the world (8,848 meters). The total area of Nepal is 147,181 square kilometers. The country is divided into three main geographical regions. The Northern Himalayan region (above 4,700 m) which covers 15% of the total land, the Middle Mountain region (above 600 to 4,700 m), which includes 68% of the country, and the Southern Plain region (70 to 600 m), covering the remaining 17%. Given its land-locked and mountainous nature, development of an information network in Nepal is occurring at a snail's pace.

Economy

Nepal is ranked among the world's poorest countries. The government is not able to mobilize funds for the development of infrastructures for information technology. While it is technically possible to expand the network to remote areas, the Nepalese government is not in a position to allocate an adequate budget especially for IT expansion. Indeed, the government does not yet have a sufficient budget for even basic needs, such as education, health, transportation, water, environment preservation, human security, and agriculture.

Many countries and international non-government organizations (INGOs) have provided significant financial contributions for the development of information and telecommunication systems in Nepal. However, the development of information technology in Nepal is still at a basic level. Financial aid provided from foreign agencies is helping to set-up a computerized environment and make the people eligible to operate the system but only in very limited regions. The government needs to make continuous efforts and receive vast financial support even to introduce technical knowledge and provide computer equipment to all regions. Employees cannot afford money for computer training from their own pocket.

Poverty

Nepal has widespread poverty. The total population of Nepal is around 26 million (Government of Nepal 2007); gross national income per capita is only US$400 (World Bank 2009). About 40% of the total population is living below the poverty line and 84% of the population live in rural areas where poverty is more prevalent and severe. The poverty rate in the mid-western and far-western mountain regions greatly exceeds the national average. There are large differences in living standards between those in the capital area and the rest of the country. Most rural people depend on subsistence agriculture for their livelihood. While the nationwide adult literacy rate is around 56.5%, most people living in rural areas are illiterate. Unless there are significant efforts to eradicate poverty and alleviate illiteracy, the possibility of introducing IT and establishing information networks in the rural areas is minimal.

Telephone Service

There are 656,070 fixed-line telephones in Nepal (Nepal Telecom 2007) and most urban areas have telephone service of reasonable quality. However, the distribution of telephone lines is very uneven. The capital region has a penetration of around 25% while other regions have far fewer. Of the 3,914 village development committees, around 30% still have no telephone service. The rural regions where telephone service is available still have the least number of telephone lines. In some mountain areas, a single telephone line has to serve an entire district. Most of the remote regions are not yet provided with private telephone lines. In some places, people have to walk for 2 or 3 days to access a phone call. With this low penetration of phone lines, few people can communicate with others even though information and communication services are already launched in their region.

Because of the rugged mountainous topography, most remote regions are served by wireless systems with solar power supply. Cellular Mobile phone service started distribution in Nepal from 1999. Though the service is still limited to main cities, the number of *mobile phone* users is rising *rapidly*. There were 936,482 mobile phone subscribers in 2006 (*Kathmandu Post* 2006). This rose to 1,219,000 subscribers by 2007 (Nepal Telecom 2007).

Electricity Service

Nepal is considered as very rich in water resources. However, only 40% of the total population has access to electricity at present and a large number of people in the rural areas are deprived of electricity. More than 80% of villagers rely on kerosene, wood, and batteries as alternatives to electricity. The Nepal Electricity Authority (NEA) has not been able to generate adequate electricity to meet the demand. It is a challenging issue for Nepal to expand electricity in the rural regions.

Some of the international organizations are helping the government to some extent to expand access to rural electricity by funding renewable energy projects, extending the integrated grid, fostering cooperative-based development, and strengthening the distribution network of the NEA. However, the high cost of extending distribution facilities in rural areas has discouraged NEA and other private investors to promote the rural electrification in wide areas. As electricity is used to operate computers and communication equipment, it is difficult to provide information network expansion to those regions where electrical service is not available.

IT Service

The computer was introduced to Nepal in 1971. Utilization of computer technology increased only slowly over the last 20 years. However, since 1991, there has been a marked increase in the computer market. A private company launched Internet and email service in 1995. During the last few years, there has been rapid development in information and communication networks. As of 2007, there were around 249,400 Internet users out of a total population of 25,874,519, representing an increased penetration five times greater than that in 2002 (Internet World Stats 2008). Now, around 50% of volts direct current have connectivity for both voice and Internet access. Nonetheless, more than 95% of users are found in major cities and people in the more remote regions still need to wait many years to get service in their regions. Only a small portion of the population in these areas is familiar with computers, networking, Internet, intranet, and email. Most of the households, even those located in urban areas, have no financial capacity to buy a computer. There are millions of people in the remote regions of Nepal who have never seen a computer.

Computerization

Due to the large number of rural people in Nepal who have never seen a computer, the likelihood of them using a computer in their work is low. In urban areas, private enterprises and only a few centers of government institutions have limited computerization. Most of the employees working in government institutions have not gained even the basic knowledge of operating the computer. So providing them with computers makes little sense. Most of the computers currently placed in government offices and government schools in rural areas are used only for typing, making nice printouts, and playing games. The problem goes beyond the provision of the hardware. There is a lack of computer experts and operators able to provide technical assistance. There is also a language barrier to implement a computerized system in Nepal. Nepali font has not yet been standardized in a computer system.

Difficulty in Implementation of New Technology

While there has been rapid development of IT in the world, much of it has passed by Nepal. Nepalese people only hear about the new technologies and may not see them implemented. Those that have connectivity are getting only common services like Internet, email, and Web hosting from IT service providers. Internet, GPS, and Geographic Information Services through cellular mobile phones are not available, even though these are common in developed countries.

Risk in Investment

Given the high operating cost and poor return on investment, private organizations are facing problems in even continuing IT service in existing regions. Low penetration of computers in rural regions and the corresponding low level of computer education discourages service providers from investing in those regions. Consequently, IT services in Nepal are concentrated in major cities. One reason for the problem in expanding an information network to rural areas is the high risk nature of the investment.

There is little doubt that IT services help develop public awareness, raise living standards, build a knowledge-based society, improve agricultural productivity, and stimulate economic development. However, application of IT in agriculture will be delayed vastly unless service for rural areas and computer literacy of the people is improved. Therefore, there is great potential for the promotion of future development through cross-border collaboration in this arena with immediate results possible for both easier and faster services within IT and especially when focused in the field of agriculture.

AGRICULTURE OF NEPAL

Agriculture is the principal economic activity of Nepal and plays a vital role in poverty reduction. It accounts for about 33% of GDP and over 65% of the total population depends on agriculture for their livelihood. Approximately 20% of the land can actually be cultivated. Rice is the most important cereal, which is grown on more than half the cultivated land, mainly in the Terai region. Rice is also produced in the highlands during the monsoon season. At present, nearly 60% of the people are engaged in agriculture work. However, due to the lack of good agriculture skills and modern technology, traditional farming methods are still prevalent and the agriculture sector has not been able to significantly support the economic growth of the country. As the present agricultural output is not raising the income level or the living standard of the farmers, the involvement of people in agriculture within Nepal is gradually decreasing.

Higher education in Nepal does not provide adequate resources for agricultural development. There are only a few higher education institutions that offer agriculture or biotechnology programs (one public university, three private universities). Some private organizations are also involved in research and development. Modern biotechnology is being used mainly in plant tissue culture, the development of bio-fertilizers and biological controls (bio-pesticides and disease diagnosis). Current research and development related to plant disease management is also focused on biotechnology and plant pathology. IT-based services in agriculture are still new in the context of Nepal. The Nepal Agricultural Research Council, established in 1991, has a newly established Agriculture Environment Unit with the aim to introduce IT tools and system analysis in agricultural research. However, due to the current situation in Nepal as outlined earlier, implementation of a new system in agricultural modernization will be a difficult task to develop alone.

In the case of plant protection, plant diseases are generally managed by spraying chemicals. But, nowadays environmentally friendly technologies such as Integrated Pest Management including Farmers' Field School are also being used under foreign aid and government initiation. Until now, studies and research about user-oriented IT-based services such as a web-based pest control system have not been available in educational organizations or in research institutes. Although there is a strong potential for making agriculture more environmentally and economically sustainable, both with better crops and suppressing the damage of insects and diseases, development is delayed due to the lack of a skilled workforce, funding, and involvement of the private sectors and teaching institutions. Effective and immediate solutions aimed at strengthening educational facilities, conducting needed research, and assisting farmers will depend, in part, on developing collaborations with foreign institutes.

Establishing a user-friendly diagnosis system with a web database to support pest control offers one potentially effective focus for cross-border collaboration. Pest control is one of the most important factors for farmers, as it can directly affect their agricultural production. In the case of crop damage, early detection on the farm (which is often far from the farmer's residence), immediate diagnosis, and a rapid decision about treatment method are essential to minimize the crop damage. In this situation, the requirement of a system using a wireless Internet connection from a laptop computer or mobile phone for data transmission would be ideal.

The remainder of this chapter will introduce a web-based diagnosis and identification system for plant disease currently being developed at a higher education institution in Japan. This research has the potential to be used in establishing cross-border collaborations for use in Nepal and other developing countries.

INTRODUCTION TO PLANT DISEASE DIAGNOSIS

Pest control is one of the major concerns of farmers in any country. There are many cases of large-scale crop damage in past years due to the unavailability of an effective system. Despite country-level supports, global integrated pest management, and the effort of the growers, economic damage caused by pests is still unavoidable. It is estimated to be even more of an issue in the developing countries of Asia and Africa.

The term pest is used in a broad sense that includes parasitic diseases, non-parasitic diseases (caused by nutritional deficiencies, heat, water, toxic chemicals, wind), insects, weeds, birds, mammals, and other organisms (Koumpouros et al. 2004). Here the focus is on parasitic plant diseases and introduces different diagnosis methods currently in use and in the research phase. It is estimated that there are more than 50,000 plant diseases in the United States (Lemon, Hamburg, Sparling, & Choffnes 2007) and 6,000 in Japan. About 70–80% of plant diseases are caused by fungi and the rest by other microbes such as virus, bacteria, and phytoplasma (Yoneyama, Ando, & Tsuzuki 2006). It is impossible even for experts to be familiar with all of them. However, unlike human beings, not all diseases are invaded by all pathogens and every disease has specific features. In some cases these are similar to each other, which helps in the identification of the disease.

With respect to the diagnosis of plant diseases, both traditional and new techniques are in use. Obviously, Integrated Pest Management and prediction services are playing significant roles in preserving the plant and suppressing the loss of crop yield. But, the existence of disease can also depend on such factors as fertilizers and soil conditions, besides the environmental changes like temperature, humidity, and rainfall. In that sense, pesticides are considered to be indispensable and still remain dominant in use over other alternatives. At present, because of the negative effects of pesticides on human beings and the environment, farmers are seeking and, when possible, often using alternative approaches. Due to the rise in awareness about food safety, low pesticide use and organic cultivation are also becoming more popular. This highlights the importance of more accurate field diagnosis and early disease control on the part of the farmers.

The most common practice in the field diagnosis of plant disease is that growers make their own diagnosis based on their personal experience, use of a diagnosis guide book, by sending samples of the damaged crop to an extension service, or by having an expert visit the field to identify the disease should the earlier strategies not work. In the case of lab diagnosis, a specialist observes the damaged plant sample under the microscope or uses methods like Triangulation Identification for the Genetic Evaluation of Risk to identify the pathogen. Both methods have their strengths and weakness. For the immediate diagnosis on the spot, a support system with speed and accuracy is desirable and should be easy for the farmer to use. To achieve these conditions (speed and accuracy), Digitally Assisted Diagnosis (DAD) might be the perfect system.

In the early 1990s when computers became capable of transmitting images, DAD was first introduced (Holmes, Brown, & Ruhl 2000). Users seeking distance diagnosis sent digital samples through the Internet. Until now, however, diagnosis still totally depended on experts. This chapter describes a web-based interactive support system for the growers to diagnose a disease using a combination of automatic analysis of image features of the disease combined with a recognition system.

IT-RELATED DIAGNOSIS SYSTEMS

The diagnosis of disease at an early stage through the use of information technology is, to some extent, already happening. Support systems currently in use and those still in the research phase are explained below.

Remote Sensing

In the case of plant disease diagnosis, remote sensing can be classified into two parts: wide-range remote sensing and field-based remote sensing. These days field-based remote sensing is becoming widely used for early detection of plant disease. Compared to the wide-range remote sensing, it is easier to set up and also possible to observe the desired part of the plant. Visible and near infrared rays are commonly used to measure the features of disease. On the other hand, wide-range remote sensing, such as spaceborne and airborne sensing, is a highly effective method for diagnosis in the field, covering a wide area. In this case, remote sensing image works as a map of crop health. It pinpoints the location of crop stress. The system has some drawbacks. Observation is only possible in good weather, it cannot detect the damage that appears on the lower part of the plants, and it needs special arrangement with sophisticated tools and high cost. Until now, research is limited on evaluating the damage level or discriminating between the disease and non-disease area.

Expert Systems

Classical *expert systems* generally depend on textual input. Application of images in expert systems is also a good concept in diagnosis. It reduces human interaction and increases the accuracy of diagnosis. But the present research and available expert system services are not oriented to mobile terminals.

Distance Diagnosis

There are some systems developed to diagnose the disease without depending on the subjective information of farmer's observation. In this system, online transmission of digital samples was introduced. Samples include disease spot, crop pattern, and microscopic image. An expert observes the sample image and performs diagnosis based on expertise, past data, and textual information. The University of Georgia developed such a system called Distance Diagnostics through Digital Imaging (DDDI). A similar system named Distance Diagnostic and Identification System (DDIS) was developed at the University of Florida (Xin et al. 2001).

In these systems, county extension personnel serve the growers as the primary point of contact and the pathway to diagnostic specialists. County extension submits the digital sample images and information of plant damage to experts for diagnosis. An appropriate expert around the state evaluates the sample and provides diagnosis and recommendations. Kouchi Plant Protection Office Japan, also started an online diagnosis query submission service with sample images aiming at the utilization of query data and results for precise and rapid diagnosis.

When the distance is a significant obstacle, distance diagnosis offers tremendous advantages of time saving in sample delivery and response. These systems can also be used for a historical archive of submitted samples, searching, a means of communication, and educational purposes. However, as the diagnosis and identification are totally dependent on the manual work of experts, it may cause delays in decision making. As the decision is made based on qualitative analysis, in some cases, experts also may face difficulty in the identification of the disease from images due to similar symptoms of different pathogens. If automatic image processing features could be included to identify a disease within the system, it will be more efficient in time and labor saving.

Web Database

To make the diagnosis faster, research on web-based pest diagnosis using mobile devices is ongoing and some of them have been kept open for use on the web. In this system, growers in remote sites can access or search the database containing digital images and textual information about diseases and compare the visual symptoms. Shimane Agricultural Research Center and Rural Culture Association Japan, has provided simple search options by selecting the disease name or via keywords of the symptoms. The National Agricultural Research Center designed the interface of multiple search options like full text search, keyword search, and multiple database searching. A Personal Digital Assistant-based diagnosis system (Mamada, Machida, & Kouno 2001), and the integrated database system (Pathology Database) to support crop diseases (Kouno, Ayabe, Hitomi, Machida, & Moriizumi 2000) are some research examples on interface development using a web database.

This system is beneficial for getting knowledge about diseases but not sufficient for quick diagnosis. Furthermore, the interface is still not reliable for field use. In most of the web database systems presently in use, growers need to input or select the disease name or keywords about the appearance of disease-like color, shape, etc., to search. But it is difficult to express the color or shape in a common word (color vision varies on light source, background, size, direction, and eyesight) because it may vary according to the user and time (Minolta Corporation 1998). For instance, the same red color can be expressed by the terms vermillion, cinnabar, crimson, strawberry, scarlet, and others with the addition of adjectives such as bright, light, and dark. If they do not know the disease name, there is a possibility of mismatch with system keywords or the displaying of multiple results. Due to this problem, the user should repeat searching with different keywords. To avoid this kind of problem, it is desirable to use the features of diseases objectively or quantitatively.

Image Processing

At present, there is much research and real applications related to image processing in the agriculture field. But, studies on diagnosis and identification of crop diseases are very few and all of them are still in the research phase.

The application of automatic image processing in a web-based environment has great potential for providing quick and precise diagnosis. Consequently, a research plan was developed that would create an interactive environment with automatic analysis of image features to support distance diagnosis possible from the users' end. The goal was to make it possible for users to perform the diagnosis from their fields by using a mobile phone. This approach to plant disease diagnosis makes national borders largely irrelevant. It offers a way that experts located at agricultural colleges and extension units at higher education institutions in one country can assist farmers in another country.

CROSS-BORDER WEB-BASED DIAGNOSIS USING IMAGE PROCESSING

Withered area, color, shape, and texture, which represent the appearance of disease spots, are considered as the basic aspects for the diagnosis. Spots that appear on the leaf, sheath, or stem indicate the existence of disease. Some research and systems that use the image features of disease spots have been introduced above. But, using the automatic analysis of such features in a web system has not been introduced. The proposed research is focused on this concept to automate the online diagnosis of plant diseases. Furthermore, the aim is to develop a field-based system in which the mobile phone is used for sample collection and data transmission. Most mobile phones now have a digital camera attached and makers are continuing to manufacture newer models with better resolution. Mobile phone use is spreading rapidly even within developing countries. The flow of the proposed diagnosis system would be that, first, the user sets the mobile phone to close-up mode and takes a digital sample of the damaged area of the plant. This would then be sent to the server via email. Second, after finishing the processing of the image, an email from the server side is sent to the user with a link to the diagnosis result. Finally, the user checks the result from the mobile browser, to compare similar patterns and decide the disease name. The important feature of this system is the simple operation of diagnosis. The user need not have computer knowledge or any special materials. The user does not need to know the mechanism that undergirds the system and the analysis. This approach offers a potentially effective strategy for assisting farmers with pest control.

Figure 10.1 illustrates the simple structure (virtual) of the system and information flow.

Mail with an image file from the mobile is delivered to the mail server via the Internet using Simple Mail Transfer Protocol (SMTP). The mail agent program inside the server downloads the message using Point Office Protocol (POP). The program checks the mail box at every time interval. If the mail is present in the mail box, the server program reads the attached file and transfers the image to the processing unit. The extracted image features are saved in the text files and analyzed with the classification model. After completion of the diagnosis, the server program again updates the result from the web server in html format and sends a notification mail of the diagnosis at the same time with an access link to the results. Depending on the situation, additional information from the user or automatic inheritance is applied. In the case of an unsatisfactory result, a digital sample is forwarded to the experts.

Special Characteristic and Originality of the Research

Application of quantitative analysis of image features in web diagnosis is still a new concept in the agriculture field. Such analysis method of color, shape, and textures considering their synthetic relations, and application of its systematic quantification according to the relation of

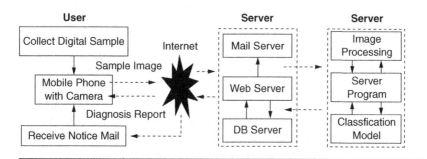

Figure 10.1 Structure of the System (Source: Authors).

growth period, infection stage, and surrounding environment, in the classification of diseases and web search shows the originality. Especially, the system that enables interactive image processing by a farmer can be considered an admirable example. After definite expression of the image features of disease, the possibility for construction of a pest control support system with quick and accurate diagnosis or identification of disease is high. If the diagnosis method with image features is established, development in mobile equipment for diagnosis purposes can also be expected.

Current Achievements and Experiments

An algorithm was developed for automatic extraction of the infected region from the image of the disease. An online method to identify the rice diseases with a unique classification method was tested by simulation. The simulation results showed the possibility of applying the method in discrimination of rice diseases. Furthermore, as part of the research, examination to characterize the reflectance features of healthy and infected regions of diseases (rice) by using hyperspectal imaging technology was conducted. Now experiments about functions of incorporating the non-image information and system operations are being conducted.

Criticism

Image processing is being used in various fields and is especially prosperous in the medical field. But, such methodology for analyzing disease features and its classification is still untapped. Possible reasons behind this might be the various restriction factors such as complexity and diversity of symptoms, changes due to photographic condition, plant growth, and environmental and chemical effects. In this research, the development of an analysis method is aimed at using the most suitable image features considering the formation and relation of such restriction factors.

Experts pointed out, "Of course, the farmer recognizes the occurrence of disease by finding spots on the leaf or withering conditions but, a digital image of a disease spot or appearance of plant disorder is not enough information for diagnosis." As is likely in human disease, it is imaginable that simply a digital image of eczema makes diagnosis possible. But in reality, both doctor (plant disease expert) and patient (farmer) are not performing diagnosis like this. Before performing the diagnosis, besides visual symptoms of the plant, it is important to know the occurrence period, distribution of plants, cultivation environment (condition of soil, fertilizer), past weather conditions, plant species, past occurrence, etc. In real diagnosis, the decision is taken under the combination of visible features (color, shape, formation) of the disease and the above factors. It is a convincible matter. To include such non-image information in the diagnosis automatically, the system is designed with GPS and data mining technologies. Implementation of these services enables automatic acquisition of past weather data, cultivation history, and other information of the particular field. At present, digital cameras and mobile phones with GPS functions are already introduced in the market.

CONCLUSION

The research outlined in this chapter has the capability to revitalize interest in agriculture. This is especially important for developing countries where agriculture is the livelihood for many people and governments are not able to devote adequate resources to the modernization of agricultural techniques. A user-friendly web-based plant diagnosis system that can be accessed through a mobile phone would allow for pest prevention and hence minimize the risk of loss in production. It also enhances the knowledge of farmers to treat the diseases, pest insects, and environmental stresses on their crops. This is vital for the socio-economic lifestyle of people in remote areas.

The principal researcher for this project is Nepalese and the higher education institution is in Japan. However, if this collaboration works well, it foreshadows the development of wider application across borders, with the goal of improving agriculture in developing countries.

REFERENCES

Gelb, E. (2008). ICT adoption for agriculture: Lessons for the future. *Agriculture Information Research, 17*(3), 3–6.

Government of Nepal (2007). *Central bureau of statistics: Population.* Retrieved October 20, 2009, from www.cbs.gov.np/#.

Holmes, G.J., Brown, E A., & Ruhl, G. (2000). What's a picture worth? The use of modern communications in diagnosing plant diseases. *Plant Disease, 84*(12), 1256–1265.

Internet World Stats (2008). *Nepal internet usage and telecommunications reports.* Bogata, Columbia: Miniwatts Marketing Group. Retrieved October 30, 2009, from www.internetworldstats.com/asia/up.htm.

Kathmandu Post (2006, December 15). Number of mobile phone users rising in Nepal.

Koumpouros, Y., Mahaman, B.D., Maliappis, M., Passam, H.C., Sideridis, A.B., & Zorkadis, V. (2004). Image processing for distance diagnosis in pest management. *Computers and Electronics in Agriculture, 44*(2), 121–131.

Kouno, T., Ayabe, M., Hitomi, H., Machida, T., & Moriizumi, S. (2000). Development of an integrated database system "PaDB" to support crop protection against diseases and insect pests. *Agricultural Information Research, 9*(1), 15–24.

Lemon, S.M., Hamburg, M.A., Sparling, P.F., & Choffnes, E.R. (2007). Global infectious disease surveillance and detection: Assessing the challenges—Finding solutions [Workshop Summary]. Washington, DC: National Academies Press.

Mamada, Y., Machida, T., & Kouno, T. (2001). Development of PDA based support system to diagnose crop disease. *Agricultural Information Research, 10*(1), 13–24.

Minolta Corporation (1998). *Precise color communication. Color control from feeling to instrumentation.* Osaka, Japan: Minolta Corporation.

Nepal Telecom (2007). *Annual report 2007.* Kathmanda, Nepal: Nepal Doorsanchar Company Limited. Retrieved October 30, 2009, from www.ntc.net.np/publication/annualreport/ntcAnnual2007.pdf.

World Bank (2009). *Gross national income per capita 2008. Atlas methods and PPP.* Retrieved October 30, 2009, from http://siteresources.worldbank.org/DATASTATISTICS/Resources/GNIPC.pdf.

Xin, J., Beck, H.W., Halsey, L.A., Fletcher, J.H., Zazueta, F.S., & Momol, T. (2001). Development of a distance diagnostic and identification system for plant, insect, and disease problems. *Applied Engineering in Agriculture, 17*(4), 561–565.

Yoneyama, S., Ando, K., & Tsuzuki, T. (2006). *Appearance of plant diseases and pests, and selection of pesticides.* Tokyo, Japan: Rural Culture Association.

Part V
Partnerships in Pursuit of Benefits beyond the Campus

11

REGION-WIDE EDUCATION FOR SUSTAINABLE DEVELOPMENT NETWORKS OF UNIVERSITIES IN THE ASIA-PACIFIC[1]

KO NOMURA, YOSHIHIRO NATORI, AND OSAMU ABE

Following the definition of sustainable development by the World Commission on Environment and Development (WCED), education for sustainable development (ESD) reorients education to address multi-disciplinary issues to ensure that present-day development does not compromise the ability of future generations to meet their own needs. This multi-disciplinary focus encompasses the environment, economy, and society at large. To effectively engage in ESD, higher education institutions (HEIs) must reconsider their programs, operation, research, and public outreach. In particular, HEIs' role to educate and train future professionals and leaders in many sectors of society is critical in realizing sustainable development. This consideration is timely. The increase in the number of institutes embarking on higher education for sustainable development (HESD) has led to the development of various HESD networks/forums. Importantly, many of these are international networks that operate as cross-border partnerships.

The aim of this chapter is to understand the role and promise of international networks as a model of cross-border collaboration in higher education. These networks consist of (a) *agencies* that undertake initiatives and contribute their own resources for network development, and (b) other *participants*, who are members of these agencies. An underlying principle is that collective actions of the network need not be based on an equal contribution of all actors.

HEIs become *participants* because they expect to receive a variety of benefits. In the case of international networks, they may want to enhance global perspectives related to sustainable development, further environmental conservation, or express concerns for the global South. For example, WCED, which highlights needs of the world's poor, views the reduction of poverty as a precondition for environmentally sound development (WCED 1987: 44, 69). To understand the development of HESD networks, it is important to examine why HEIs become members, with particular attention to perceived benefits of that participation.

The aims and expectations of the *agencies* are sometimes unclear. One exception might be in the case of international organizations (particularly the United Nations) whose participation has lent credibility to issues related to sustainability. Indeed, the concept of sustainable development has grown largely in the context of international policy negotiations and conventions, by significantly incorporating the interests of developing countries. WCED was set up as an outcome of the 1982 Nairobi conference. The UN Conference on Environment and Development (Rio Summit, 1992) and the World Summit on Sustainable Development (WSSD or Johannesburg Summit, 2002) disseminated the concept worldwide. This global process led UN agencies to take leadership in international actions on sustainable development. Furthermore, the 2005 declaration of the UN Decade of ESD (UNDESD) further encouraged international ESD efforts, with the UN Educational, Scientific, and Cultural Organization (UNESCO) taking the leading role. However, little attention has been paid to how and why agencies develop international HESD networks in general. Even in the case of international organizations, one often has to examine the process carefully to identify the real agencies behind the scenes since the UN consists of collective entities of nation states.

The emergence of international HESD networks suggests their importance. However, it remains necessary to study agencies' motivations to form the networks, as well as the members' expectations of (potential) benefits from the networks. In addition it is important to consider the challenges such networks encounter before considering them as models of cross-border HEI collaboration.

To that end, this chapter examines a prominent example of an international HESD network: the Promotion of Sustainability in Postgraduate Education and Research Network, or ProSPER.Net. ProSPER.Net is a network of postgraduate institutes in the Asia-Pacific region to promote education and research in the field of sustainability, consisting of 18 universities (as of December 2008). In other words, this is a cross-border HEI collaboration conducted through networking instead of one-on-one communication. Particular emphasis will be placed on the role of the agency due to its importance as a source of financial resources.

The meaning of "network" needs to be clarified before approaching the case study. Multiple terms can be used to express the linking of institutes, e.g., forums, coalitions, and alliances/confederations (see Eccleston 1996). Regardless of the term used by the organization itself, this chapter uses "networks" to refer to associations among HEIs that meet three conditions: (a) they exchange information actively, (b) they set up a coordinating secretariat, and (c) they hold regular personal contacts.

The information and the data for this chapter were gathered through a literature review, informal interviews, and participant observations, as discussed below. A literature survey related to ProSPER.Net was conducted and then supplemented with unpublished documents collected through personal communications. The informal interviews were conducted by the authors with policy makers and HEI staff members involved in ProSPER.Net. Lastly, data were collected through participatory observation. The access needed for the observations was possible since one of the authors is on the management side of the network (i.e., *agency*) and the other authors are affiliated with institutes that are members of the network (i.e., *participants*). Accordingly, subjective views from both perspectives are those of the authors unless other sources of information are indicated.

To situate the case of ProSPER.Net the chapter first outlines crossborder efforts on HESD, worldwide and in the Asia-Pacific more specifically. Then the development of ProSPER.Net is examined, followed by an analysis of the aims and expectations of the agency. The concluding section discusses the achievements of the network (i.e., benefits of forming a network) and the challenges it faces for further development.

HISTORICAL DEVELOPMENT OF ESD NETWORKS IN THE WORLD AND THE ASIA-PACIFIC REGION

This section introduces five major international HESD networks and their parent organizations: the Association of University Leaders for a Sustainable Future (ULSF) based on the Talloire Declaration; the International Association of Universities (IAU); Co-operation Program in Europe for Research on Nature and Industry through Coordinated University Studies (COPERNICUS); the Global Higher Education for Sustainability Partnership (GHESP) consisting of ULSF, IAU, and

COPERNICUS; and the Baltic University Program (BUP). They are followed by several HESD networks in the Asia-Pacific.

HEIs, particularly European and American universities, initiated international efforts on ESD in the early 1990s. The Talloire Declaration in 1990 is the first official international statement by HEIs to specifically commit to the issue of sustainability. It was the result of a conference of university leaders held at the Tufts University European Center in Talloire, France. The 22 vice-chancellors, presidents, and rectors who gathered at the conference made a consensus statement of 10 key actions for HEIs to contribute to ESD and environmental literacy. The Talloire declaration has now been signed by more than 370 HEIs around the world (as of October 7, 2008). As is stated in the declaration, ULSF was created in 1992 as a secretariat for the signatory institutes to continue this momentum. ULSF helps the signatory HEIs on the implementation of the declaration through information sharing such as publications, research, and assessment.

IAU, the UNESCO-based worldwide association of HEIs, is also developing international HESD networks. Ninety international university leaders participated at the IAU's ninth round table in 1993 which resulted in the adaptation of the Kyoto Declaration on Sustainable Development, an action plan for individual HEIs to follow. Since then, IAU has provided a forum for international cooperation and a clearing house for information among member HEIs. These include offline efforts such as organizing the Prague conference ("Education for a sustainable future: shaping the practical role of higher education for sustainable development") with Charles University in Prague in 2003, attended by almost 130 higher education representatives from around the world. Their online efforts include dissemination of educational materials as well as information on various initiatives of the member HEIs (e.g., their ESD courses) and related events.

COPERNICUS was established in 1988 by the predecessor of the European Universities Association: the Association of European Universities (CRE). Its "COPERNICUS-Campus" is a European network to share knowledge and expertise to facilitate HEIs' efforts to contribute to sustainable development. Its Charter for Sustainable Development was created in 1994, and is now signed by over 300 university leaders in 37 European countries.

ULSF, IAU, and COPERNICUS-Campus formed GHESP in 2000 together with UNESCO, in response to Chapter 36 of Agenda 21 ("Education, Public Awareness and Training"). GHESP made a memorandum of understanding and an action plan to undertake joint actions in the area of HESD with four objectives: to promote better understanding and more effective implementation of HESD; to identify, share, and disseminate effective strategies, models, and good practices for promoting HESD; to make recommendations on HESD; and to work closely with the UN system to develop and implement the action plan. The GHESP partners (IAU, ULSF, COPERNICUS-Campus, and UNESCO) adopted the Lüneburg Declaration on HESD at the International COPERNICUS Conference in October 2001, which resulted in the development of a "Type II Partnership" initiative as a major higher education outcome of the WSSD in 2002. At the WSSD, the United Nations University (UNU), the GHESP partners, UNESCO, and other foremost learning and scientific world organizations signed the "Ubuntu Declaration" to emphasize the role of education, science, and technology and the importance of partnership for achieving sustainable development. The GHESP partners have tried to assist implementation of HESD by producing such materials as an action-oriented toolkit, assessment tool, and an online resources database. GHESP also has joint publications on the theme of HESD in the 2002 *Higher Education Policy* and *International Journal of Sustainability in Higher Education*.

BUP is a very successful network of about 225 HEIs from all 14 Baltic Sea countries in the field of research and education for sustainable development and democracy. BUP was initiated by Uppsala University (Sweden) in 1991, which now hosts the BUP Secretariat. The Swedish Ministry of Education is the leading financial contributor to BUP, followed by the Uppsala University and government institutes, such as the Swedish Institute and Swedish International Development Cooperation Agency (BUP 2007). This initiative was a response to the social changes in the Baltic region at that time, such as the independence of three Baltic states and the end of the Cold War, as well as the common environmental concerns of nations surrounding the Baltic Sea.

This social and environmental background is reflected in the BUP's three courses at the undergraduate and the postgraduate levels respectively. They include "A sustainable Baltic region" and "The Baltic sea region area studies" (undergraduate courses) and "Sustainable water management" (graduate course). At present almost 10,000 students participate in these courses each year. Students at each member university form study groups according to the courses, each of which is supported by a mentor. Technology is actively used to aid their studies utilizing teleconference, video programs, and various online databases. Many educational materials have also been produced and staff/student exchange has been active as well.

While ULSF, IAU, COPERNICUS, GHESP, and BUP are important and leading international HESD networks, it may be worthwhile to note two things about these networks. First, the institutes that became "agencies" to form these networks (and financially support these networks) are either several HEIs themselves or international/national educational organizations such as UNESCO, CRE, and the Swedish Ministry of Education. In other words, these agencies are from the "education sector." Second, these networks are dominated by institutes from outside the Asia-Pacific, although the geographical coverage of these networks altogether is global.[2] Among 375 signatory HEIs of the Talloires Declaration, only 17 institutes are from the Asia-Pacific (while more than 140 signatories are in the United States and 52 are in Brazil). IAU often counts its members (more than 600 institutes: 23% of them from Asia-Pacific) (IAU 2008) as involved in the Kyoto Declaration, but the "impact of the Kyoto Declaration is difficult to understand, as there are no signatories" (Wright 2002: 208).

This does not mean that Asian HEIs are not interested in making HESD networks; in fact, they are emerging. One prominent example is ProSPER.Net, which is the focus of this chapter. Another notable example is the United Nations Environment Programme (UNEP) Asia-Pacific Regional University Consortium (RUC) formed in 2003 under the aegis of the UNEP Regional Office for Asia and the Pacific in Bangkok (UNEP-Bangkok). This consortium currently comprises the Asian Institute of Technology, Griffith University (Australia), Nanyang Technological University (Singapore), Tongji University (China), UNU, University of New South Wales (Australia), Wollongong University (Australia), and Yale University (USA). It aims at fostering multi-disciplinary academic and research development through joint activities and serving as a resource base of expertise for the activities and programs of UNEP in the Asia-Pacific. As a part of the RUC's programs, UNEP-Bangkok and Tongji University (China) cooperate to develop courses on sustainable development.

Given that ProSPER.Net started with strong support and the initiative of the Japanese Ministry of the Environment (examined later), it is interesting to note here that *environmental* institutes such as the Environment Ministry and UNEP have taken a lead in making HESD networks in the Asia-Pacific, unlike IAU, ULSF, COPERNICUS-Campus, and GHESP. In other words, these networks are responding to social demands on HEIs from outside the education sector. One exception would be UNESCO, an educational institute, which has initiated the Asia-Pacific Regional Network of Teacher Education Institutes for ESD (ESD-Net) since 2006 to coordinate efforts by member institutes to reorient their curricula for ESD by having a training workshop to help make ESD action plans at member institutes and online-based information sharing (e.g., e-list and online discussion sessions). Nevertheless, the salient presence of environmental institutes acting in the agency role can be regarded as a regional characteristic of the development of HESD networks in the Asia-Pacific.

THE DEVELOPMENT AND OUTLINE OF PROSPER.NET

ProSPER.Net is a network of HEIs in Asia and the Pacific that is committed to work together to integrate sustainable development into postgraduate courses and curricula. This alliance is an effort of the UNU's Institute of Advanced Studies (UNU-IAS) located in Yokohama, Japan, under its ESD program, which started in response to the declaration of the UN Decade of ESD.

The "formal" preparation of ProSPER.Net started in 2007, with the first meeting held in November to develop the concept and the Charter. There were participants from 11 HEIs in Asia and the Pacific at this first meeting. The second meeting was held in March 2008, and participants proposed joint activities (described later) and developed the network Bylaws. Following these two meetings, ProSPER.Net was formally launched in June 2008. The inauguration was accompanied by the first General Assembly and Board meeting, held in conjunction with Hokkaido University's "Sustainability Weeks 2008"—the celebratory activities leading to the G8 Hokkaido Toyako Summit in July 2008 (Hokkaido University is a member of ProSPER.Net).

The governing and management structure of ProSPER.Net is stipulated in its Charter and Bylaws. The annual General Assembly elect the Board members. The Board "shall serve as the executive body acting on behalf of the General Assembly" (UNU-IAS 2008d: 2); or "the governance and management functions are vested upon the Board" (UNU-IAS 2008e: 3). UNU-IAS "shall serve as the Secretariat of the network" (UNU-IAS 2008e: 3). The secretariat is responsible for coordination and arrangement of any relevant network-related meetings and network-related communications (UNU-IAS 2008d). Now the Board members are the representatives of RMIT University, Tongji University, TERI University, Hokkaido University, University of Tokyo, Universiti Sains Malaysia (USM), Asian Institute of Technology (AIT), Yonsei University, and the University of the South Pacific. They were selected at the first General Assembly held on June 20, 2008 with three criteria presented by UNU-IAS: active in the development of joint projects; extent of involvement in the development of the network (i.e., participants from the early inception period); and geographical distribution.

Since the network's first meeting in 2007, the number of participating HEIs has grown to 18 (they are the founding members of the network). The membership covers nine countries in the region, in addition to two regional universities in Asia and the Pacific (Table 11.1).

The range of the network's activities is wide, reaching from annual colloquia to faculty exchange schemes aimed at knowledge sharing. At the first meeting in 2007, participants brought proposals for joint projects, including such ideas as promoting graduate students' engagement with sustainable development issues, faculty and teacher training, training of government officials, case studies on sustainable development, summer school, and community engagement (UNU-IAS 2007a). In meetings during 2008, these proposals were categorized into four focal themes: faculty development, networking, and mobility; student development, networking, and mobility; curriculum development and delivery; and program support development (UNU-IAS 2008f).

Then, three joint projects were selected from these proposals. They were: (1) curriculum development and delivery of the school of public policy and sustainable development; (2) sustainable development integration in business school curricula; and (3) training on sustainable development for educators and researchers. This is particularly due to interest within the Japanese Ministry of the Environment in funding these programs via UNU-IAS from April 2008 (UNU-IAS 2008f). The main reason for the Ministry's support, it appeared, was that the Ministry thought the proposed activities were likely to result in concrete achievements such as curriculum and training sessions.

Table 11.1 ProSPER.Net Members

Participants from the First Meeting	From the Second Meeting (*) and After
RMIT University, Australia	Shinshu University, Japan
Tongji University, China	Iwate University, Japan
TERI University, India	Okayama University, Japan*
Universitas Gadjah Mada, Indonesia	Rikkyo University, Japan
Hokkaido University, Japan	Chulalongkorn University, Thailand
Nagoya University, Japan	University of South Pacific (Regional)*
University of Tokyo, Japan	
Universiti Sains Malaysia, Malaysia	
University of the Philippines, Philippines	
Yonsei University, Republic of Korea	
Asian Institute of Technology (AIT/ Regional)	
Miyagi University of Education, Japan (as an observer in the first meeting)	

Source: Authors.

Among the next batch of projects, two new joint-project proposals were identified in relation to the interests of the Ministry of the Environment Japan. They were "summer schools for graduate students in sustainable development" and "establishing ESD guidelines" for HEIs. UNU-IAS suggested the allocation of funds for these projects at the meeting, and the Ministry stated that it "wished ProSPER.Net to continue considering the two emerging joint projects—summer schools and ESD guidelines—as the Ministry might be able to consider committing resources in the future" at the first Board meeting (UNU-IAS 2008a: 2). At the second Board meeting in November 2008, a representative from the Ministry called for these new projects to be prepared to be in time for submission to the Japanese Ministry of Finance as a part of the Ministry's next year's budget, illustrating the Ministry's continuous interests in and support of these projects (UNU-IAS 2008c: 9). Also, at the second Board meeting, UNU-IAS introduced the idea of having another project called "reorienting engineering education," with possible collaboration with the UN Industrial Development Organization and UNEP-Paris (UNU-IAS 2008c: 8).

THE AIMS AND EXPECTATIONS OF THE AGENCY

The Japanese Ministry of the Environment played a critical role through its sponsorship of ProSPER.Net, working through UNU-IAS. In the Preamble of the ProSPER.Net Charter, three international initiatives are stated. One is UNDESD (to which UNU-IAS responded by making the ESD program). The others are the Asia-Pacific Forum for Environment and Development (APFED; eminent persons' forum) and the Environment Congress for Asia and the Pacific (ECOASIA; informal environmental ministerial meeting in the Asia-Pacific), both of which "have recognized the importance of networks of HESD" (UNU-IAS 2008e: 1). APFED and ECOASIA are not only regional "environmental" meetings but also they are funded and managed by the Japanese Ministry of the Environment and its affiliated organizations. UNDESD is a result of the Japanese proposal at WSSD in 2002 and the Ministry played a pivotal role in making the proposal (Nomura & Abe 2009). The other related international initiatives of (higher) education are not mentioned here.

How did the Ministry come to be involved in the creation of this HESD network? First of all, UNU-IAS's ESD program needed to engage in HESD, because higher education is identified as one of the five focal areas of the program (the former senior officer of UNU-IAS, personal communication, January 27, 2009). So, with reference to the preceding efforts by UNU and UNEP-Bangkok, the senior officer dispatched from the Ministry to the Program at that time suggested and discussed with colleagues about the idea of forming networks (the former senior officer of UNU-IAS, personal communication, January 27, 2009; a senior staff member of the Environmental Education Office of the Ministry, personal communication, January 26, 2009). At the same time, the Ministry's Office of Environmental Education was planning to engage in HESD within Japan, which later resulted in a consortium of HEIs called "Environmental Leadership Initiatives for Asian Sustainability" (ELIAS). The main aim of ELIAS is to develop human resources in Japan who can take leadership in the field of sustainable development in the Asia-Pacific. Therefore, the Ministry was supportive of the idea of ProSPER.Net, a postgraduate international network on ESD in the Asia-Pacific, as it could make a synergetic link with ELIAS in Japan. In fact, the Office of Environmental Education claims ProSPER.Net as one of the three projects of ELIAS (a senior staff member of the Environmental Education Office of the Ministry, personal communication, January 26, 2009).

This relationship with the Ministry's project was critical in strengthening the Office's budgetary request to the Ministry of Finance for increasing the financial contribution to UNU-IAS for ProSPER.Net (the former senior officer of UNU-IAS, personal communication, January 27, 2009). It is also significant to note here that the promotion of ESD in general is one of the important issues for the Ministry of the Environment. This is because, as mentioned earlier, the Ministry is the major actor of the Japanese proposal of UNDESD at the WSSD (Nomura & Abe 2009). Support via UNU-IAS is a much easier way for the Ministry to work with institutes in other Asia-Pacific countries. Accordingly, the Ministry has motivation to support UNU-IAS's ESD program to make a regional contribution to the success of UNDESD, even though the name of the Ministry is not up front.

The significance of the role of the Ministry can be seen from its contributions to ProSPER.Net management and activities. The funds to implement ProSPER.Net activities are currently fully provided from the Ministry's Office of Environmental Education via UNU-IAS. Accordingly, the Ministry has strong leverage in identifying the prioritized joint activities (while there are other ideas as mentioned earlier) by promising funds to those they find most interesting. About seven to eight million yen is provided from UNU-IAS to implement each of the three prioritized projects respectively. In addition, the Ministry introduced other funding sources and expressed its intention to promote ProSPER.Net diplomatically to other governments (UNU-IAS 2008f).

This also suggests the Ministry is playing a vital role in mobilizing resources to substantiate network activities.

One can also see the Ministry's influence from the aspect of human resources for the development and management of ProSPER.Net. Normally, a senior official of the Ministry is dispatched to the ESD section of UNU-IAS, which is the network secretariat. Inclusive of this, the salary of all the staff members of the program is provided by the Ministry. In fact, the entire budget concerning the UNU-IAS's ESD program is provided by the Ministry (about 150 million Japanese yen for fiscal year 2008, including the budget for ProSPER.Net; see Ministry of the Environment 2007). Given that UNU-IAS started ESD activities when the Ministry started to fund its ESD program in fiscal year 2003, one may say that the Ministry itself started the program.

The selection of network members also illustrates the Ministry's influence. Many of these members are like-minded professionals who have often collaborated with the Ministry/UNU. Hence, this international HESD network started based on the same "epistemic community."[3] The current senior officer at the UNU-IAS's ESD program (i.e., an author of this chapter) recalls that the UNU-IAS/the Ministry first invited the HEIs involved in its RCE (Regional Centers of Expertise) project, which is a network of multi-stakeholders, mobilized to deliver ESD to local and regional communities. (UNU has acknowledged more than 60 RCEs around the world until the end of 2008. UNU-IAS plays a secretarial role for this project as its service center from 2006. The Ministry of the Environment has financially supported this project through UNU-IAS.) They include Miyagi University of Education, Yonsei University, Universitas Gadjah Mada, USM, University of the Philippines, and the University of the South Pacific. These consist of more than one-third of its members.

Second, many of them overlap with the institutes that have often collaborated with UNEP-Bangkok, to which the Ministry normally dispatches a senior staff member. They include AIT and Tongji University (China) as mentioned earlier. Third, the human relations between the officers at UNU-IAS/Ministry of the Environment and ESD academics brought their affiliate universities into the membership. RMIT University was contacted by UNU-IAS, because a distinguished figure in the field of environmental education was there, who has had experience in collaboration with UNU-IAS/the Ministry. The leading figure of Rikkyo University (i.e., an author of this chapter) has been involved in the Ministry's environmental education/ESD policy process for a long time. Nagoya University has several former staff members of the Ministry, which would have facilitated the communication between the University and the Ministry of the Environment and UNU-IAS.

A few universities without significant collaboration experiences with UNU-IAS were also invited, because they are playing an important role in other related networks. They include the University of Tokyo. It takes a leading role in the sustainability research network called "Integrated Research System for Sustainability Science (IR3S)," an alliance comprising five universities (with six other supporting universities), supported by a funding scheme of the Japanese Ministry of Education, Culture, Sports, Science, and Technology. However, without having any significant public relations activities to call for its memberships so far, one can say most of the participants are involved because they have had, and they are likely to further develop, a collaborative relationship with the UNU-IAS/the Ministry.

In addition, the concept of ProSPER.Net was developed with an academic from the same epistemic community. The concept paper was drafted by a visiting fellow of UNU-IAS and Professor at AIT. He was chosen because he was the coordinator of UNU-IAS's RCE project in Asia (the former senior officer of UNU-IAS, personal communication, January 27, 2009). He has long working relations not only with the Ministry of the Environment Japan but also with the senior staff members of the UNU-IAS's ESD program, which assured the quality and range of the issues covered to meet the Ministry's expectation.

ACHIEVEMENTS AND CHALLENGES

Most HESD declarations, such as the COPERNICUS Charter mentioned above, call for the development of partnerships between institutes and individuals (Wright 2004: 16). Then, what have been the achievements of ProSPER.Net? The network's concept paper says the "strategy optimizes utilization of resources as well as reduces or eliminates duplications. The 'sharing of resources and knowledge' and 'learning from each other' approaches are important ingredients of success" (UNU-IAS 2007b: 4). In other words, *sharing resources through joint activities* and *information sharing* are the two major objectives to be achieved.

One of the main means of information exchange is face-to-face meetings. In the preparatory phase, two meetings were held in November 2007 and March 2008, respectively. They were followed by the first General Assembly and Board meeting in June 2008, and the second Board meeting in November 2008. A meeting on joint activities was held a day before the first General Assembly. As is mentioned later, small-scale meetings are held according to the joint projects. These frequent meetings can be considered to have contributed to information sharing among members. Additionally, email is used to exchange ideas among members and the secretariat is preparing a newsletter and planning a website (UNU-IAS 2008a: 2).

ProSPER.Net is bringing significant benefits to the members in terms of another objective of the network: sharing resources through joint activities. Now there are three projects going on as mentioned earlier. The lead institute for the development of business school curricula is AIT. The main participants in the project are USM, Shinshu University, Yonsei University, and Universitas Gadjah Mada. This project aims at forming an HEI consortium to mainstream sustainability issues in their curricula, teaching, and learning. Each member HEI has activities such as creating new courses on related topics (e.g., social business and poverty reduction at AIT, sustainable development and East Asian business at a graduate school of Yonsei, and leadership for sustainable development for the masters of management at Gadjah Mada), curriculum development (e.g., MBA curriculum on sustainable development at USM), and case studies by Shinshu University. They have held several workshops, often involving non-ProSPER.Net members, in addition to daily communication through emailing and other means, for sharing information, knowledge, and experiences. Shared information is brought back to member HEIs to improve their activities.

TERI University leads the program in public policy and sustainable development in collaboration with AIT, Tongji University, USM, University of the South Pacific, and University of Tokyo. Its target is mid-career government officials. The project is currently aiming to launch an online pilot program on sustainable development practice as a first step, setting its long-term goals to provide a diploma from a ProSPER.Net consortium. As for the curriculum, three fully developed course modules are planned to be available online during July and August 2009 over a 2–4 week period, to be followed by the second and the third cycle of curriculum delivery. Students completing three separate course modules over the 1 year period will be eligible for the awarding of a Diploma (TERI University 2008: 6). For developing this project, an inception workshop involving non-ProSPER.Net members was held. The pilot courses curriculum involves three topics: resource efficiency and sustainable development; economic tools for sustainable development; and tools and framework for sustainable development.

The lead institute for training of educators (and researchers) on sustainable development is USM (Malaysia). It collaborates with Hokkaido University, University of Tokyo, AIT, Yonsei University, and TERI University. Its goal is to develop a generic model for teaching postgraduate educators and researchers in the field of sustainable development. Meetings and workshops were held to develop a model and a manual for it. Testing of the model at network members' institutes and the evaluation/refinement of the model are to be followed to finalize it.

Given that these projects were chosen from the proposals made by member HEIs themselves and involve many of them, one can say that ProSPER.Net is contributing to *sharing resources through joint activities.*

Additionally, three new projects are now being considered as mentioned earlier. One of them, the development of a ProSPER.Net summer school, is to involve another three ideas out of the nine ideas of joint activities raised by participants at the first meeting in November 2008 (UNU-IAS 2008b: 8).[4] Also, it was discussed by the members that elements of other joint project ideas were already incorporated into the three joint projects funded by the Ministry of the Environment Japan (UNU-IAS 2008b: 9).

There are also benefits to members that are not actively involved in the joint projects. For example, a representative of Rikkyo University (i.e., an author of this chapter) made efforts to bring the University into the network in order to stimulate the action of the University leaders (e.g., the president and vice-president) in the field of ESD, as well as to strengthen the profile of the University. While it may be too early to think about the benefits of becoming a part of the network, he regards participation in ProSPER.Net as encouraging University decision makers to apply to the Ministry of the Environment's ELIAS program in the next fiscal year. The vice-president of Iwate University regards that, while their focus has been put on the undergraduate courses, information concerning the postgraduate courses collected via ProSPER.Net has been conducive to improving their undergraduate ESD programs (personal communication, January 26, 2009). These cases suggest that participation in the network can provide inspiration and motivation to pursue environmental and sustainability initiatives and constitutes a commitment to which the institution can be held accountable over time, which are mentioned as one of the five institutional benefits in signing the Talloires Declaration ("Benefits to signing" n.d.). The establishment of the "Prosper.Net-Scopus Young Scientist Award in Sustainable Development" in 2008 in collaboration with an international publisher will also encourage the ESD research in the region. (The award is to be given annually to a young scientist or researcher in the region who has made significant contributions in the field of sustainable development.) The leading figure of Okayama University said the University will ask for the collaboration of the network members for the fund it mobilized for HESD (personal communication, January 30, 2009).

From the viewpoint of the agency (including one of the authors of this chapter), a major challenge for the further development of the network is how to expand the network, particularly by involving other major HEIs in the region. The exchange of information should increase and potential synergies can develop as the number of participants grows. However, it is often difficult for latecomers to be assimilated in an existing community and gain certain benefits. This is particularly true when the available resources (particularly from the Japanese Ministry of the Environment) are limited, putting a ceiling on the number and scale of joint projects (a senior staff member of the Environmental Education Office of the Ministry, personal communication, January 26, 2009). This is related to the limit on the scope of the network; it is now difficult for the network to embark on other aspects of HEIs than postgraduate courses (the former senior officer of UNU-IAS, personal communication, January 27, 2009; the vice-president of Iwate University, personal communication, January 26, 2009). Accordingly, the agency is now planning to mobilize resources from the governments in the region as a request from the Japanese Ministry of the Environment at such multi-lateral meetings as ECOASIA or bilateral meetings, while asking for an increase in the contributions of each member HEI.

In addition, since the network itself is new, it is regarded as important to further clarify its strategies for its effective development. In the second Board meeting, the representative from UNU-IAS mentioned that "sharing information and experiences might not be the main problem. They should also worry about what should be the procedure to generate new ideas in the long-term and that there is a need to better delineate ProSPER.Net's strategies" (UNU-IAS 2008c: 5).

CONCLUSION

ProSPER.Net has contributed to the development of a cross-boarder collaboration in the field of education for sustainable development in the Asia-Pacific. It has brought about not only the sharing of information and experiences in this emerging field but also the implementation of joint projects based on members' interests and expertise. The case of ProSPER.Net provides a model of collaboration in higher education with the following features: (1) collaboration is based on a *network*; (2) the network was formed by the leadership of an *agency* that was *not a higher education institution* and *not from the education sector*. In other words, this case illustrates that HEI collaborations can be developed by those outside of the higher education sector when they contribute their resources to form HEI networks.

A major promise of this model is that HEI collaborations can be made and utilized to cope with emerging social issues, if an institute in a given sector provides resources. European and American cases introduced in this chapter are the networks initiated by HEIs (i.e., some of the participants) themselves, educational agencies (e.g., Ministry of Education), and the United Nations. However, in Asian cases, "environmental" organizations have formed HEI networks. Besides, the case of ProSPER.Net shows that a Ministry of one country with resources can take the lead in forming cross-border HEI networks by making the most of its "epistemic communities."

A lesson from this model is that the commitment of the agency, particularly in resources contribution, is critical in developing networks and HEI collaborations. ProSPER.Net activities have so far been dependent on the Ministry's contribution.

On the other hand, this resource dependency on the agency also creates a major challenge for the further development of ProSPER.Net. The scope and scale of activities, as well as the number of participants, may not go beyond the interests and resources of the Ministry of the Environment Japan. In order to consider the future of ProSPER.Net, one may want to study a similar case in a sense that the resources and initiatives for the management and activities of HESD networks depend on a few agencies. One suggestion might be BUP, to which the Swedish government and Uppsala University are the major financial contributors, which may provide useful information to consider the future of ProSPER.Net.

Because ProSPER.Net is a new network, lessons from the existing HEIs/HESD networks are in fact important to cope with the challenges it faces. Such networks may include domestic as well as cross-border networks. As for domestic networks, they include the Environmental Association for Universities and Colleges in the UK and the Association for the Advancement of Sustainability in Higher Education in the U.S. and Canada. Despite several challenges facing the network, the case of ProSPER.Net is suggestive as a model of promoting cross-border HEI collaboration to cope with emerging important social issues such as sustainability.

NOTES

1. The views and opinions expressed in this chapter are solely those of the authors, and do not necessarily reflect those of the institutes the authors belong to. This

chapter uses the term ESD to refer to sustainability education in general, instead of such terms as "education for sustainability" (EfS) and "education for sustainable future" (EfSF). This is mainly because this chapter often refers to the several initiatives made by the United Nations, who tend to use the term ESD.

2. The Swansea Declaration (1993) of the Association of Commonwealth Universities (ACU), which is another important international HESD declaration, was adopted with the participation of a considerable number of HEIs from the Asian Commonwealth nations. It is arguable, however, if they formed a "HESD network" afterwards unlike the ones introduced here.

3. An epistemic community is "a network of professionals with recognized expertise and competence in a particular domain and an authoritative claim to policy-relevant knowledge within that domain or issue-area" (Haas 1992: 3). Members of this community share not only a set of principled and causal beliefs but also notions of validity and policy enterprise. Epistemic communities are used to explain international policy coordination. They articulate "the cause-and-effect relationships of complex problems, helping states identify their interests, framing the issues for collective debate, proposing specific policies, and identifying salient points for negotiation" (Haas 1992: 2).

4. Among the nine ideas of joint projects, "promotion of graduate students' engagement with sustainable development issues," "community engagement," and "faculty collaboration" were considered to be involved in this summer school project. RMIT University and Tongji are in charge of developing the concept paper for the summer school project.

REFERENCES

Baltic University Program (2007). *The Baltic University program: Annual report 2006*. Retrieved March 10, 2009, from www.balticuniv.uu.se/publications/AnnualReport06.pdf.

Benefits to signing (n.d.). Retrieved March 10, 2009, from www.ulsf.org/programs_talloires_benefits.html.

Eccleston, B. (1996). Does North–South collaboration enhance NGO influence on deforestation policies in Malaysia and Indonesia? In D. Potter (Ed.), *NGOs and environmental policies: Asia and Africa* (pp. 66–89). London: Frank Cass.

Haas, P.M. (1992). Introduction: Epistemic communities and international policy coordination. *International Organization, 46*(1), 1–35.

International Association of Universities (2008). *International Association of Universities: Members*. Retrieved March 10, 2009, from www.unesco.org/iau/members_friends/index.html.

Ministry of the Environment (2007). *Heisei 20 Nendo Kankyo-sho Yosan-an Jikoubetsuhyo* [Budget plan for the fiscal year 2008 by items: Ministry of the Environment]. Tokyo, Japan: Ministry of the Environment. Retrieved March 10, 2009, from www.env.go.jp/guide/budget/h20/h20-ann.pdf.

Nomura, K., & Abe, O. (2009). The movement of education for sustainable development in Japan: A political perspective. *Environmental education research, 15*(4), 483–496.

TERI University (2008, July). Updated concept document on the collaborative initiative for the design and delivery of an online pilot program on "Sustainable Development Practice" (Leading to a Future Diploma Program) at TERI University, New Delhi (India) as an Activity of ProSPER.Net. Revised Proposal submitted through ProSPER.Net to Environmental Policy bureau, Ministry of the Environment, Government of Japan.

UNU-IAS (2007a, November). *Minutes: Meeting of heads of higher education institutions in the Asia-Pacific region on postgraduate sustainable development education and research.* Retrieved January 5, 2009, from United Nations University-Institute of Advanced Studies (UNU-IAS), Yokohama, Japan, www.ias.unu.edu/resource_centre/Minutes%20of%20November%20ProSPER%20Net%20meeting.pdf.

UNU-IAS (2007b). *Promotion of sustainability in postgraduate education and research through networking (Concept paper).* ProSPER.Net/GA1/2, ProSPER.Net/Board1/2. Retrieved January 5, 2009, from United Nations University-Institute of Advanced Studies (UNU-IAS), www.ias.unu.edu/resource_centre/ProSPER.Net%20Concept%20paper.pdf.

UNU-IAS (2008a). Minutes: First ProSPER.Net board meeting. Draft (unpublished).

UNU-IAS (2008b). Minutes: ProSPER.Net meeting on joint activities. Draft (unpublished).

UNU-IAS (2008c). *Minutes: Second ProSPER.Net board meeting.* Retrieved January 20, 2009, from www.ias.unu.edu/resource_centre/2nd_Prosper_Net_Board_Meeting_Minutes.pdf.

UNU-IAS (2008d). *Promotion of sustainability in postgraduate education and research network: By-laws.* ProSPER.Net/GA1/4. ProSPER.Net/Board1/4. Retrieved January 5, 2009, from United Nations University-Institute of Advanced Studies (UNU-IAS), www.ias.unu.edu/resource_centre/ProSPER%20Net%20By%20laws.pdf.

UNU-IAS (2008e). *Promotion of sustainability in postgraduate education and research network: Charter.* ProSPER.Net/GA1/3. Retrieved January 5, 2009, from United Nations University-Institute of Advanced Studies (UNU-IAS), www.ias.unu.edu/resource_centre/ProSPER%20Net%20Charter.pdf.

UNU-IAS (2008f, March). *Summary minutes: ProSPER.Net research and organizational meeting.* Retrieved January 5, 2009, from United Nations University-Institute of Advanced Studies (UNU-IAS), Yokohama, Japan, www.ias.unu.edu/resource_centre/Minutes%20of%20ProSPERNet%20March%202008%20meeting.pdf.

World Commission on Environment and Development (WCED) (1987). *Our common future*. Oxford: Oxford University Press.

Wright, T.S.A. (2002). Definitions and frameworks for environmental sustainability in higher education. *International Journal of Sustainability in Higher Education, 3*(3), 203–220.

Wright, T.S.A. (2004). The evolution of sustainability declarations in higher education. In P.B. Corcoran and A.E.J. Wals (Eds.), *Higher education and the challenge of sustainability: Problematics, promise, and practice* (pp. 7–19). Dordrecht, the Netherlands: Kluwer Academic Publishers.

12

CROSS-BORDER COLLABORATION IN THE SERVICE OF HUMAN CAPACITY DEVELOPMENT

CHRISTOPHER S. COLLINS

Brilliant theorists of economics do not find it worthwhile to spend time discussing issues of poverty and hunger. These economists ... rarely reflect on the origin and development of poverty and hunger. As a result, poverty continues.

(Yunus 2003: 35)

Today's economic circumstances make higher education a more compelling need in developing countries than it has ever been.

(UN Millennium Project Task Force 2005: 90)

INTRODUCTION

In January 2009, the magazine *African Executive* featured an article with the title, "African Universities Must Fight Poverty." Upon first glance, the article may appear non sequitur; could a diagnosis for some of the most impoverished areas of the world be a healthy dose of universities? The article expands the concept by asserting, "Africa needs a strong pan-continental community of researchers to discover resourceful, timely ways to deal with poverty's many causes" (Muchie 2009). It is not that university research will be an instant cure or the missing link for poverty reduction, but more so, it is a long-term contributor and creator of new forms of knowledge. Cross-border collaborations in university science and technology research in the service of human capacity have demonstrated the ability of the university to be positioned as one element of poverty reduction.

Universities around the globe are seeking to collaborate across borders. This occurs in various forms of cross-border supply, including students, faculty, programs, and other ways. For several decades, intergovernmental organizations (IGOs), including the World Bank, International Monetary Fund (IMF), and World Trade Organization (WTO) have been the center of cross-border collaboration on development projects ranging from infrastructure (roads, dams, and electricity) to health and education. Higher education falls under the purview of these IGOs. In fact, the WTO has included higher education as a tradable commodity that must be regulated by trade agreements. While previous IMF and World Bank policies limited lending for higher education (Collins & Rhoads 2008), the World Bank now offers loans for higher education. These loans focus on building human capacity, and many are specifically directed toward university research with science and technology.

During the last decade, international organizations have identified the importance of university science and technology in the knowledge economy, in development, and ultimately in poverty reduction. This chapter evaluates IGOs as a center of cross-border collaboration. With the emergence of the knowledge economy as a backdrop, higher education plays a key role in building human capacity and ultimately in reducing poverty in developing countries. These concepts are linked through an exploration of World Bank policies in higher education lending, an overview of the knowledge economy and poverty reduction, and an evaluation of cross-border collaborations in university science and technology research in two Bank loan recipients: Thailand and Uganda.

POVERTY

A primary goal of IGOs that engage in international development is to reduce poverty. There are several means by which this happens, including a broad focus on economic growth and a more narrow focus on human capacity building. In order to study human capacity building and higher education, it is essential to understand poverty. The World Bank and other international and regional development banks consider poverty reduction to be a primary mission. However, as Yunus (2003) noted, the assumption that economic prosperity will curtail poverty does not diagnose the primary issue.

The idea that economic growth contributes to the reduction of poverty has been criticized as being a mutated version of trickledown economics (Stiglitz 2002). With trickledown economics, it is expected that income will eventually move from the wealthy to the poor. However, this method allows for greater income inequality, instead leading to an increase in poverty. Elkins (1992) demonstrated that in areas of India, economic growth resulting from development initiatives (e.g., building dams) occurred in conjunction with increased poverty. While economic growth occurred with the stated goal of reducing poverty, the beneficiaries were few, and inequality and poverty increased. In this example, poverty reduction was considered a byproduct of economic growth, instead of a primary goal. As such, the latent outcome of economic growth was an increase in poverty—opposite of the original intent. In order to re-envision poverty reduction as a primary goal instead of a byproduct, we need an operational definition of poverty and an overview of its global status.

The literature suggests two convergent points that can contribute to the reduction of poverty: advancing scientific and technical knowledge, and enhancing self-sufficiency. On the first point, Sachs (2005) identified "knowledge capital" as one of the six major kinds of capital that the poor lack. Sachs defines knowledge capital as "the scientific and technological know-how that raises productivity in business output and the promotion of physical and natural capital" (2005: 244–245). Ideas and knowledge can be shared and utilized over and over again. Natural resources are not the catalyst for growth. Instead, the knowledge of how to use such resources can have a tangible impact. The academic community is one location where knowledge development in science and technology can occur (industry is another location for this kind of development).

The second point, self-sufficiency, is identified as a necessary element for poverty reduction. Easterly (2006) called this "homegrown development," and cautioned that "aid cannot achieve the end of poverty ... only homegrown development based on the dynamism of individuals and firms in free markets can do that" (368). The salient concept of self-sufficiency is deeply connected to knowledge creation and distribution. Knowledge created in developed countries by the private sector in response to market demands will rarely meet the challenges presented by developing countries (Easterly 2006). The chief operators charged with reducing global poverty have been rooted in the thought of development economics. The field of development economics emerged after World War II as an afterthought to reconstructing the main tenets of economic theory. A primary criticism of development economics theory and practice is that it is not rooted in the culture of that which it is attempting to assist. Africa is now poorer than it was during the late 1960s, when the IMF and the World Bank first arrived. Yunus (2003) wrote, "Concepts, institutions, and analytical frames—the conditions—that created poverty cannot end poverty" (2003: 250).

THE KNOWLEDGE ECONOMY

Research and literature on higher education and poverty is steeped in the notion that we are living in an increasingly knowledge-based society. The recent focus on poverty reduction in connection to higher education has risen in conjunction with an interest in knowledge and the economy. However, knowledge, economics, and education are not newly compatible components of growth and development. In 1810, a Prussian educational philosopher founded the University of Berlin and put into practice a model of integrating research as a vital component of teaching. With an emphasis on science, Humboldt attempted to position the university to contribute more directly to economy and society (Ruegg 2004). Scientific discoveries have since sparked innovations in the industrial and agricultural arena, producing knowledge and improving techniques in various fields. German universities produced knowledge for chemical and pharmaceutical industries from the late nineteenth century onward (Mowery & Rosenberg 1998).

In the United States, the Morrill Land Grant Acts of 1862 and 1890 provided colleges and universities with land in exchange for their commitment to pursuing agriculture and other applied sciences; the Hatch Act of 1887 funded agricultural research to assist rural communities in developing better farm practices (MacGarvie & Furman 2005). Both acts represented the U.S. government's interest in using higher education to benefit the larger population through the development and dissemination of knowledge. The emphasis on the contribution of knowledge accumulation to the expansion of gross domestic product reflects a particular model of growth in economic theory (Lucas 1998; Romer 1989). Yusuf (2007) argued that "most of the technological advances that have economic consequences can be traced indirectly or directly to universities, either through the training provided, the knowledge spillovers, or the actual research conducted" (9).

Major segments of national economies have shifted from being industrial based to knowledge based, as driven by the scientific and technological advances, as in wealthy countries like Germany, Japan, the United Kingdom, and the United States, among others. The industrial-based economy has not disappeared, but a new form of the global economy, which more often assumes a dominant position, has emerged. To a large extent, the new knowledge-based economy reflects the growing power of computerized, network-based processes connected to the production and management of information and/or knowledge. An emerging group of descriptors have come to represent this worldwide transformation, including expressions such as "new economy," "information age," "network society," "knowledge society," and so forth (Carnoy, Castells, Cohen, & Cardoso 1993; Castells 1996, 1997; Morrow & Torres 2000; Peters & Besley 2006; Slaughter & Rhoades 2004; Stromquist 2002; World Bank 2002). This global economic transformation is closely tied to changes in the university, whereby science and technology, along with research and development, assume central importance (Calderone & Rhoads 2005; Geiger 2004). Although the transformation of economies and key institutions such as the university impact all nations of the world, such a shift is far more prominent in the wealthier nations, where the most advanced forms of science and technology exist.

Slaughter and Rhoades described the new economy as an environment that "treats advanced knowledge as raw material that can be claimed through legal devices, owned, and marketed as products or services" (2004: 15). As a result, it is difficult to separate universities from this new economy, since they are key locations of knowledge creation. In addition to contributing to the knowledge economy, universities, in fact, helped to create it. This is evident at universities in the United States based on the number of patents created, the number of publications produced, and the high rate of technology transfer (Slaughter & Rhoades 2004). Consequently, it is essential to study the role of the university in developing nations' quest for economic development.

Only in recent years have IGOs come to see the university as a critical player in economic development in the Third World. However, before IGOs contributed to linking higher education and knowledge development, two schools of thought over two distinct historical periods had a negative impact on university systems in developing countries: (1) the funding of vocational education to the exclusion of other forms of higher education during the infrastructure drive of the 1950s, and (2) the focus on primary education during the structural adjustment drive of the 1980s.

During the first period, in the 1950s, development agencies focused on the potential success of building a modern commercial sector alongside a labor-intensive sector to expand productivity. It was an industrialization strategy intended to lead to social and economic progress. Rostow (1960) presented five stages of economic growth that captured the approach to development at the time. The stages included traditional society, preconditions for takeoff, takeoff, the drive toward maturity, and the age of high mass consumption. Following the development experience of the West, he claimed that every society can fit into one of these stages. As developing societies were in the earlier stages, according to this model, vocational education was seen as the most useful investment in terms of training (i.e., manual, practical, and usually non-academic training). The focus on vocational education was exclusive, and IGOs including the World Bank, did not lend any money for the support of university education.

The second period, which arose primarily during the 1980s, was characterized by the advance of neoliberalism. There was an emphasis on structural adjustment policies, privatization, and the reduction of public expenditures. While this model of development was most prevalent during the Thatcher–Reagan alliance, it still remains as a dominant policy for the IMF and the World Bank. Under structural adjustment programs, public expenditures were reduced. At the same time, a rate of return analysis was employed to measure the impact of education. Psacharopoulos (1981, 1987, 1988), an economist for the World Bank, found that primary education had a better rate of return for a developing government's investment. As a result, primary education received the majority of funding and attention. On the other hand, higher education was characterized as a personal responsibility and considered only to be beneficial to the individual student, which substantiated a required reduction in state support. Peters and Besley (2006) described the structural adjustment policies of neoliberalism as "disastrous" for the Third World and for higher education. However, it is important to note that these two schools of thought preceded IGO emphasis on the knowledge economy and its connection to higher education.

Today, the dominant position of development organizations tends to identify higher education as a greater priority. The significant role of higher education in the knowledge economy is increasingly seen as important by national governments and development agencies. A progression of seminal works from various agencies has shown university science and technology research as a major contributor to the knowledge economy, and, in turn, poverty reduction (OECD 1996: UN Millennium Project Task Force 2005; World Bank 2002).

The World Bank published a major report, *Constructing Knowledge Societies: New Challenges for Tertiary Education* (2002), to describe how universities can increase a country's research capacity and its ability to participate in the knowledge-based global economy. The report described the potential of higher education to enhance economic growth and reduce poverty. With the observation that developing countries may be further marginalized without the opportunity to create knowledge through university education, the Bank departed from the previous position that higher education did not provide a good return on a country's investment. This shift reflected a growing consensus that university education has an important role to play in the development of a knowledge economy. The Bank emphasized expanding a country's capacity for participation in an "increasingly knowledge-based world economy" (World Bank 2002: 2). The report also sought to address the mounting criticism of the Bank's policies toward higher or tertiary education, noting that there is an increasing perception among clients that the World Bank is not doing enough in this sector of education. The report noted that it "became necessary to revisit the Bank's policies and experience regarding tertiary education in light of the changes in the world environment and the persistence of the traditional problems of tertiary education in developing and transition countries" (World Bank 2002: 2). Although the discourse of casting potential policy errors simply as "perceptions" of clients seemed somewhat calculated, the Bank nonetheless appeared ready to direct greater attention, and, most importantly, money, to higher education in the developing world.

A 2005 report by the United Nations Millennium Project Task Force, titled *Innovation: Applying Knowledge in Development*, is the most poignant work that links higher education to development and poverty reduction. The report highlighted that science, technology, and ingenuity have helped to lessen poverty and hunger and promote economic growth in regions such as Southeast Asia. In addition, the report underscored that the donor community, until recently, has overemphasized primary and secondary schooling. The current state of affairs has highlighted the difficulty of achieving universal primary education without higher education training, and the overemphasis has weakened development by creating the false bifurcation of mutually exclusive goals between primary and higher education. Although higher education provides expertise to all sectors of society and the economy, the UN report focused on science and technology. Although the immense potential of universities to develop technology was acknowledged, it highlighted that many universities in developing countries cannot meet the challenge due to, "Outdated curricula, under motivated faculty, poor management, and a continuous struggle for funds have undermined the capacity of universities to play their roles as engines of community or regional development" (UN Millennium Project Task Force 2005: 90).

Once development agencies and the donor community make the commitment to fund higher education, there are specific ways in which a healthy university system can promote economic growth and reduce poverty. For example, universities can assist in the growth of business and industrial firms and contribute to economic revival and high-tech development in their surrounding regions. Connections with business and industry should not be limited to the model of quantifying everything of value as a private good. As outlined by Slaughter and Rhoades (2004), there is a fine line in technology transfer when public research becomes private, profitable knowledge. However, in order for technology in developing countries to become useful, it must transfer to industry outside the university. Knowledge should be considered a public good, as advocated by Stiglitz (1999), ex-chief economist of the World Bank. Universities can also be incorporated into the public sector by conducting research and development for industry. In the West, these types of initiatives are often referred to as academic capitalism, where the academy is seen as a potential medium to generate income through new circuits of knowledge (Slaughter & Rhoades 2004). The UN Task Force argued that in developing countries, universities should engage in these academic ventures that promote societal benefits and "ensure that students study the relationships between science, technology, innovation, and development, so that they are sensitive to societal needs" (UN Millennium Project Task Force 2005: 93).

The United Nations Educational, Scientific, and Cultural Organization (UNESCO) *Science Report* (2005) noted, "it is now customary to affirm that knowledge, education, science, technology and innovation have become the prime drivers of progress that is itself targeting that most cherished of goals, the knowledge society" (2–3). While the world devoted 1.7% of the GDP to Research and Development, this global statistic conceals the vast discrepancy between developed and developing countries. The divide is highlighted by the fact that the majority of the world lives in developing and less-developed countries (80.6% of the population), where only 22.2% of the gross expenditure on research and development (GERD) is spent, as noted in Table 12.1.

The report reveals similar discrepancies in scientific publications, patents, and high-tech imports, including pharmaceuticals. As a result, the report called for developing and developed countries alike to seek a clear vision for the improvement of the various components of a strong science and technology system, primarily through universities.

Table 12.1 Key Indicators on World GDP, Population, and GERD, 2002

	GDP (in Billions)	% World GDP	Population (in Millions)	% World Population	GERD (in Billions)	% World GERD	% GERD	GERD per Inhabitant
World	47,599.4	100	6,176.2	100	829.9	100	1.7	134.4
Developed Countries	28,256.5	59.4	1,195.1	19.3	645.8	77.8	2.3	540.4
Developing Countries	18,606.5	39.1	4,294.2	69.5	183.6	22.1	1	42.8
Less-developed Countries	736.4	1.5	686.9	11.1	0.5	0.1	0.1	0.7

Source: UNESCO 2005.

Notes
GDP: gross domestic product; GERD: gross expenditure on research and development.

However, many university systems (among other public services) in developing countries have yet to recover from the structural adjustment programs of the IMF and the World Bank (Peters & Besley 2006).

Many developing countries are home to universities that are in a state of crisis (Task Force on Higher Education and Society 2000). These universities suffer from a lack of physical infrastructure and human resources. A 2005 report by the Commission for Africa titled *Our Common Interest* highlighted the fact that university research capacity has declined. The Commission wrote, "Africa needs higher education and research institutes that attract students, researchers and teachers to study and work in Africa—at present there are more African scientists and engineers working in the USA than in Africa" (2005: 34). The Commission added, "Scientific skills and knowledge enable countries to find their own solutions to their own problems … critically, they unlock the potential of innovation and technology to accelerate economic growth, and enter the global economy" (2005: 138). The idea of promoting science and technological research likely applies to other developing regions, not just Africa, in the call to produce locally relevant solutions to social problems.

The literature suggests that the ability to produce locally and globally relevant solutions will elevate poorer countries to become active participants in the global knowledge economy. Until this comes to fruition, these countries are relegated to remain consumers in a new era of intellectual domination. However, the existing body of literature lacks a thorough analysis of the impact of structural adjustment policies on the current state of affairs for universities in developing countries, evaluation of the educational policy shifts by IGOs and international donors, and an appraisal of the commitment by universities in wealthy nations to utilize universities to reduce global poverty in connection to building human capacity.

LOAN COLLABORATION

The educational policies and practices of the World Bank have been intensely debated over the last two decades. The rate of return analysis, which evaluated the utility of an education based on an individual's productivity, was considered by many to be a very narrow approach to education as it yielded a great deal of support for primary education and disinvestment in higher education (Heyneman 1999, 2003; Birdsall 1996). The policy, which has been argued extensively on all sides, was featured in a moderated debate in the *Comparative Education Review* in 2006. Critique of the Bank's work in education led some to hold the

Bank responsible for the struggling higher education sector in developing countries (Caffentzis 2000; Goldman 2005; Pincus & Winters 2002).

While the critiques consider the impact of the Bank's former policies and practices, the Bank's new wave of publications and loans place a high value on university support, especially in the area of science and technology. Evidence of this trend has been demonstrated in new lending for higher education, despite the lack of a formal statement concerning the effects of an absence of higher education lending of the past (Collins & Rhoads 2008). While the long-term focus of the Bank and the impact of the new interest is yet to be seen, concrete moves by the organization link university science and technology to knowledge production, and ultimately poverty reduction.

Due to conflicting agendas and loan conditions, the method of intergovernmental collaboration via World Bank loans has a varied past. However, in a move toward engaging the knowledge economy, the Bank has displayed some evidence of a shift in policy that includes loan projects that support science and technology infrastructure, teaching, and research in the university setting. Table 12.2 shows a list of Bank loans since 2005 that are specifically for the areas of science, technology, and higher education.

A cursory survey of the projects and loans that link science, technology, university education, and the knowledge economy reveal some concrete commitments. Historically, Bank involvement in the area of

Table 12.2 Bank Loans for the Knowledge Economy

Year	Country	Project	US$ Million	% Higher Education
2008	Chile	Promoting Innovation and Competitiveness Project	70	40
2008	Tanzania	Science and Technology Higher Education Program	100	88
2007	Nigeria	Nigeria Federal Science and Technical Education	200	50
2006	Uganda	Millennium Science Initiative	33	65
2005	Romania	Knowledge Economy Project	60	21
2005	Croatia	Science and Technology Project	47	0
2005	Chile	Tertiary Education Finance	100	90
2005	Indonesia	Higher Education for Relevance and Efficiency	114	99
2005	Mexico	Innovation for Competitiveness	441	70

Source: Author.

higher education prior to the early 1990s was non-existent (Collins & Rhoads 2008).

To evaluate the role of science and technology in developing countries, Thailand and Uganda were selected as research sites, both countries with Bank lending experience. While Thailand's Bank loan had just been completed, Uganda's was just beginning. In addition to a review of all relevant loan documents and education goals published by each respective country, 26 interviews were conducted with Ministry of Education officials, World Bank staff, and university professors. Uganda and Thailand were purposefully selected, as both countries have received loans from the Bank in order to develop university science and technology.

Additionally, several universities receiving Bank support were visited, allowing for interviews of faculty and staff involved in Bank-related initiatives, observation of laboratories and equipment, and tours of the campuses. Makerere University, Uganda Christian University, Kyambogo University, and Nkumba University in Uganda and Chulalongkorn University, Thammasat University, Mahidol University, and the Rajamangala University of Technology in Thailand are among the universities that were visited. All of the interviews were recorded (with permission), transcribed verbatim, and coded to evaluate the goals of Uganda and Thailand for their university science and technology programs in comparison with Bank initiatives and support. The data were analyzed to draw conclusions about the opinions of the work of the Bank in these countries, and the effectiveness of past and current projects.

Thailand

The Universities Science and Engineering Education Project (USEEP) was a US$143 million loan committed to advancing Thai universities and their ability to contribute to the knowledge economy. Prior to its approval in 1997, several years were spent in preparation for the project. During the preparation period, Thailand reported shortages of scientists and engineers. The Project Information Document (World Bank 1996) recorded that international indicators showed that Thailand's scientific and technical manpower was "13 per 10,000, as compared to Korea's 37 per 10,000" (1). The government responded with an initiative to increase the number of graduates in science and engineering. However, at the time, only "24 per cent of engineering and 31 per cent of science faculty held a doctorate degree" (World Bank 1996: 2). Lack of modern equipment was another factor that affected the quality of teaching and inhibited research. In collaboration with the World Bank, the following loan objectives to improve science and engineering programs at 20 public universities were identified:

1. Strengthen the teaching capacities of faculty
2. Upgrade the content of existing programs in science and engineering
3. Modernize Laboratories
4. Improve the utilization of resources in departments of engineering and science.

(World Bank 1996: 2)

To meet these objectives, the loan funded a project that would provide short-term training for faculty, finance small-scale research projects, and procure equipment to upgrade laboratories. The project was designed to improve the quality of science and engineering programs, thereby supplying more scientists and engineers to the industry, and thus enhancing the industry's "capacity to handle more advanced production technologies" (World Bank 1996: 4). Intended to produce a long-term result of enhanced capacity for Thailand's technological industry, the project ultimately sought for greater participation in the knowledge economy.

Completed in 2003, the project was able to support enhancements at 20 public universities. According to the report that evaluated the project outcomes, the project met and even exceeded its objectives. In terms of the teaching capabilities of faculty, "2,836 science faculty and 805 engineering faculty participated in training for curriculum development, teaching methodologies, research methodologies, and technical support" (World Bank 2004: 4). The Bank found that the outcomes for this component were satisfactory. The second component, which enhanced the content of existing programs for science and engineering of "3,000 engineering and science course/modules," was also found to be satisfactory (World Bank 2004: 5). The third and most complex aspect of the project involved the modernization of university laboratories.

The completion report identified over "38,000 items that were ordered and delivered to 295 different laboratories on the 20 campuses" (World Bank 2004: 5). The Bank assessment report also considered the final component was satisfactory, as a system to establish the sustainability of the equipment, its maintenance, and procurement for future replacement was established. At the conclusion of the report, the Bank included a section called "Ratings for Achievement of Objectives/ Outputs of Components" in which they rank poverty reduction as "substantial" (three out of four) and institutional development as "high" (four out of four). The report also incorporated comments from the borrower, which included both praise for the World Bank and concern about the procurement of equipment.

This theme also emerged in many of the interviews. A high-ranking official in the Ministry of Education commented that "The World Bank project helped in speeding up the improvement of quality. I think it helped to some degree, but I also think there is a lack of continuation." However, the official went on to say that "Once their investment was made, it became stagnant ... We are trying to develop and expand at a moderate speed ... so I think at this moment, we will try to rely on our own resources." This particular comment is representative of the belief that the loan had moderate success, but that there is perhaps more value in Thailand proceeding without collaborating through loans from the World Bank. However, several officials identified the Asian Development Bank as a potential partner for this type of collaboration.

Much of Thailand's population still exists in poverty. The degree of stratification is great, and the government struggles to be competitive in a region that also struggles with poverty. As the development of scientific and technological knowledge is a prominent goal for the country, the USEEP loan was one of several methods employed to advance that goal. Several high-ranking officials in the Ministry of Education spoke of the significance of research, development, agriculture, and the importance of the university in each area. One official mentioned:

> We only have 20 researchers per 10,000 in Thailand, but the United States has more than 200. We have to continue to improve science programs for better research ... to produce goods and services that increase the standard of living for everyone.

An official from the Thai Higher Education Commission also stated:

> The main idea is to improve the faculty of science/engineering to modernize and produce undergraduates with skills. We have a high interest in research, to transfer technology, to collaborate to produce some goods and services, and to commercialize technology.

There was a strong belief in the potential for research, knowledge creation, and distribution to make contributions to the country's human capacity for these types of roles.

As with many poverty reduction strategies, there are many complexities and barriers. Following a coup in 2006, Thailand is currently facing political unrest. During the life of the USEEP loan, the country experienced an economic crisis. These barriers were cause for major setbacks, but, overall, the leaders in the Ministry of Education and other parts of the government recognize the connection between poverty reduction, the knowledge economy, and the university's role as an incubator for knowledge economy.

Uganda

The Millennium Science Initiative Project (MSI) was approved in 2006. Currently, the project is underway in the amount of US$33 million. This is the second major project that Uganda has had with the Bank for the development of university education. During the appraisal stage for the loan, the World Bank prepared a Project Information Document in which Uganda was identified as having what they called "a historical neglect of science and technology" (World Bank 2006: 2). The document continues to say, "In Uganda, neglect of science and technology has created a disconnect between the country's needs and its ability to meet them" (2). Interestingly, the Bank document recognizes the importance of science and technology, while also acknowledging that enrollments went from fewer than 25,000 in 1990 to almost 110,000 in 2004. The document does not, however, include any reference to the Bank's role in causing the predicament. Other problem areas were mentioned, such as poor wages for professors, large teaching loads, and the faculty student ratio of 1 to 200.

Through a Poverty Eradication Plan (PEAP) established in 1997, the government is actively working to alleviate some of these issues. This plan was established on four pillars to help Uganda become a modern economy: creating a framework for economic growth and transformation, ensuring good governance and security, directly increasing the ability of the poor to raise their incomes, and directly increasing the quality of the life of the poor. The MSI project has two objectives that align with Uganda's PEAP: (1) enhancing productivity, competitiveness, and income by increasing the amount and quality of skills available to the labor market in areas critical to private-sector growth; and (2) improving human development by reforming higher education curricula through greater emphasis on science and technology (World Bank 2006: 4–5).

In order to fulfill these objectives, the project has two components: (1) a competitive fund to support research, education, and training in science and engineering, as well as linkages to the private sector; and (2) an outreach, policy, and institutional strengthening component

(World Bank 2006: 8–9). Essentially, the first component includes a fund that will provide grants to: (1) individuals or teams who are emerging young investigators at universities or research institutes, (2) those boosting undergraduate programs in the sciences (laboratory equipment, texts, etc.), and (3) those seeking to form partnerships with industry. The second component involves marketing campaigns like a National Science Week, and strengthening the Ugandan Council for Science and Technology through reorganization and improved science policies (this Council is similar in mission to the National Science Foundation in the United States).

It appears that the government of Uganda has made concrete links between the development of science and technology, university education, and poverty reduction. However, the National Council of Higher Education reported that 85% of university enrollment is in arts and humanities, with only 15% in science and technology. The Ugandan government recognizes the imbalance, as too few students are engaged in subjects that will promote poverty reduction. As a result, the government offers scholarships of up to 70% for students willing to major in science and technology. A high-ranking official in the Ministry of Education stated that in the few years this program has been in place, the number of students studying science and technology has increased to 20%.

The professors, researchers, and education officials interviewed have high hopes for this project, but also for the development of human capacity around science and technology. The urgency and articulation of these needs were very clear in almost every interview. In terms of self-reliance, one professor stated:

> You need to have some highly trained persons in math or physics and to use them to build the capacity and best practices. This is often cheaper than saying that we'll depend on foreign personnel to do high level research.

The professor went on to note that, "Having the right sort of human resources would allow Ugandans to engage with science, technology, and engineering." He gave the example of being able to build roads independently of foreign contractors to highlight his point. This type of sentiment is directly linked to the idea that developing countries are often relegated to consumers or patrons in the knowledge economy instead of producers.

In developing countries like Uganda, there is a struggle over where to allocate money in developing human capacity. Due to limited resources, the basic education and rate of return analysis debate is still alive. One higher education official stated, "You cannot survive on basic education alone because we know that in higher education we find invention and creation—we know that." In terms of production, the official asked: "How many sacks of coffee do you think it takes to get a vehicle? We are not selling processed coffee, it is raw because we do not have the technology and production, and therefore we cannot reap the benefits."

University education and especially research, however, are certainly more expensive than basic education, which is why there is a great value in explaining the connections between university research in science and technology with human capacity building and poverty reduction. One scientist in Uganda noted that, "Research is expensive, but as a scientist, I've always told colleagues that it's very, very dangerous for you to do a cost–benefit analysis for research because you may never do the research." The scientist noted that a coffee variety developed in the 1960s is now in every household. The scientist went on to explain that, "As this was being developed, a lot of money went in the lab and the research. That is coffee, but let's talk of a vaccine." In terms of research and money to develop something that could save generations of people, it is difficult to find a price tag. He went on to say, "There is a lot of research and money to develop vaccines for HIV/ AIDS, but once a breakthrough comes, the impact will be felt for generations." The point of the explanation was summarized in his final comments, connected to evaluation structures:

> So if you do a cost–benefit and you start seeing we are spending $50 million in this project, that contributes to curing AIDS and will save millions of lives, then you can understand. So I've always discouraged a cost–benefit analysis.

The MSI is what one researcher called a "significant departure" from what the World Bank has done in Uganda in the past. As evidence, the researcher cited that funding was allocated to universities as opposed to basic education, fewer conditions or strings were attached to the loan, and the process was much more collaborative.

CONCLUSION

Cross-border collaboration through grants or lending can help to jump-start some of these processes, but increased national debt and consequences for lending often cause hesitation. Thailand and Uganda, in particular, appear to be at a crossroads with Bank lending, but in different ways. Thailand is moving toward self-reliance and regional lending, while Uganda continues to struggle with the remaining tensions of previous Bank policies that operated very differently from the MSI. Loans from development banks are an effective way to increase the commitment to human capacity building in science and technology. However, the type of lending is a critical question in the process. International development organizations have been criticized for creating the current poverty-stricken conditions that are in many countries today, and are still questioned as to whether or not they can reverse the process.

Lending and collaboration to build a country's human capacity for research and knowledge production in science and technology certainly have been shown to have great potential for solving poverty-related problems. The move of the World Bank to lending for universities and the knowledge economy is a positive step toward supporting this aspect of development. Other aspects necessary to make this component effective include collaboration that places a high value on homegrown development and universities that have strong connections to the community, in terms of distributing knowledge and transferring technology. In terms of lending, the right balance must constantly be sought to create accountability without micromanagement and to ensure loan expectations match the country's goals for growth and development.

REFERENCES

Birdsall, N. (1996). Public spending on higher education in developing countries: Too much or too little? *Economics of Education Review, 15*(4), 407–419.

Caffentzis, G. (2000). The World Bank and education in Africa. In S. Federici, G. Caffentzis, & O. Alidou (Eds.), *A thousand flowers: Social struggles against structural adjustment in African universities* (pp. 3–18). Lenton, NJ: Africa World Press.

Calderone, S., & Rhoads, R.A. (2005). Challenging the mythology of the "disappearing nation-state": A case study of competitive advantage through state–university collaboration. *Education and Society, 23*(1), 5–23.

Carnoy, M., Castells, M., Cohen, S.S., & Cardoso, F. (1993). *The new global economy in the information age: Reflections on our changing world.* University Park: Pennsylvania State University Press.

Castells, M. (1996). *The rise of the network society.* Boston, MA: Blackwell.

Castells, M. (1997). *The power of identity.* Boston, MA: Blackwell.

Collins, C.S. & Rhoads, R.A. (2008). The World Bank and higher education in the developing world: The cases of Uganda and Thailand. In D.P. Baker and A.W. Wiseman (Eds.), *The worldwide transformation of higher education: Volume 9, The international perspectives on education and society series* (pp. 177–221). Oxford, UK: Elsevier.

Commission for Africa (2005). *Our common interest*. Retrieved March 1, 2007, from www.commissionforafrica.org.

Easterly, W. (2006). *The white man's burden: Why the west's efforts to aid the rest have done so much ill and so little good*. New York: Penguin Press.

Elkins, P. (1992). *The new world order: Grassroots movement for global change*. New York: Routledge.

Geiger, R.L. (2004). *Knowledge and money: Research universities and the paradox of the marketplace*. Stanford, CA: Stanford University Press.

Goldman, M. (2005). *Imperial nature: The World Bank and struggles for social justice in the age of globalization*. New Haven, CT: Yale University Press.

Heyneman, S.P. (1999). Development aid in education: A personal view. *International Journal of Educational Development, 19*(3), 183–190.

Heyneman, S.P. (2003). The history and problems in the making of education policy at the World Bank 1960–2000. *International Journal of Educational Development, 23*(3), 315–337.

Lucas, R. (1998). On the mechanics of economic development. *Journal of Monetary Economics, 22*(1), 3–42.

MacGarvie, M., & Furman, J. (2005). *Early academic science and the birth of the industrial research laboratories in the U.S. pharmaceutical industry* (Working Paper 11,470). Cambridge, MA: National Bureau of Economic Development.

Morrow, R., & Torres, C.A. (2000). The state, globalization, and educational policy. In N.C. Burbules & C.A. Torres (Eds.), *Globalization and education: Critical perspectives* (pp. 27–56). New York: Routledge.

Mowery, D., & Rosenberg, N. (1998). *Paths of innovation: Technological change in 20th century America*. New York: Cambridge University Press.

Muchie, M. (2009, January). African universities must fight poverty. *African Executive*. Retrieved January 31, 2009, from: www.africanexecutive.com.

OECD (1996). *The knowledge-based economy*. Paris: OECD.

Peters, M.A., & Besley, A.C.T. (2006). *Building knowledge cultures: Education and development in the age of knowledge capitalism*. London: Rowman & Littlefield Publishers.

Pincus, J.R., & Winters, J.A. (2002). Reinventing the World Bank. In J.R. Pincus & J.A. Winters (Eds.), *Reinventing the World Bank* (pp. 1–25). Ithaca, NY: Cornell University Press.

Psacharopoulos, G. (1981). The World Bank in the world of education: Some policy changes some remnants. *Comparative Education, 17*(2), 141–145.

Psacharopoulos, G. (1987). *Economics of education: Research and studies*. Oxford, UK: Pergamon Press.

Psacharopoulos, G. (1988). Education and development: A review. *Research Observer, 3*(1), 99–116.

Romer, P.M. (1989). *Human capital and growth: Theory and Evidence* (Working Paper 3,173). Cambridge, MA: National Bureau of Economic Research.

Rostow, W.W. (1960). *The stages of economic growth: A non-communist manifesto.* Cambridge, UK: Cambridge University Press.

Ruegg, W. (2004). *Universities in the nineteenth and early twentieth centuries (1800–1945): Volume 3.* Cambridge, UK: Cambridge University Press.

Sachs, J.D. (2005). *The end of poverty: Economic possibilities of our time.* New York: Penguin Books.

Slaughter, S., & Rhoades, G. (2004). *Academic capitalism and the new economy: Markets, state and higher education.* Baltimore, MD: Johns Hopkins University Press.

Stiglitz, J.E. (1999). Knowledge as a global public good. In I. Kaul, I. Grunberg, & M. Stern (Eds.), *Global public goods* (pp. 308–326). New York: Oxford University Press.

Stiglitz, J.E. (2002). *Globalization and its discontents.* New York: W.W. Norton and Company.

Stromquist, N.P. (2002). *Education in a globalized world: The connectivity of economic power, technology, and knowledge.* New York: Rowman & Littlefield Publishers.

Task Force on Higher Education and Society (2000). *Higher education in developing countries: Peril and promise.* Washington, DC: World Bank.

UN Millennium Project Task Force (2005). *Innovation: Applying knowledge in development.* London: Earthscan.

UNESCO (2005). *Science Report.* Paris: UNESCO.

World Bank (1996). *Thailand universities sciences and engineering education project information document.* Washington, DC: World Bank.

World Bank (2002). *Constructing knowledge societies: New challenges for tertiary education.* Washington, DC: World Bank.

World Bank (2004). *Thailand universities sciences and engineering education information completion report.* Washington, DC: World Bank.

World Bank (2006). *Uganda millennium science initiative project information document.* Washington, DC: World Bank.

Yunus, M. (2003). *Banker to the poor.* New York: Public Affairs.

Yusuf, S. (2007). University–industry links: Policy dimensions. In S. Yusuf & K. Nabeshima (Eds.), *How universities promote economic growth* (pp. 1–26). Washington, DC: World Bank.

13

CROSS-BORDER COLLABORATION FOR INCLUSIVE AND SUSTAINABLE HIGHER EDUCATION

Searching for Priorities

JOUKO SARVI[1]

Demand for regional cooperation and integration has increased considerably in recent years in Asia and the Pacific region in order to support social and economic development and reduce poverty. Strategies focusing on inclusive and sustainable development have become increasingly important for poverty reduction in individual developing countries and to regional and subregional cooperation efforts.

Developing countries in the region share the challenge of making social and economic development more inclusive. Public policies need to focus on inclusiveness to create opportunities for everyone, particularly the poorest, provide a safety net for those who fall on hard times, and achieve other important social and economic objectives in society. The policies that best address these issues are often national in scope, but the challenges also have important regional dimensions (Asian Development Bank [ADB] 2008b).

While most Asian economies have made remarkable progress in reducing poverty, benefits have failed to reach significant numbers of people. Progress has lagged in some countries, especially on non-income measures. Sharp income disparities have emerged within some countries. Economic growth and development in the region have been far from inclusive. The gap between the rich and poor has widened in recent years (ADB 2008b, 2007a). Most recently, the impact of the global economic downturn has further highlighted the income ine-qualities and the risks they pose for social and economic development globally and in the region (International Labor Organization [ILO] 2008b).

As economies in the region have grown larger and more complex, they also have become more integrated through various forms of eco-nomic and social exchange (ADB 2008b). Higher education is envisaged to have an increasingly important role in developing human resources and contributing toward increased movement of people, students, and the workforce in the region. In order to fulfill this role in an inclusive and sustainable manner, higher education must be equitable in terms of access and financing mechanisms, and of good quality. Countries in the region seek increasing cross-border collaboration in both higher educa-tion and labor markets. In doing so, they sometimes look to interna-tional development organizations, such as the Asian Development Bank (ADB) and the World Bank, for financial and technical assistance.

In its long-term strategic framework, *Strategy 2020*, the ADB focuses on five core operation areas (including the education sector) that are essential to sustaining development and growth and providing access to economic opportunities—the pillars of inclusive growth (ADB 2008d). Inclusive development and growth require continuous devel-opment of an adequate human resource base. The current economic downturn has only served to further confirm the importance of sup-porting inclusiveness through education in the region. Education of good quality, and equitable access to it, will continue to be important to social and economic development in the region. Demand also is increasing for pursuing regional cooperation and cross-border collabo-ration in the sector, particularly in higher education.

ADB's strategic study of the education sector in Asia and the Pacific region (ADB 2008a) provides a systematic analysis of education and human capital development challenges and presents strategic recom-mendations for ADB operations in the education sector. It helps ensure that ADB's operations continue to respond effectively to developing countries' needs that arise from evolving labor markets and rapid eco-nomic and social development.

Resource requirements and development needs in higher education are expected to increase significantly over the next decade due to system expansion and development pressure. While economic circum-stances may challenge the investment scenario in the short term in some parts of the region, it is reasonable to assume that, overall, invest-ment in higher education will continue to increase due to a strong demand.

The rapid economic development in many parts of the region has influenced the type of knowledge and skills needed. This transformation will continue, at a slower pace during the economic slowdown. Nonetheless, there will continue to be an increasing need for workers with higher-level technical, managerial, and administrative skills than education systems in the region have been able to meet. Skill shortages have become widespread in the region and have affected the economic development in the region.

The shortage of adequately educated and trained workers has continued to be a major bottleneck to growth and economic expansion in the region. While the skills shortage has particularly affected multinational companies operating in the region, it has increasingly undermined expansion and operation of local companies (ILO 2008a). The shortage persists despite the slowdown in economic activity across the region ("You still can't get the staff" 2008).

TRENDS IN CROSS-BORDER COLLABORATION IN HIGHER EDUCATION ACROSS ASIA

Regional collaboration on various development agendas, including higher education, often center on the Association of Southeast Asian Nations (ASEAN), which has a long history and well-developed framework for regional cooperation (ADB 2008b). The ASEAN University Network, which was established in 1995 and involves 20 leading universities, is an example of networks pursuing the aim of student and teacher exchanges, joint development of study programs, and networking among departments and faculties (see www.aun-sec.org).

ADB provides support to cross-border collaboration efforts in the Greater Mekong Subregion (GMS), such as through the implementation of the GMS Human Resource Development (HRD) Strategic Framework and Action Plan. Overall, the plan aims to strengthen cooperation among the GMS countries through national and subregional HRD networks, and the Plan implementation will also be mainstreamed into the programs and budgets of relevant ministries in GMS countries. The education sector is one of the key sectors in the Plan that incorporates initiatives for standards and accreditation as well as for curriculum harmonization in selected subject areas (ADB 2008c).

The internationalization of higher education and the prevalence of cross-border higher education have rapidly increased. Between 2000 and 2006, the number of students enrolled in higher education institutions outside their own countries (worldwide) rose more than 50%. In particular, students from Asian countries have contributed to this trend. One reason for this trend is the growth in global multinational professional career demands: students sense that time spent studying abroad may increase their chances of getting jobs in multinational companies. But for students from the developing world, poor-quality higher education and a lack of student places in their home country are stronger factors for their desire to study abroad ("The future is another country" 2009).

Currently the picture is mixed in terms of the contribution of the global international higher education markets to regional or subregional cross-border collaboration. Universities in developed countries have rushed to set up their "hubs" or outposts abroad. However, the financing of these partnerships remains largely uncharted terrain (Lewin 2008) and, so far, has produced unclear results. Universities in the region that have been active in partnering with hubs in developed country universities are themselves increasingly pursuing cross-border collaborations. They aspire eventually to become regional hubs in higher education; i.e., providing higher education to students from neighboring countries and setting up institutions across borders (ADB 2008a; Kapur & Crowley 2008; UNESCO 2006).

While there is a high demand for quantitative expansion and diversification of higher education in the region, there is also an increasing concern about concurrently ensuring good-quality higher education and equitable access to it, and about cost efficiency and sustainable financing of higher education. It is reasonable to anticipate that the current economic downturn may further highlight these concerns. To effectively support the development of these dimensions, it is important to improve the understanding and awareness of their intertwined relationships. For example, appropriate financing arrangements through cost sharing and partnerships can contribute not only to cost efficiency and financial sustainability of higher education, but also help to facilitate equitable access and improve quality and relevance of higher education (Sarvi 2008). How are we to ensure that the rapid quantitative expansion of higher education will not undermine these other important dimensions? How are we to ensure that higher education will be inclusive, and will contribute to inclusive development and growth in the region?

CROSS-BORDER COLLABORATION IN QUALITY ASSURANCE IN HIGHER EDUCATION—CHALLENGES AND OPPORTUNITIES

In recent years, encouraging initiatives have emerged in cross-border collaboration for quality assurance in higher education in the region.

The Southeast Asian Ministers of Education Organization (SEAMEO) is an international and intergovernmental organization for regional cooperation in education, science, and culture. It currently has 11 member countries and eight associate member countries. Over the past three decades, SEAMEO has developed a range of specialist centers, one of them being the Regional Center for Higher Education and Development (RIIHED) in Bangkok, which specializes in regional cooperation in higher education development (see www.seameo.org). RIIHED's objectives are to foster efficiency and effectiveness of higher education in SEAMEO member countries through research and professional development activities. RIIHED also aims to serve as the regional center and clearing-house for the exchange and dissemination of information and research findings on higher education planning and management.

Compatibility in higher education qualifications, common frameworks for quality assurance, and standardization of curricula are key elements of the long-term vision of RIIHED. RIIHED seeks to become the prime mover in promoting policy initiative for the establishment of a common higher education space and higher education harmonization in the Southeast Asia region. To this end, RIIHED has recently led knowledge-sharing and capacity-development activities that draw on studies undertaken in five ASEAN countries (namely Malaysia, Indonesia, the Philippines, Thailand, and Vietnam) and on experiences in other parts of the world, such as the Bologna process for higher education harmonization in Europe.

The Asia-Pacific Quality Network (APQN) is another example of a network that promotes regional and cross-border collaboration aimed at building capacity and strengthening quality assurance in higher education. The mission of APQN is to enhance the quality of higher education in Asia and the Pacific region through strengthening the work of quality assurance agencies and extending cooperation among them. To achieve its mission, APQN promotes good practice in higher education quality assurance by providing information and expertise to governments and quality assurance agencies in the region, supporting cross-border cooperation between quality assurance agencies, assisting its members in determining standards of institutions operating across national borders, facilitating recognition of qualifications, and enhancing the mobility of students between institutions and member states (APQN 2008).

APQN has 57 member agencies and institutions (plus another six observers) from 27 countries. These countries include those which are members of SEAMEO and the ASEAN University Network; however,

APQN members include agencies and institutions in countries beyond Southeast Asia. The APQN secretariat has been hosted by the Australian Universities Quality Agency but, starting from 2009, the Secretariat will be based at the Shanghai Education Evaluation Institute (Pijano 2009). APQN has jointly produced with UNESCO a toolkit for regulating the quality of cross-border education (UNESCO and APQN 2007). APQN is a partner in the Brisbane Communiqué process and, in support of the process, APQN carried out a scoping study of quality assurance arrangements in higher education in the Asia-Pacific region (APQN 2008, see www.apqn.org).

The Brisbane Communiqué, which was launched at the inaugural Asia-Pacific Education Ministers' Meeting in Brisbane, Australia in 2006, has been signed now by more than 50 countries. The Communiqué promotes collaboration for the recognition and quality of education in Asia and the Pacific region. The Communiqué process promotes development of quality assurance frameworks for the region linked with international standards. In support of this, the process has included studies and workshops on quality assurance and recognition of qualifications in higher education (see www.brisbanecommunique. deewr.gov.au).

Given the increasing expectations of higher education in developing human resources and contributing toward the movement of people, students, and the workforce in the region, the demand for cross-border collaboration in higher education quality assurance is also likely to increase. Particularly, Southeast Asian countries are proactively contributing to this field as members in the collaborative networks of SEAMEO–RIIHED, APQN, and the Brisbane Communiqué process.

On one hand, systems and resources in the education sector vary markedly among countries in the region. Therefore, quality assurance and harmonization of higher education can be a serious challenge even across the Southeast Asia subregion, which already has well-established regional cooperation spearheaded by SEAMEO. On the other hand, as SEAMEO member countries are also members of ASEAN (which promotes a coherent framework for economic cooperation between these countries) and the ASEAN University Network, it is reasonable to assume that cross-border cooperation efforts in higher education may have more potential in this subregion than in other subregions of Asia where no such established cooperation frameworks or specialist centers for higher education cooperation are operating. It will be important to share with countries in other subregions the experiences and lessons gained in cross-border collaboration in higher education quality assurance in the Southeast subregion.

PRIORITIES FOR CROSS-BORDER COLLABORATION IN FINANCING AND PARTNERSHIPS IN HIGHER EDUCATION

Costs per student in higher education are much higher than in primary and secondary education. This has a range of implications for strategic planning and financing in the education sector and, therefore, deserves to be included in the agenda of cross-border collaboration. On average, low-income countries spend 34 times more per higher education student than they spend per primary education student, and 14 times more than they spend per secondary education student. The analogous figures for high-income countries are 1.8 and 1.4 (ADB 2008a; Glewwe & Kremer 2005).

In developing countries, sudden and large shifts of government funding toward higher education can jeopardize adequate government financing of lower subsectors of education. It is important to mitigate this risk. It can be particularly important during the current economic downturn when public budgets for basic and secondary education in many poorer developing countries have come under intense pressure. Cross-border collaboration can play an important and productive role in sharing strategies for financing and cost sharing in higher education.

Over the decades, the debate surrounding investment in higher education has evolved through several stages. Earlier, in the absence of robust economic rate of return models, wider considerations of social interest and equity dominated the debate. When the concepts and models of education as a social and private investment—and the rate of return to that investment, were developed—the social rate of return to basic education was found to be considerably higher in most countries than the rate of return to higher education. Private returns to higher education were much greater than the social returns. In light of this, reallocation of more public spending to basic education became an important priority. Additionally, the development framework of the Millennium Development Goals contributed to this priority setting. Stronger emphasis on cost-recovery measures, such as tuition fees and student loans, was advocated for higher education. More recently, particularly in the context of education's key role in supporting the development toward knowledge-based economies, major external benefits that are crucial for knowledge-driven economic and social development are seen as arising from investment in higher education. It is recognized that social benefits of higher education may have been underestimated in the earlier rate of return models. However, the arguments in favor of cost sharing for higher education financing have remained (Woodhall 2007).

Meaningful financing schemes involving cost sharing and partnerships are important in higher education. It is important to encourage the development of appropriate policies and strategies to address these issues, not only in individual developing countries, but also through cross-border collaborations. This helps ensure that governments share their lessons and experiences of balancing their resources among basic, secondary, and higher education rather than disproportionately allocating funds to higher education (where cost recovery from beneficiaries is more justified). Furthermore, appropriate cost sharing and partnerships in higher education are important not only from the perspective of encouraging cost efficiency and sustainability of financing, but also from the perspective that they can effectively support the improvement of equitable access, quality, and relevance of higher education.

The question is not whether increased investment in higher education is justified, but, rather:

> What is the government's role in ensuring that a sufficient number of higher education graduates are available, that they have received higher education of good quality and relevance, and that higher education is inclusive based on equitable access and does not merely serve the upper income groups?

Governments should focus their role on creating a supportive policy environment for private sector provision, determining and assessing standards of performance, setting broad national policies, and developing an accreditation mechanism (ADB 2003).

Cost sharing in higher education has continued to be a politically sensitive issue in many developed and developing countries. It seems that the use of politically "correct" terminology has made a difference in the debates. The concept of cost sharing has attracted greater support than other economic concepts, such as "cost recovery" or "user charges," and especially much greater support than "tuition fees." Cost sharing in higher education is generally increasing and many different economic and political arguments or mix of arguments (e.g., economic arguments mixed with equity and efficiency arguments) have been used to support cost sharing in higher education (Johnston 2004; Woodhall 2007). Cross-border collaboration can play an important role in reducing the political sensitivity of cost sharing by improving awareness and clarity of key concepts and strategies, and their relevance to the circumstances of developing countries in the region.

In the context of limited public resources and the increasing demand for higher education, two strategies have usually been pursued: (a) more resources have been mobilized, principally by introducing or raising tuition fees as a way of increasing cost sharing; (b) additional private resources have been sought through commercialization of research and other private use of institutional facilities and staff. However, the limitations of these strategies have become more evident as the demand for higher education has accelerated. There is an increasing need to pursue innovation in higher education financing (Salmi & Hauptman 2006).

Lessons learned from innovative financing underline the importance of pursuing multiple sources of funding and a mix of allocation mechanisms. This approach has facilitated flexibility, which can be necessary when governments and institutions consider a response in the context of limited public resources and increasing demand for higher education, particularly while being cognizant of access, equity, and quality concerns. While the use of a mix of allocation mechanisms provides greater potential, it requires careful consideration since there is a risk that one mechanism may undermine the success of other important objectives. Allocation mechanisms, which have a longer-term perspective and therefore allow higher education institutions to plan and implement their investment and reform in a more strategic way, have proven to be more appropriate than annual allocation mechanisms (Salmi & Hauptman 2006). It is important to include knowledge sharing of these lessons in the agenda of cross-border collaboration in order to encourage governments and other stakeholders in developing countries in the region to search for innovative solutions in higher education financing, and to raise awareness of the real potential and possible risks of such solutions.

Limited public resources and dissatisfaction with the quality and relevance of public higher education has resulted in the rapid growth of private higher education. Therefore, private financing and public–private partnerships in higher education are also important focus areas for capacity development through cross-border collaboration in the region. Governments have found the private sector useful in helping to increase the level of financial resources committed to the higher education sector through such strategies as private philanthropic support of education programs or infrastructure. Additionally, private resources often focus on providing additional inputs (such as learning materials, infrastructure, IT, training) aimed at improving the quality of education delivered in government institutions. Increased private involvement can help with upgrading pedagogical and technological skills and knowledge in higher education and improving management, including financial management, in higher education institutions. Private sector provision of higher education can supplement the limited capacity of government institutions to absorb growth in higher education enrollments. Governments may opt to publicly fund students in private universities, which can result in lower per-student cost than in the public sector (Fielden & LaRocque 2008; LaRocque 2007a; Hahn 2007).

To successfully adopt these approaches, governments will need the knowledge and capacity to build the necessary regulatory frameworks, investors will need to undertake market research at the country level, and higher education institutions will need knowledge and capacity to build business relationships with the private sector (Hahn 2007). Too often, government regulation appears to discourage private investment without any commensurate gain in the quality of education. Government funding policies generally favor public provision over private provision, despite the adverse equity and efficiency impact this can have on the sector and the lack of any public rationale for such a distinction (Fielden & LaRocque 2008; ADB 2007b).

Philanthropic foundations can contribute to higher education partnerships by promoting new development approaches and paradigms. International philanthropic foundations are steadily expanding their portfolios for higher education, albeit mostly in developing regions outside Asia and the Pacific region thus far (Marten & Witten 2008; Loren & Ateinza 2006). Proactive cross-border collaboration can play an important role in raising awareness of the partnership potential with philanthropic foundations and in attracting the foundations to become partners in higher education in the region. The range of options and the potential for financing partnerships in higher education in the regional context warrants further exploration. Higher education provision through regional or subregional hubs can help to reduce the burden on individual countries in responding to the increasing demand for higher education. From a financing perspective, particular interest also would be in hubs pursuing the role of cross-border collaboration established primarily through the organic growth of leading universities in the region, or through other means (e.g., through strengthening university networks or twinning arrangements between universities in the region and universities in developed countries) (Sarvi 2008).

CROSS-BORDER COLLABORATION FOR DIVERSIFICATION: SCIENCE AND TECHNOLOGY IN HIGHER EDUCATION

As higher education expands and develops, increasingly a wider range of institutions emerge in the sector that caters to the different needs of an ever more diverse group of students. At its most simple level, this diversification can be defined between public and private higher education providers, or by program type or funding source. Other levels of differentiation include traditional and research universities, polytechnics, technical institutes, open learning institutes, and community colleges (UNESCO 2006).

Diversification occurs as countries respond to social and economic demand for higher education, including specific demands for improving access, equity, and quality and relevance of higher education. Obviously, diversification provides challenges as well as opportunities for partnerships; e.g., in quality assurance and financing in higher education, particularly as the range of higher education stakeholders expands with diversification. One increasingly important area of diversification relates to the anticipated role of higher education in supporting science and technology development in the region.

Cross-border collaboration can be an important and effective platform for sharing experiences and knowledge about the potential as well as the obvious limitations of higher education in supporting the development of science and technology. Capacity in science and technology can be developed in at least two basic ways. One is through improving science and technology in secondary and higher education, as well as through building a labor force with stronger skills that can support the development of more technology-based business and industry. Another is through using universities to serve as incubators of innovation and fuel the development of new business and industry (ADB 2008a).

Enrollment data from the region suggest that one area of attention would be measures to encourage enrollments in fields that most directly contribute to scientific and technological innovation. However, just encouraging enrollment growth in these fields will not be enough. Once enrolled, students must have a meaningful program of study and research. Development of indigenous capacity is important in many developing countries in the region to support such a program through university–industry partnerships and through linkages with regional or subregional cross-border research networks (ADB 2006, 2008a; LaRocque 2007a).

While more higher education in science and technology across the region is widely supported, the role of higher education institutions in fostering innovation and technological change is less clear. Investment in university-based science and technology can be questioned on the grounds that the development of science and technology is not an outcome of just one sector, but the convergence of sectoral inputs with many other factors. Thus, the linear model is increasingly challenged; i.e., a model which assumes that by developing good teaching in the sciences and spending more on research—particularly at university-based basic research centers—advanced technology will be developed, disseminated, and commercialized by business and industry in ways that promote national economic development. This model is increasingly criticized because the principal factors that promote technological development are not the activities of universities, science ministries, or specialized institutes. Development of productive technologies is more often the outcome of industrial and trade policies that promote in-house research and development by business and industry, taxation policies, fiscal policy, and even foreign policy (ADB 2006, 2008a; LaRocque 2007b).

Cross-border collaboration will be important to share experiences and raise awareness of both supply and demand-side strategies for improving science and technology, and the potential and limitations of the support from higher education. While the value of these strategies should be assessed in the context of each country, there obviously are important common areas and opportunities for joint efforts (at least in subregional frameworks) for improving science and technology relevant for economies in a particular subregion. Supply-side strategies aim to support innovation through increasing the capacity of higher education institutions to produce more graduates in advanced training in science and technology fields. Demand-side strategies aim to support innovation through a favorable regulatory framework and tax structure, strong protection of intellectual property, and access to capital in order to support entrepreneurial use of innovative thinking (ADB 2008c).

CONCLUSIONS

Cross-border collaboration can play an important and effective role in helping universities draw on lessons about the potential opportunities and risks associated with higher education development in the region. While there is a high demand for quantitative expansion of higher education and increasingly for its diversification in the region, there is also an increasing concern about concurrently ensuring good-quality higher education and equitable access to it, and about cost efficiency and sustainable financing of higher education. Cross-border collaboration can help to address these issues in a balanced manner and ensure that the rapid quantitative expansion will not undermine the other equally important dimensions in higher education. Furthermore, the important role of higher education's contribution to inclusive development and growth in the region should be part of the agenda of cross-border collaboration. The economic downturn in 2009 further increased the demand for addressing these issues through cross-border collaboration.

In recent years, encouraging cross-border collaboration has emerged as part of higher education quality assurance issues, particularly in the Southeast Asia subregion where several collaborative cross-border networks for economic and social development are well established. It will be important to share these experiences with other countries in the region. Cost sharing in higher education, innovative higher education financing mechanisms, and partnerships in higher education all can contribute not only to more cost efficient and financially sustainable higher education, but also to the improvement of quality, relevance, and equity in higher education. Raising more awareness of the potential and experiences in these development issues is part of the important agenda for cross-border collaboration in higher education.

Cross-border collaboration can be an important and effective platform for sharing experiences and raising awareness, not only for improved science and technology, but also in identifying the limitations of higher education in supporting science and technology.

Given the increasing expectations regarding the role higher education should play in the human resources development plans of many countries, the demand for cross-border collaboration in higher education is likely to increase. In order to fulfill this role in an inclusive and sustainable manner, higher education institutions must provide equitable access, sensible financing mechanisms, and quality instruction. Coordination of cross-border collaboration is important to ensure synergies and effectiveness of these efforts. ADB is keen to support cross-border collaboration for sharing experiences and knowledge in these issues, and for developing the necessary capacity of line ministries, higher education institutions, and other stakeholders of higher education in the region.

NOTE

1. The author is Practice Leader (Education Sector) at the Asian Development Bank (ADB). The views expressed in this chapter are those of the author and do not necessarily reflect the views and policies of ADB's management, Board of Directors, or the governments they represent.

REFERENCES

Asian Development Bank (2003). *Education. Our framework. Policies and strategies*. Manila, the Philippines: ADB.
Asian Development Bank (2006). *Project completion report on the science and*

technology personnel development project in Sri Lanka. Manila, the Philippines: ADB.

Asian Development Bank (2007a). *Key indicators 2007: Inequality in Asia.* Manila, the Philippines: ADB.

Asian Development Bank (2007b). *Public-private partnership handbook.* Manila, the Philippines: ADB.

Asian Development Bank (2008a). *Education and skills: Strategies for accelerated development in Asia and the Pacific.* Manila, the Philippines: ADB.

Asian Development Bank (2008b). *Emerging Asian regionalism: A partnership for shared prosperity.* Manila, the Philippines: ADB.

Asian Development Bank (2008c). *Greater Mekong Sub-region: Regional cooperation operations business plan 2009-2011.* Manila, the Philippines: ADB.

Asian Development Bank (2008d). *Strategy 2020: The long term strategic framework of the Asian Development Bank 2008-2020.* Manila, the Philippines: ADB.

Asia Pacific Quality Network (2008). *APQN annual report 2006-2007.* Melbourne, Australia: APQN.

Fielden, J., & LaRocque, N. (2008). *The evolving regulatory context for private education in emerging economies.* Washington, DC: International Finance Corporation.

Glewwe, P., & Kremer, M. (2005). *Schools, teachers, and education outcomes in developing countries.* Harvard University Working Paper in Handbook on the Economics of Education. Cambridge, MA: Harvard University.

Hahn, R. (2007). *The global state of higher education and the rise of private finance.* Issue Brief. Washington, DC: Institute for Higher Education Policy. Retrieved November 20, 2009, from www.case.org/files/AsiaPacific/PDF/Global_State_of_Higher_Education.pdf.

International Labor Organization (2008a). *Labor and social trends in ASEAN 2008: Driving competitiveness and prosperity with decent work.* Bangkok, Thailand: ILO Regional Office for Asia and the Pacific.

International Labor Organization (2008b). *World of work report: Income inequalities in the age of financial globalization.* Geneva, Switzerland: ILO International Institute for Labor Studies.

Johnston, D.B. (2004). The economics and politics of cost sharing in higher education: Comparative perspective. *Economics of Education Review, 23* (4), 403-410.

Kapur, D., & Crowley, M. (2008). *Beyond the ABCs: Higher education and developing countries* (Working Paper No. 139). Washington, DC: Center for Global Development. Retrieved November 20, 2009, from www.eldis.org/cf/rdr/?doc=35501&em=040608=educ.

LaRocque, N. (2007a). *The role of education in supporting the development of science, technology, and innovation in developing member countries.* Manila, the Philippines: ADB.

LaRocque, N. (2007b). *Study on science and technology: Constraints to development.* Manila, the Philippines: ADB.

Lewin, T. (2008, February 10). Universities rush to set up outposts abroad. *New York Times*, A1.

Loren, R., & Ateinza, J. (2006). *International grant-making update 2006: A snapshot of U.S. foundation trends.* Washington, DC: Foundation Center and the Council on Foundations.

Marten, R., & Witten, J. (2008). *Transforming development? The role of philanthropic foundations in international development cooperation* (Research Paper series No. 10). Berlin, Germany: Global Public Policy Institute.

Pijano, C.V. (2009, January 19). Lessons learned and new challenges for quality assurance in the Asia-Pacific Region. Presentation made at the Asian Development Bank, Manila, the Philippines.

Salmi, J., & Hauptman, A. (2006). *Innovations in tertiary education financing: A comparative evaluation of allocation mechanisms* (World Bank Paper series No. 4). Washington, DC: World Bank. Retrieved November 20, 2009, from http://siteresources.worldbank.org/EDUCATION/Resources/278200-1099079877269/547664-1099079956815/Innovations_TertiaryEd_Financing.pdf.

Sarvi, J. (2008, September 26). Higher education in Asia and the Pacific region: Issues of financing and partnerships, particularly from the perspective of access, equity, quality, and diversity of higher education. Paper presented at UNESCO's Asia-Pacific Sub-regional Preparatory Conference for the 2009 World Conference on Higher Education, Macao.

Southeast Asian Ministers of Education Organization (2008). *Accomplishment report FY 2006/2007.* Bangkok, Thailand: SEAMEO Secretariat.

The future is another country (2009, January 3). *The Economist, 390*(8612), 43–44.

UNESCO (2006). *Higher education in South-East Asia.* Bangkok, Thailand: UNESCO Asia and Pacific Regional Bureau for Education.

UNESCO, & Asia-Pacific Quality Network (2007). *Toolkit: Regulating the quality of cross-border education.* Bangkok, Thailand: UNESCO.

Woodhall, M. (2007). *Funding higher education: The contribution of economic thinking to debate and policy development* (World Bank Working Paper series No. 8). Washington, DC: World Bank. Retrieved November 20, 2009, from http://siteresources.worldbank.org/EDUCATION/Resources/278200-1099079877269/547664-1099079956815/Funding_HigheRed_wps8.pdf.

You still can't get the staff (2008, November 20). *The Economist, 389*(8607), 75–76.

Part VI
Conclusion

14

THE FUTURE OF CROSS-BORDER
PARTNERSHIPS IN HIGHER EDUCATION

DAVID W. CHAPMAN AND ROBIN SAKAMOTO

International partnerships are not a new concept in higher education. Students have been crossing borders to pursue their education for centuries. Of growing interest but less widely understood is the movement of higher education programs and institutions across borders and the broadening nature of the activities underway within these collaborations. The preceding chapters have provided examples and analysis of (a) collaborations that moved campuses instead of students across borders, (b) collaborations that extended partnership activities beyond classroom instruction, to such things as research, faculty development, quality assurance, (c) collaborations that employed cross-border partnerships to advance fields of practice in areas as diverse as health care, business administration, and agriculture, and (d) collaborations that were undertaken to achieve larger societal goals, such as poverty reduction, sustainable development, and greater equity in the distribution of societal benefits.

The preceding chapters support eight general observations about the rise of cross-border programs in higher education.

- More recent forms of cross-border collaboration are taking on greater complexity as they involve a wider set of goals, activities, and organizational structures. While these partnerships can offer multiple payoffs, they often yield unanticipated cross impacts due, in large part, to the greater-than-anticipated complexity associated with working across cultures, institutional policies, and national legal systems.

- There is no one dominant model of cross-border partnership in higher education. The collaborations discussed in this volume reflect initiatives across a variety of content areas, undertaken for different reasons. The positive side of this diversity is the creativity and obvious effort that has been invested to adjust higher education partnerships to the particular contexts, interests, and needs of institutional partners. The downside of such variety is that lessons may not travel well. Experiences of one partnership can only be generalized to other collaborations with great caution.
- As collaborations move beyond just an instructional focus, both higher education institutions and governments have less experience on which to draw to guide their actions and decisions. As Al-Barwani et al. found in the Oman case, cross-border partnerships can inadvertently end up conflicting with government initiatives.
- Institutional identity is often deeply woven into cross-border partnerships. Participation in these programs often conveys a forward-looking, international perspective. The risk is that enthusiasm for the symbolic benefits may overshadow and mask operational problems that need attention.
- While programs mostly rise and fall with the fate of their champions, there are good examples of how strategic leadership can guide champion-based partnerships to more sustainable institutional relationships.
- University partnerships often start as bottom-up initiatives, championed by individuals who are often motivated by friendships and personal professional linkages. This was well illustrated in the case studies offered by Austin and Foxcroft and by Shivnan and Hill. However, as such cross-border partnerships are increasingly seen by governments as a means of promoting a larger collective agenda, as illustrated by Fong and Postiglione, this has led both to more support for and more oversight of these programs.
- Those establishing cross-border programs need to plan for a long time frame. Payoffs often emerge only slowly, as initial misunderstandings and misjudgments get sorted out and as institutional players become better acquainted. Quick return on investment may be elusive.
- Cross-border partnerships are a further example of how higher education institutions are evolving from just centers of higher learning to serve as vehicles to further broader social policy,

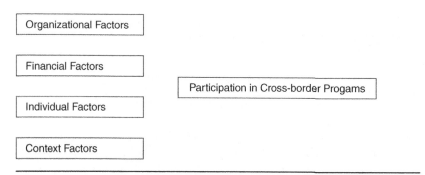

Figure 14.1 Framework of Factors Related to Higher Education Institutions' Participation in Cross-border Partnerships (Source: Authors).

points well illustrated by the Sarvi, Nomura et al., and Collins chapters.

The framework introduced in Chapter 1 offers a useful scaffold for examining the expansion in cross-border programs into these domains (Figure 14.1).

ORGANIZATIONAL FACTORS

New forms of cross-border partnership have necessitated new organizational arrangements, as colleges and universities launch programs and construct campuses in foreign settings. The cross-border campuses of institutions that operate as public universities in their home country may be legally constituted as private institutions in the partner country. Laws that regulate land rights, quality assurance, awarding of degrees, treatment of human subjects in research studies, and intellectual property rights at home and abroad can be very different. Educators' notions of what constitute appropriate faculty responsibilities, workload, and pedagogy can lead to misunderstandings that fuel tension. Institutional policies that have evolved from substantial experience may be deemed curious and irrelevant by international partners who operate from the lens of their own history and experience.

The insight, flexibility, and wisdom with which college administrators and participating faculty members cope with these differences will largely shape the quality and persistence of the relationship. Many of these issues can be anticipated and addressed in advance; some will only emerge as programs are implemented. None of these issues necessarily needs to thwart the development of strong cross-border partnerships. The problems tend to come when higher education institutions on both sides of a partnership ground their collaborations on wishful thinking and overly optimistic expectations.

FINANCIAL FACTORS

Financial return is generally not the only motivation in the move of colleges and universities to enter into cross-border partnerships, but few institutions can afford to ignore this dimension. As cross-border collaborations involve more complex sets of activities that, in turn, involve greater upfront investment in on-site facilities and staffing, financial risks increase and are harder for partners to anticipate and manage. Money matters. Regardless of other benefits that flow from cross-border partnerships, the financial dimension has to be considered.

Generally speaking, unless there is a financial advantage to all parties in the cross-border collaboration, shared commitment and the sustainability of the program will be at risk, as illustrated by Lane in his chapter on joint ventures in Malaysia. At the same time, as both Lane and Croom discussed, partnership arrangements increasingly involve more substantial up-front investments in physical infrastructure and on-site staff, introducing new levels of financial risk. Although revenue generation is a dominant rationale for the expansion of branch campuses, long-term profits can be an iffy proposition when a regional economy declines or national political alliances shift.

The lure of *external* funding for cross-border programs is powerful, Collins points out the risk posed by dependency on funding from international organizations that sometimes have short attention spans. Equally problematic is when external funding comes with strings attached. Funding agencies have their own agendas, as illustrated by Collins, writing about the World Bank, Sarvi, writing about the Asian Development Bank, and Nomura et al. looking at the role of a government ministry in supporting a cross-border collaboration. The tendency for funding to be allotted primarily to projects that correspond to the agenda of the funder is hardly surprising, but sometimes problematic.

INDIVIDUAL FACTORS

Individual faculty champions are still important to the creation and continuation of cross-border programs, but less than they used to be. New levels of interest on the part of university administrators, national governments, and international organizations in initiating and promoting partnerships aimed at a broader array of activities have, at times, eclipsed the importance of the champion role. A related consideration, though, is that when cross-border partnerships that address activities that go well beyond instructional programming do emerge from the energy of individual champions, institutional leaders need to be alert in assessing the different opportunities and risks associated with such efforts.

CONTEXT FACTORS

Context factors can both encourage and constrain cross-border collaborations. On the positive side, the wider prevalence of technology has fueled the growth of cross-border partnerships in two ways. Communications technology has made it easier and less expensive for partners to stay in close touch. Consultation among partners can be more frequent and travel costs are dramatically reduced. The application of new technologies has become a focus of some cross-border collaborations. For example, while the use of computer-based online instruction linking campuses is now commonplace, the emergence of more cutting-edge applications are illustrated by Maharjan and Sakamoto's discussion of diagnosing plant diseases via cell phone photography. More generally, as discussed by Vincent-Lancrin, technology has provided new modalities for engaging researchers across countries and institutions. On the negative side, new forms of cross-border partnership raise questions about operating in multiple legal jurisdictions, pose new considerations of political stability, and introduce levels of complexity previously not encountered.

One of the biggest changes in the context in which cross-border programs operate is, as Knight points out, the inclusion of higher education in GATS. This has pushed higher education toward being seen and treated as a commodity. One consequence of this shift is that cross-border higher education is big money. As such, it is attracting the attention of new audiences who see this as a new area of international commerce. This, in turn, is triggering new considerations about quality control, regulation, and scale.

CONCLUSION

As borders become less relevant in the delivery of higher education, the nature of cross-border partnerships in higher education is changing. Benefits of such collaborations can be significant, but cannot be assumed. Done well, such collaborations provide a significant source of innovative thinking, creative sharing, and, possibly, economic return. However, there are also risks. As cross-border collaborations become more institutionalized, require more upfront investment, and take on greater complexity, the consequences of champions losing interest, disagreement emerging among partner institutions, and regulatory, political, and economic changes in the larger environment increase. Nonetheless, the move toward expanding cross-border partnerships in higher education will continue. The message from this volume is that colleges and universities that want to get in the game or expand their profile in cross-border collaboration need to understand the changing nature of both the payoffs and the risks, plan more strategically than in the past, and take a long view.

CONTRIBUTORS

Osamu Abe is Professor at the College of Sociology and Graduate School of Intercultural Communication, Rikkyo University (Japan) where he also serves as the Director of the Education for Sustainable Development Research Center. He is Chairman of the Board of the Japan Council on the UN Decade of ESD (ESD-J), President of the Japanese Society of Environmental Education, and a member of the Commission on Education and Communication of the World Conservation Union (IUCN).

Thuwayba Al-Barwani is Dean of the College of Education at Sultan Qaboos University in Oman. She is a member of the State Council (Parliament) and previously served as Deputy Minister for Social Development. She earned a bachelor's degree in English Literature and Language from Kuwait University, and an MA and PhD in Curriculum and Instruction from the State University of New York at Albany (USA).

Hana Ameen is Advisor for Academic Affairs in the Office of the Minister, Ministry of Higher Education in the Sultanate of Oman. She earned both a BA and a MA degree in statistics from Baghdad University and a PhD in statistics from Newcastle upon Tyne University (UK). She is a member of the Academic Council for Education Colleges, and a member of the Board of Trustees of Colleges of Technology in the Sultanate of Oman.

Ann E. Austin is Professor of Higher, Adult, and Lifelong Education and Director of the Global Institute for Higher Education at Michigan State University. Her research concerns organizational change, faculty careers and professional development, doctoral education, and teaching and learning issues. She was a Fulbright Fellow (South Africa, 1998), the 2001–2002 President of ASHE, and is currently the co-principal investigator of the Center for the Integration of Research, Teaching, and Learning (CIRTL), a National Science Foundation-funded Center focused on preparing doctoral students for faculty positions in STEM fields.

David W. Chapman is the Birkmaier Professor of Educational Leadership in the Department of Organizational Leadership, Policy, and Development at the University of Minnesota. His specialization is in international development assistance. He has worked on development assistance activities in over 45 countries and has authored or edited 10 books and over 125 book chapters and journal articles, many of them on issues related to the development of education systems in international settings.

Christopher S. Collins is Associate Director for the Globalization and Higher Education Research Center (GHERC) and a Research Associate for the UCLA Higher Education Research Institute (HERI) at the University of California, Los Angeles. He serves as the Editor for *InterActions: UCLA Journal of Education and Information Studies.* His research interests include higher education policy, as it relates to human capacity building and international development initiatives.

Patricia W. Croom is Associate Director for International Admissions at Michigan State University. Her research focuses on the globalization of higher education, with an emphasis on partnership models and international branch campuses. She is a frequent presenter at NAFSA: Association of International Educators as well as the American Association of Collegiate Registrars and Admissions Officers (AACRAO). She is a past recipient of both Fulbright and DAAD awards in Japan and Germany, respectively.

Peter Fong teaches in the School of Economics and Finance of the University of Hong Kong and runs cross-national programs in business and public affairs for the University of Hong Kong.

Cheryl Foxcroft is Professor of Psychology and Senior Director, Higher Education Access and Development Services at Nelson Mandela Metropolitan University in Port Elizabeth, South Africa. She was President of the Psychological Society of South Africa (2005–2006), serves on the Council of the International Test

Commission (2000–present), and serves on project teams of Higher Education South Africa and SANTED related to access, admission requirements, benchmark tests, and student retention.

Martha N. Hill is Dean of the School of Nursing and Professor of Nursing, Medicine, and Public Health at the Johns Hopkins University. Dr. Hill served as president of the American Heart Association from 1997–1998, and is a Fellow in the American Academy of Nursing, a member of the Research!America Board of Directors, and a member of the Institute of Medicine (IOM) of the National Academy of Sciences and the IOM Council.

Jane Knight is an Adjunct Professor at Ontario Institute for Studies in Education at the University of Toronto (Canada). She is the author/editor of many publications on internationalization concepts and strategies, quality assurance, institutional management, mobility, cross-border education, the General Agreement on Trade in Services (GATS), and capacity building. In the last 10 years she has taken a leadership role in working with international teams on four regional studies on internationalization of higher education in Europe/North America, Asia-Pacific, Latin America, and Africa.

Jason E. Lane is Assistant Professor in the Department of Educational Administration and Policy Studies at the University at Albany, State University of New York (U.S.A.), where he also holds an appointment in the Comparative and International Education Policy Program and the Rockefeller College Public Policy Program. His research focuses on government planning and policy, institutional capacity building, and accountability. He is currently investigating the development of international branch campuses.

Gauri Maharjan is a graduate student of the United Graduate School of Agriculture, Iwate University (Japan). He previously worked 8 years in an instructional technology company in Nepal. His specialty is agricultural informatics. His research interest is in utilization of instructional technology in agriculture and rural development.

Yoshihiro Natori currently works for the United Nations University-Institute of Advanced Studies (UNU-IAS) (Japan) where he is responsible for the Education for Sustainable Development Program. He has previously worked as Director of the Wildlife

Division of the Japanese Ministry of the Environment, at the Nature Conservation Bureau and the Global Environment Department of the Japanese Environment Agency, at the Embassy of Japan in Kenya, and at the Regional Office for Asia and the Pacific of the United Nations Environment Program based in Thailand.

Ko Nomura is an Associate Professor in the Graduate School of Environmental Studies of Nagoya University (Japan). His research interests have been in the fields of environmental politics and environmental education in East Asia, particularly the role of environmental non-governmental organizations. He has held positions as a researcher at the Institute for Global Environmental Strategies and at the ESD Research Center, Rikkyo University, Japan. He has also worked on development assistance activities in Southeast Asia, particularly Indonesia.

Gerard Postiglione is Professor of Education and Head of the Division of Policy, Administration, and Social Science in the Faculty of Education at the University of Hong Kong. He has published widely on issues of higher education across Asia.

Robin Sakamoto is Professor in the Faculty of Foreign Studies at Kyorin University as well as a lecturer at the University of Tokyo. She also serves as the editor of the *Journal of Intercultural Communication* for SIETAR-Japan. She serves annually on the staff of the Japan Education Forum, which looks at multi-organizational collaboration in educational development. Most recently, she has worked in development assistance activities internationally in Uganda and the Ukraine.

Jouko Sarvi is currently Education Lead in the Regional and Sustainable Development Department of the Asian Development Bank (ADB) (Manila). He is responsible for education sector policy and strategy development at ADB, and serves as a Coordinator of ADB's community of practice in education. He has worked previously at ADB as a Senior Education Specialist in the South Asia Operations Department of ADB and as Senior Adviser at Cambridge Education Consultants (UK).

Jane C. Shivnan is the Executive Director at the Institute for Johns Hopkins Nursing (IJHN) in Baltimore, Maryland, a joint initiative of the Johns Hopkins University School of Nursing and the Johns Hopkins Hospital Department of Nursing. In her current role she is responsible for planning, developing, implementing, and evaluating the continuing education activities of IJHN. As Director of the Office of Global Nursing within IJHN, she is responsible for facilitating the international education of nursing students, and facilitating faculty and staff involvement in international nursing activities.

Stéphan Vincent-Lancrin is an Analyst with the OECD Centre for Educational Research and Innovation (Directorate for Education) where his work focuses on internationalization of higher education, e-learning, international quality assurance, knowledge management, and learning cities and regions. He co-authored the recent OECD/CERI publications on internationalization and trade in higher education and on e-learning in tertiary education. Prior to joining the OECD, he was a lecturer and researcher in economics at the University of Paris-Nanterre and the London School of Economics.

INDEX

Note: Page numbers in *italics* denote tables, those in **bold** denote figures or illustrations.

Made in the USA
Coppell, TX
01 October 2021